FLIGHT TO ST ANTONY

Why did they have to ditch at night?

An aviation mystery by

Tony Blackman

Flight to St Antony ISBN 978-0-9553856-6-7, 0-9553856-6-0
First Published 2008
© 2008 by Anthony Blackman. All rights reserved.
Blackman Associates
24 Crowsport
Hamble
Southampton SO31 4HG

Previous books by the same Author

A Flight Too Far
ISBN 978-0-9553856-3-6, 0-9553856-3-6
Published Blackman Associates

The Final Flight
ISBN 978-0-9553856-0-5, 0-9553856-0-1
Published Blackman Associates

The Right Choice
ISBN 978-0-9553856-2-9, 0-9553856-2-8
Published Blackman Associates

Flight Testing to Win (Autobiography)
ISBN 978-0-9553856-4-3, 0-9553856-4-4
Published Blackman Associates September 2005

Vulcan Test Pilot
ISBN 1-904943-888
Published Grub Street June 2007

To Margaret, my long suffering wife, without whose first class ideas, enormous help, continuous encouragement and amazing editing skills, this book would never have seen the light of day.

Acknowledgements

This book could not have been completed without the help of specialist advisers. I should like to acknowledge with thanks the support and advice I have received from Richard James of the UK Air Accident Investigation Board Flight Recorder section. Also enormous help from Chris and Louise Payne, Andrew McClymont, Peter Cox, Chris Hodgkinson, Kay Lindars and many others. I must apologise to those who I inadvertently have not mentioned.

Despite all the help I have received, there will inevitably be inaccuracies, errors and omissions in the book for which I must be held entirely responsible.

Author's Note

This book, *Flight to St Antony*, was completed in draft before the accident to the British Airways twin engined Boeing 777 airliner G-YMMM took place at Heathrow on 17 January 2008, though the opportunity has now been taken to refer briefly to the incident in this story. Publication took place before the Air Accident Investigation Branch had issued a definitive report and therefore the cause of the accident was not known when the book was printed.

Flight to St Antony is also about a landing accident to a large fictional twin engined airliner, not dissimilar to the Boeing 777, after a long flight. However, there is no suggestion in any way that the accident described in this book has any relation to the accident at Heathrow.

The technology of the book in certain ways is ahead of current aircraft but, interestingly, has strong affiliations with the Avro Vulcan bomber built many years ago in which I spent many happy hours testing and developing.

Anthony L Blackman OBE, M.A., F.R.Ae.S

About the Author

Tony Blackman was educated at Oundle School and Trinity College Cambridge, where he obtained an honours degree in Physics. After joining the Royal Air Force, he learnt to fly, trained as a test pilot and then joined A.V.Roe and Co.Ltd where he became Chief Test Pilot.

Tony was an expert in aviation electronics and was invited by Smiths Industries to join their Aerospace Board, initially as Technical Operations Director. He helped develop the then new large electronic displays and Flight Management Systems.

After leaving Smiths Industries, he was invited to join the Board of the UK Civil Aviation Authority as Technical Member.

Tony is a Fellow of the American Society of Experimental Test Pilots, a Fellow of the Royal Institute of Navigation and a Liveryman of the Guild of Air Pilots and Air Navigators.

He now lives in Hamble writing books and spends his spare time designing and maintaining databases on the internet.

DRAMATIS PERSONAE

Given Name	Family Name	Description
Peter	**Talbert**	**Aviation Insurance Investigator, Narrator of Book**
Alvin	Goddard	*Dark Blue Diving* instructor
Becky	Samuels	Worldwide Manager, St Antony
Ben	Masters	Head of Police, St Antony
Beverley		*Discover St Antony* agent
Brian	Matthews	Daily Mail Reporter
Bill	Dawson	Chief Technical Pilot, Worldwide Airlines
Bob	Furness	Head AAIB, UK
Charles	Hendrick	Chief Pilot, Worldwide Airlines
Charles	Prentice	Rescued passenger
Charlotte		Cabin Supervisor Alpha Delta
Cindy	Smart	Reporter, St Antony *Announcer*
David	Winston	Deputy Chief Pilot, Worldwide Airlines
Debbie	Braxton	Hospital Administrator
Dick	Bartholomew	Head of Immigration, St Antony
Dorothy	Henshaw	UK High Commission Consular Official, St Antony
Eldine	Roach	Skipper *Red Snapper*
Frank	Westbourne	Owner and CEO, West Atlantic Airways
Geoffrey	Hudson	Jackson Turner's man
Gretchen		Stewardess in charge economy section, Alpha Delta
Graham	Prince	AAIB Inspector
Harry	Markov	ITAC Engineer
Helen	Partridge	Cabin Crew Alpha Delta
Henry	Thompson	Alpha Delta crew chief
Ian	Somerton	NTSB accredited representative
Jackson	Turner	Jacko, boss of drug running organisation
Jane	Brown	Worldwide Airlines First Officer G-WWAD
Janet	Johnson	Worldwide Scheduling Clerk
Jearl	Sobers	Ben Master's secretary.

Flight to St Antony

Jeremy	Brock	Rescued passenger
Jill	Jenkins	Peter's London secretary
Jim	Scott	Worldwide Airlines Captain G-WWAD
Jimmy	Benson	ITAC Electrical design engineer
Joel	Davis	Skipper of *Blue Lobster*
John	Southern	Hull Claims Insurance executive
Joseph	Benjamin	St Antony accident investigator
Ken	Bradley	Worldwide Airlines first officer
Linda	Sutcliffe	Cabin crew Alpha Delta
Mandy	Arrowsmith	Peter Talbert's ex-girl friend, lawyer
Margaret	Proudfoot	Rescued passenger
Mary	Turner	Charles Hendrick's secretary
Michael	Longshaw	Passenger in Alpha Delta
Michael	Noble	Seattle editor of Aviation Week
Mike	Mansell	Insurance executive, Australia
Moira		Cabin staff, Worldwide Airways
Pamela	Westbourne	Frank Westbourne's wife
Philip	Smithson	Owner, *Dark Blue Diving*
Reggie	Pendlebury	Wing Commander, UK High Commission
Ricardo	Gonzales	Worldwide Dispatcher
Rick	Welcome	St Antony policeman
Roger	O'Kane	ITAC Avionics engineer
Ronald	Raycroft	ITAC Accident Liaison
Rupert	Stanton	Doctor, St Antony
Sandy	Thomas	Worldwide chief dispatcher
Stan	Bellow	Worldwide Maintenance Chief
Stanley	Carstairs	AAIB engineer
Susan	Brown	Frank Westbourne's secretary
Thomas	Smith	Jacko's man
Tim	Hardcastle	SATCO St Antony
Toby	Makepeace	Survivor
Tom	Falconbury	AAIB Inspector
Tracey	Stapleton	TV interviewer
Vincent	Greene	Engineering Chief, St Antony ATC
Wendy		Cabin Attendant, ITAC 831
Yvonne		Gatwick air traffic recorder

ACRONYMS AND DEFINITIONS

Acronym or Expression	In full or explanation
AAIB	Air Accident Investigation Branch
Alternator	An electrical generator producing alternating current/AC
ADD	Acceptable Deferred Defect on airliner
ADS C	Automatic satellite position reporting
APU	Auxiliary Power Unit (jet engine)
ATC	Air Traffic Control
BAA	British Airports Authority
CAA	UK Civil Aviation Authority
CASA	Civil Air Safety Agency, Australia
CVR	Cockpit Voice Recorder, one of the two crash recorders
EASA	European Aviation Safety Agency
ELT	Emergency Locator Transmitter
ETOPS	Extended Range Twin Engined Operations.
FAA	Federal Aviation Agency
FDR	Flight Data Recorder, one of the two crash recorders
FMS	Flight Management System
FUGRO	Specialist underwater recovery firm
GAPAN	Guild of Air Pilots and Air Navigators
GPS	Global Positioning System
HF	High Frequency aircraft radio communication
ICAO	International Civil Aviation Organisation
ITAC	Independant Transport Aircraft Company
MAYDAY	Extreme Emergency distress call
NTSB	National Transportation Safety Board
NUBEC	New Bristol Engine company
NWIA	New World International Airlines
PA	Aircraft Public Address System
PAN	Emergency distress call
QAR	Quick Access Recorder, airline maintenance
RIB	Rigid Inflatable Boat
ROV	Remote Observation Vehicle
SRG	Safety Regulation Group, UK CAA, Gatwick
TCAS	Traffic and Conflict Alerting System
TRU	Transformer Rectifier Unit
VHF	Very High Frequency radio for communications

LONDON (GATWICK) --- St ANTONY
3,620 nautical miles

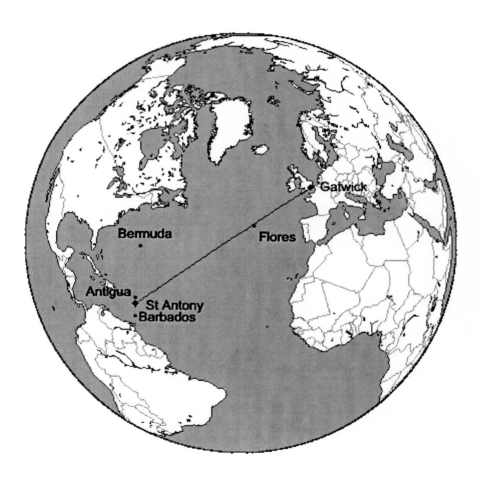

Flight to St Antony

Prologue

"We may have to ditch." Gretchen had taken her portable oxygen mask off to talk to Helen and Linda at the rear of the aircraft and Helen could see she was ashen faced. "Charlotte has just seen the Captain and told me. We've got to get the passengers to put their life jackets on now. The PA system isn't working so you'll have to tell them all individually ."

Helen looked at Gretchen who was in charge of the economy section of the aircraft.

"OK. How much time have we got? It's going to be difficult while they're still using oxygen masks."

"About thirty minutes Charlotte said. The Captain is still hoping to make St Antony but he thinks we need to be ready for ditching as we may not make it."

For a brief moment Helen considered their predicament. It was bad enough that they'd had to shut down an engine but to have had a pressurisation failure as well didn't seem fair. Gretchen had told them earlier that they would be diverting to St Antony instead of going to Barbados but now they were having to think about ditching. None of it made sense. Clearly it wasn't their day. Something else must have gone wrong.

She knew that there wouldn't be time for everyone to put their lifejackets on when the aircraft started descending. Gretchen was right. They needed to start putting them on straightaway. She saw Linda, who together with her looked after the rear cabin and the rear doors in the event of an evacuation, going quickly to her side of the aircraft and Helen immediately started briefing her own passengers, commencing from the rear.

Helen realised it was going to be very difficult to get everything done in time if they were really going to ditch, since they were still at twenty thousand feet and were all having to use oxygen masks to breath. Without the passenger address system working they were going to have to tell all the passengers what was happening, row by row. She took her mask off and spoke as quickly as she dared to each row on the possibility of ditching, and showed them where their life jackets were, told them to put them on but warned them, whatever happened, not to inflate them inside the aircraft.

She couldn't wait at each row to check that the life jackets had been put on correctly and she just hoped that they had all paid attention to the briefing at the beginning of the flight. She took deep breaths from her mask as she went from row to row. She was having to work both sides of the aisle on her side of the aircraft for the twelve rows in the section which she and Linda covered. When she got to the front of her cabin she decided to remind everybody how to put on life jackets by facing them as she put her own on.

As she went to the back of the aircraft she looked at her watch and reckoned there might only be about ten minutes left before they landed or had to ditch. She wasn't surprised to hear the engine note change and to feel the increasing pressure on her ears as the aircraft began to descend. She started checking at each row that they had got their life jackets on and, because time was so short, took the emergency sheet from the seat pocket in front of the passenger nearest to her in each row and made sure that they could all see the correct bracing position. She was very worried as some passengers were having trouble getting the life jackets on with the oxygen masks in the way so she told them all to forget about the oxygen masks since they were now much lower and asked the passengers who had been successful to help their neighbours. She took her own mask off to emphasise the point.

Back at the front of the cabin she glanced at her watch again and reckoned there could only be two or three minutes left before landing or ditching. She went quickly to the cabin attendant's seat next to the rear door and, as she sat down, tried to remind herself what she had to do. Besides helping the passengers out of the door and into the slideraft, she had to take an emergency pack with her and also the locator beacon which transmitted its position to the emergency global satellite system. She got them both down next to her and decided to switch on the beacon so she wouldn't forget.

Helen heard the note of the engine falter. She looked for runway lights through the window but saw none and realised that the ditching was really going to happen. She yelled "Brace, Brace" and then went to the brace position herself. She felt a shudder as the aircraft touched the water and then there was a sickening bang as it veered to the right. Just for a moment she was frozen wondering what was going to happen next and then remembered that every moment counted. She unbuckled her straps, rushed to the door, pulled the lever and thanked God as the door opened automatically into the darkness outside. There was an inrush of damp air from the black void. She could hear the air inflating the slideraft but she decided to pull the manual inflation lever to be sure. In fact she had to search to find it as the only illumination was the cabin emergency lighting which had come on as the aircraft ditched. She sensed that the water must be very close, only a few feet below the door sill.

The passengers started coming towards her and she could hear Linda yelling through the megaphone for people to leave the aircraft by the rear. She pushed the first man out of the aircraft and he fell into the water. The slideraft must have been slightly to one side. She tried to shout 'inflate' but the next passenger, a lady, got in the way as she jumped out, but this time Helen could hear the passenger dropping into the slideraft. The passengers now seemed to pour out, most stepping into the slideraft since the water level was now only just below the door opening. A few still missed and fell into the water.

Suddenly the exit was blocked as two men fought each other to get out; one hit the other very hard on the side of the head so that he fell whimpering, blocking the door opening. Helen drew back as the man who had struck the blow tried to climb out over the almost unconscious body but there wasn't enough room. He had to be helped by Helen to push the man into the slideraft. Once the body was in the life raft the man was able to get out and the struggling passengers behind immediately forced their way through.

Helen felt people pushing and hitting her and she realised that more and more passengers were beginning to struggle to get to the door and get out but all she could do was to assist each one through the door into the slideraft.

To her horror she could feel that the aircraft was rapidly going nose down and she found that she had to stand on the side of the seat in front of the door to hold her position. The water was beginning to pour over the side of the door and the entrance was now almost completely blocked by the slideraft. She could hear shouts of pain and screaming from the passengers as they realised that they might not escape in time. They were now fighting for their lives to get out. There was nothing she could do to calm things down and she concentrated on getting as many as she could safely out of the aircraft. It was very difficult with the slideraft blocking the door and it was necessary to push the raft back for each passenger to scramble out.

Water was now pouring into the aircraft through the door opening. She looked across to Linda's side and saw that there the water was cascading in and there was no hope of getting out.

Helen realised that the plane was about to sink and that she would have to leave to look after the slideraft even though there were going to be a lot of passengers left behind. She grabbed the emergency kit and the locator beacon and threw them into the slideraft. She knew it was imperative to release the slideraft from the aircraft and she had to push a man back to reach sideways to the bottom of the door to find and lift the flap which covered the separation handle. She just managed to force herself up and over into the slideraft as the side of the aircraft door sank beneath her with the water pouring in.

Helen looked back at the aircraft with its tail pointing vertically up to the sky and even in the almost pitch darkness she realised that no-one else would be able to get out as the water poured in. She looked with horror and disbelief as the aircraft slowly started to submerge with water now completely covering the rear door from which she had escaped, trapping the passengers inside but she could do nothing and there was no time to look. As she inflated her life jacket she saw to her dismay the line attaching the life raft to the plane tighten and then she remembered she had been taught that there was an open hook knife attached to the slideraft to cut the line. To her amazement she could feel the knife in the dark and somehow she managed to cut the line, just as the aircraft disappeared under the water.

But events were still crowding in on her and there was so much to think about. She picked up the locator beacon and threw into the water hoping it was working. She tore open the emergency pack and found the torch. She was able to find the flares and thankfully managed to get one to ignite and shoot up into the night sky, illuminating the terrible scene.

She stopped for a moment and looked round. There seemed to be a lot of passengers in the life raft but she could also see some people in the water, clinging on to the rope attached to the outside of the raft. She shouted at a male passenger to help her drag one man in but they were only just strong enough between them and even then they could not have managed except the man they were rescuing still had enough strength to be able to help. She decided she had better light another flare and then she shouted at some other passengers who were not hurt to try to drag survivors in the water into the slideraft but really it was an almost impossible task. The people in the water were too heavy with their soaking clothes and were seemingly too weak to help themselves, so that only the lightest were able to be pulled in.

Out of the corner of her eye she saw a flare and thankfully realised that there was another slideraft out there, almost certainly Linda. Suddenly she heard the sound of a boat's engine and saw some navigation lights coming towards them. She shone the torch towards the navigation lights and a searchlight appeared. There were some men in the oncoming boat which she recognised as a fishing trawler and somehow she managed to help them tie the boat alongside the slideraft without trapping the people in the water. But still she couldn't stop as the passengers needed help clambering up the steps attached to the fishing boat to get onto its deck. Then one of the crew stepped down into the slide raft to help her lift some of the weak and unconscious passengers into the boat.

Finally it was done and she and the crewman were alone but when she came to the steps she found she wasn't strong enough to climb up and the crewman had to help and push her up the steps until another crewman dragged her in.

She sat breathless and exhausted on the deck for a few minutes but as she started to recover she saw that the passengers needed assistance with blankets and towels which the boat's crew had produced. Somehow she found some strength and made herself help with the blankets but she barely knew what she was doing. Finally one of the crew sat her down and for a few minutes she was dead to the world.

DAY 1

The wind was whistling past my face and goggles as I skied down the slope turning and twisting, trying to avoid the moguls and other dangerous, but well marked, mounds of snow. My phone started to vibrate and then, thankfully, it stopped. I pulled up at the bottom of the slope and the phone started to vibrate again. I slowly started to take my gloves and goggles off, trying to reach the phone but it again stopped. Finally I got it out and looked at the caller. It had been from John Southern of Hull Claims Insurance in England. From experience of earlier aircraft accidents, I wasn't sure I wanted to talk to him. A message came through which I didn't bother to check since I was sure it would just be telling me that John had called. I reset my phone intending to call him when I had finished skiing but the phone rang again and this time I managed to answer it.

"Peter, where are you? The ringing tone sounded funny. Have you heard?"

"John, I'm skiing in the Snowy Mountains in Australia and am about to go up in the ski lift. I've heard nothing and from your tone, I'm not sure I want to."

"Peter, we're in trouble. A Worldwide Airlines aircraft has just landed in the water in the Caribbean near St Antony and we're insuring the hull."

"John, slow down for a moment. If I understand what you're saying, an aircraft has ditched and your firm, Hull Claims, are liable. What sort of aircraft? Did anyone survive? What about the passengers, the crew?"

"Don't know the aircraft yet but we insure all the Worldwide aircraft. Apparently some passengers escaped."

"How do you know? When did it happen?"

"Six or seven hours ago. Not sure exactly. Just heard on the radio and the only information I'm getting is from CNN. Haven't heard any real details. I told you. It only happened a few hours ago. The airline hasn't called me yet."

"Well there's nothing I can do here, but thank you for letting me know."

John's voice went up an octave. "But we need you to go to St Antony and find out what happened, look after our interests."

"You're jumping the gun, John. Anyway, whatever happened you people are going to have to pay up. Don't waste your money on me."

"Peter, you're wrong. It's not as simple as that. For the airline to get the full amount for which the aircraft is insured, it has to show that it has been operated correctly within the rules. Furthermore, the aircraft must have been maintained correctly. It could be that we may only be liable for part of the full amount. We have to have someone on the spot during the accident investigation who understands how Hull Claims might be affected. That's why we want you to go to St Antony."

"Why don't you go and get some more details John and then you can call me when I'm in my hotel; it's the Rydges Hotel in Thredbo, New South Wales."

"How long are you going to be in Australia? This could be terrible for us."

I didn't feel too sympathetic though I felt horrified just by the idea of such an accident. The thought of an airliner crashing into the sea full of passengers was too horrible to contemplate and yet apparently this had actually happened, and at night. If anybody had escaped it would be a miracle, unbelievable.

Insurance companies like Hull Claims are very professional and would have taken into account all the risks and, if necessary, have laid off some of their potential liabilities. However, I made most of my living working for insurance companies so I couldn't be too detached. I decided to cut my skiing short and go back to the hotel, a few hundred yards away, so I could get an update from John. I skied down the access slope to the side of the hotel where I removed my skis and went up on the special elevator reserved for skiers.

In spite of my desire not to get involved prematurely, I found myself doing some sums. The aircraft must have ditched on Tuesday, St Antony time, at night, about 2000 hours. I was amazed that anyone could have been saved in the dark. As far as I knew there had never been another airliner ditching at night and, if it was the twin engined ITAC 831, then the whole thing seemed even more unlikely, since inevitably one of the engines would hit the water first and the aircraft would be uncontrollable, almost certainly breaking up and probably somersaulting. The pilots must have done a superb job, not to mention the cabin staff faced with a virtually impossible situation.

Aircraft designers have to fit the aircraft with life rafts to be used in the case of ditching but in fact it is only really possible to visualise the life rafts being any good if the accident happens slowly, like an aircraft overshooting a runway and going in to the water, as might be imagined at airfields like Hong Kong. In fact the life rafts double as escape chutes, one for each emergency exit, which extend in the event of an emergency evacuation of the aircraft on the ground, hence the name sliderafts.

I switched my TV to CNN as I was getting ready for a shower. The newscaster was talking to a very businesslike looking lady in St Antony who turned out to be CNN's local reporter. She seemed to be standing on a beach in the dark with lights illuminating the water breaking on the sands. It must have been quite warm there as she was only wearing what looked like a thin blouse and short skirt.

"All we know so far is that a Worldwide Airlines aircraft has landed in the water not far off the shore trying to land at Nelson airport. The coastguard centre in Cape Harbour has told us that there are some survivors being rescued by fishing boats."

"Carol," that appeared to be the name of the reporter, "what happened?"

"According to air traffic control at Nelson airport, the aircraft called them when they were about 90 miles away saying that they were trying to land at Nelson but might have to ditch. The airport radar tracked them in and then, when the aircraft was about five miles from the coast, the pilot made an emergency call saying they couldn't make it and that they were going to have to land in the water. The tower told the coastguards who had already been alerted, and that was it."

"Did the pilots say what the problem was?"

"Don't know. If they did, then air traffic haven't told us."

"Carol, do you know what type of aircraft it was?"

"No. There is going to be a media briefing by air traffic later on. I'm not sure when."

The interview ended not leaving the viewers a lot wiser. There wasn't much more I could do until more details arrived. My guess was that we wouldn't get a lot more information until it got light in St Antony in a couple of hours. I tried to work on some reports that I needed to complete on other jobs but it was difficult to concentrate. I gave up after a bit and decided to go down to the bar where I ordered a Coopers Pale Ale and a smoked salmon salad. I asked for CNN to be selected but apparently that wasn't possible as it was necessary to watch the end of an Australian football match, Swans versus St Kilda, which puzzled me for a bit since I didn't know there was another St Kilda apart from the one off the Scottish Hebrides. I went over to a table in the corner of the room where I could see a screen and started my salad. The football game must have ended and the barman must have relented as I suddenly noticed that CNN was now on the screen. There were only a few months left before the US Presidential election so this was clearly exercising CNN and, presumably, the viewers, judging by what seemed to be unending political coverage of who the candidates might be and how each one was performing. Luckily, text messages were appearing all the time at the bottom of the screen, most of them relating to the accident in St Antony.

Apparently one fishing boat had returned to Paradise Harbour with forty one survivors who had been rushed to Cape Harbour hospital. There were two other boats still searching. Another message said that the aircraft took off with 245 passengers and crew from Gatwick and that it had been going to Barbados. There was still no mention of the type of aircraft but as it was a Worldwide one I knew that it had to be an Independant Transport Aircraft Company aircraft manufactured in Seattle, either a four engined 798 or the twin engined 831.

The accident sounded unbelievable. It seemed incredible that it actually had to ditch and not land at Nelson when it was so close. I racked my brains trying to think of a reason for the aircraft having to land on the water. It shouldn't have been short of fuel. Maybe there was a flying control failure of some sort, the aircraft was very advanced technically. But really, it just didn't make sense. Perhaps they had had a fuel leak. Surely they must have said something. I knew I would have to be patient and wait for the news to dribble in slowly from St Antony. There must have been a failure of some type, but why hadn't the pilot told someone?

The political briefing on the forthcoming United States election finally came to an end and the newsreader said that they were going back to St Antony to get the latest news. Carol appeared again.

"We have just heard that a second fishing boat has reached Paradise Harbour with sixteen survivors. It is just beginning to get light here and a coastguard helicopter is going to start searching. A Royal Navy minesweeper, which is visiting St Antony, has also just left Cape Harbour to help with the search for survivors and dead bodies."

"Any official statements yet, Carol, from air traffic or from the airline?"

"The Prime Minister of St Antony is making a statement in half an hour at eight o'clock."

I looked at my watch. It was 2030 Australian EST time, 1130 UK summer time and 0730 St Antony time. It should be broad daylight off the coast there and by now hopefully more survivors were being found. My phone rang, it was John again.

"They've got fifty seven survivors, Peter."

"So I've just seen on CNN here. Any other news? Aircraft type?"

"The UK Minister of Transport is making a statement at nine o'clock."

"What are the BBC and Sky saying?"

"Not very much at the moment as everyone is short of information. Hopefully Worldwide will be saying something very soon. Are you going to help us, Peter?"

"If you think I can. I'm planning to come home on Friday."

"Why don't you go straight to St Antony?"

"Thanks a lot. I've got my life to lead, John. I've got things I must attend to. Do you know if the St Antony government have asked for help from AAIB? If they have, I can't possibly go until I've spoken to AAIB as well as Worldwide."

"You can do all that over the phone, can't you?"

"Possibly. But we don't know yet if AAIB is involved as well as the airline. You may have to help me with the phoning. Will let you know."

"When will you be there?"

"John, I've just said that I'll go to St Antony, but be reasonable. I don't know yet. I haven't checked the schedules but it

22

might be quicker to go through London. Mind you, nothing is quick through London these days I'm sorry to say. Anyway as I told you, I'm not sure how I'll be able to help."

The London airports had acquired a terrible reputation for long delays at check-in and security and the airports themselves still left an awful lot to be desired. Huge queues at the airline check-in desks and airport security made travelling via London at peak times very unattractive, particularly with the arrival of the latest jumbo aircraft, the Airbus 380, with at the very least one hundred more passengers then the venerable Boeing 747. Even though it sometimes took longer, I tried to avoid using London and went via Southampton to either Paris, Frankfurt or Amsterdam. My current airline booking to UK was NWIA to Frankfurt and then BE to Southampton. The Government were doing what they could to improve things but it seemed to me that the whole concept was fatally flawed, since the airport operators now made their real profit from the shopping, not from shifting passengers.

Currently there was another advantage in avoiding London since the tickets from the European carriers seemed to be considerably cheaper; strangely some of the larger UK airlines had not grasped the fact that there really was a global economy and all airlines were only an internet click away.

John said he would ring again later before I went to sleep and I got my notebook out ready to listen to the St Antony Prime Minister. He appeared with a man next to him I instantly recognised. He was Tim Hardcastle, the chief air traffic control officer at Nelson airport, St Antony, who I had met a few years previously when an aircraft disappeared going to Bermuda.[1]

The Prime Minister started by saying how sorry he was for the relatives of all the people who had died in the accident and that everything was being done to look after the survivors in the Cape Harbour hospital and nursing homes. He paid tribute to the coastguard and to the crews of the fishing boats that had rescued the survivors. He said that he wanted the cause of the accident to be found as quickly as possible and, as the aircraft was registered in the United Kingdom, he was asking the UK Government to allow their Air Accident Investigation Branch to help the St Antony

---

[1] *The Final Flight* by the same author

Ministry of Transport staff. The manufacturers of the aircraft and the engines were also sending teams out to help in the investigation.

Tim Hardcastle then started to give the facts as far as he knew them.

"The aircraft was an Independant Transport Aircraft Company 831 flown by Worldwide Airways going from London Gatwick to Barbados. The flight was designated Worldwide 442 and the registration of the aircraft was G-WWAD, Golf Whiskey Whiskey Alpha Delta. We were called by Miami Center some three hours before the aircraft ditched, telling us that Worldwide 442 was diverting to Nelson airport here at St Antony instead of going to Barbados, having had a failure of the right engine. Apparently there was something wrong with the aircraft's satellite radio as Miami centre lost contact with the plane. In due course the aircraft called Nelson approach on the normal VHF radio and we saw it on our radar fifty miles out. The pilot said he was trying to land at Nelson but might have to ditch. He then made an emergency call, when it was only four miles from the runway, saying that they were definitely ditching. The aircraft turned left and disappeared off the screen."

The reporters in the room started to ask questions. Tim dealt with them very professionally. The key answer as far as I was concerned was in response to a question asking if the Captain explained the reason for the ditching.

"No, unfortunately the pilots did not at any time indicate why they had to ditch."

There was nothing more that came out of the briefing. The important point for me was that the aircraft was an ITAC 831, which was a twin engined aircraft, and it was flying on one engine. I was wondering how I was going to be able to hear the UK Minister of Transport on the BBC when CNN announced that they would be taking the broadcast. I had another beer and sat down to wait. The Minster of Transport appeared not looking particularly smart and I had a rather difficult time trying to understand his strong Scots accent.

"We are not yet aware of all the details of this terrible accident but we are doing everything we can to help the relatives. A hot line for enquiries has been set up and the number will be on the screen at the end of this broadcast. The aircraft was on the British register

24

and, at the request of the St Antony government, a team from our Air Accident Investigation Branch is on its way to St Antony to help the local authorities."

"Minister," the interviewer started probing "the aircraft is under water. Will it be possible to establish what happened?"

"Apparently the aircraft is very close to the coast in shallow water so there should be no difficulty in finding the crash recorders to establish what went wrong and ensure that it won't happen again."

"Minister, the ITAC 831 only has two engines and one of the engines had failed. A lot of people feel that an aircraft should have at least three engines when crossing the Atlantic or the Pacific to cater for a possible engine failure."

I had to admire the Minister, he didn't hesitate, he must have been well briefed. "That's very old fashioned thinking. Aircraft with only two engines have been operating all over the world for many years because modern engines are so reliable. However, to put your mind at rest, twin engined aircraft always have to be within a safe distance from an airport and this distance is specified in the regulations and is being constantly reviewed by the certification authority."

The interviewer had also been very well briefed. "But Minister, I believe the aircraft are allowed to be well over a thousand miles away from the nearest airport. That doesn't sound too safe a distance."

"Again that's rather outmoded thinking. As I said, the engines are incredibly reliable so that a thousand miles on one engine is a trivial distance. We are taking risks all the time in our lives and the risk of a second engine failing after the first is negligible." The minister paused. "What matters now is finding out what happened so we can ensure that it never happens again and, of course, supporting the survivors and their relatives. We've given instructions to our staff in St Antony to help the airline in every way."

The interviewer gave up and CNN switched to other matters. I noticed that the Minister did not offer any government financial aid but then they never did. My phone rang almost immediately. It was John.

"Did you hear the broadcast?"

"Yes John, though I wish we had Ministers who did not have such strong accents."

John made no comment. "I thought he did rather well. It's a difficult subject. Though I have to say my sympathy has always been with the apocryphal passenger who, when he was asked why he had flown from New York in a four engined aircraft instead of coming earlier in a twin engined one replied 'because there wasn't a five engined aircraft available'."

"Well if you feel like that you shouldn't be insuring twin engined aircraft."

"Peter, it must be safer to have four engines than two, particularly on these long routes."

"Possibly John, but then it is all a matter of probability and the way twin engined aircraft are now designed ensures that they meet the required standard of safety, the certification standard if you like. They are 'safe enough'. To make them any safer would make them too expensive to operate. Safety costs money."

"Peter, that's as maybe. You understand these things better than I do. The point is we've heard the basic facts and AAIB are going out there now. We definitely want you there as well to make certain we understand all the issues."

"Look, John, I've told you. I'm not going out without the airline being aware that I shall be there and without AAIB being informed. Have you told Worldwide yet that you are asking me to act for you? And have you told AAIB? You know how strict AAIB are about releasing information. They like to keep everything to themselves. It's going to be very difficult for me to talk to them operating from here and then going direct to St Antony. I'll have to think about it overnight."

"Oh Peter, by the way," I sensed there was going to be a complication, "we're not covering the New Bristol Engine Company engines. NUBEC have a special arrangement with Worldwide which covers maintenance and includes any losses."

"That sounds as if it could be very complicated. What happens if an engine fault caused the aircraft to crash? Whose going to be responsible for settling the passenger claims?"

"We would have to pay for the hull, unless it was due to faulty maintenance or operating procedures by the airline. I expect we would have to negotiate on the personal claims."

I decided not to point out that any legal negotiation spelt interminable delays for the claimants and a bonanza for the lawyers.

Back up in my room I reviewed the situation. I had been away from the UK for two weeks instructing a batch of new pilots from New World International Airlines, based in Sydney, on the challenges and intricacies of interfacing with a modern digital flight deck. I was always very conscious that though the aircraft manufacturers did an amazing job trying to ensure that pilots would always do the right thing in failure as well as in normal conditions, an aircraft these days looked like a very advanced computer room and it was always necessary to remember that it had to be able to be flown safely by the airline's worst pilot.

It was winter in Australia but the weather in Sydney had been like a balmy English summer with temperatures around 22°C. However, the thought of living in my own home again was becoming more and more attractive and I was very conscious that I was missing the best of the summer weather in England, though I could hardly complain at the winter weather I had been experiencing.

Furthermore, I had had some bad news from England as Mandy, my girl friend of several years standing, had just sent me a long letter saying that she had decided to end our relationship. For some time we had been living together in my house at Kingston during the week and then spending most week-ends in her house in Bournemouth. She was a high powered London solicitor, very bright and very smart in every way, working in a big partnership. Perhaps she was getting fed up with my being away, travelling all over the world investigating aircraft incidents and accidents on behalf of various insurance firms or airlines. In addition, she probably wasn't exactly enamoured of some of the ladies, girls, females, whatever, I had encountered in the course of my investigations. She knew as well as I did that the associations were only in the course of business and were not lasting relationships, but in these matters I had discovered that logic very often takes a back seat. I had tried ringing her in her office before leaving Sydney so that we could discuss the matter but she wouldn't accept my call.

It didn't help that one of the girls I had met, Liz Ward, was an Australian who Mandy had met in London when Liz had come to the UK to give evidence at a Public Inquiry.[2] Perhaps I had been unwise mentioning that I was going to see her again. In fact I had had dinner with her and her husband Mike a few days previously in their spectacular house at Darling Point overlooking Sydney harbour. When the Inquiry had finished she had set up a very expensive fashion house in Sydney based on clothes she designed herself and Mike, after emigrating from the UK to marry Liz, now had his own aviation insurance business. I wasn't sure how Liz was going to manage in three months time when their baby was due but that was definitely SEP, someone else's problem.

I had tried to ring Mandy again without success when I got to Thredbo, where I was now taking a couple of days off before returning to England. I wondered whether the fact that the divorce with my long separated wife Diana had finally come through after several years might have brought matters to a head. Perhaps I should have proposed straightaway when we knew about the divorce, but I seem to remember I was very busy at the time. Not that that was a satisfactory reason these days with Skype and global emails. All very unromantic I realised ruefully; after all 'where there's a will there's a way', as Mandy would have realised. Perhaps subconsciously I wasn't sure about settling down. Maybe Mandy, very understandably, felt unhappy that I hadn't proposed or, possibly, she was expecting me to at any moment and she realised she would be forced to make her mind up whether to get married or not and she couldn't face up to it. There could of course be an entirely different explanation in that she had found someone else. It was all too difficult and I decided to try to put the whole thing out of my mind, certainly until I got home.

This ditching near St Antony was for me an amazing coincidence because the NWIA pilots I had been teaching were about to take their technical examination on the 831 and the subject of twin engined operation had come up.

In a way it was a bit incongruous for me, not even a current airline pilot, to be instructing NWIA aircrew since they had their own instructors. However, I had built up a reputation in the specialist airline world, discussing how the new flight decks were in some ways very challenging should anything out of the ordinary

---

[2] *A Flight Too Far* by the same author

ever go wrong, notwithstanding the enormous care the designers took in catering for malfunctions. In addition, I was now quite well known as a private investigator of aircraft accidents, representing airlines or insurance companies. People liked to question me on the lessons learnt from these occurrences. In some ways, being a freelance instructor and investigator gave me a wider experience of airlines and aircraft than the airlines' own staff.

At my last lesson we had discussed the subject of operating twin engined aircraft over very long distances, as NWIA had to do flying across the Pacific. As the interview with the Minister had clearly demonstrated, the general public accepted that flying four engined aircraft across the world was an acceptable risk but people were worried doing the same thing if the aircraft only had two engines. The subject, as usual in the aviation world, had an acronym, ETOPS, Extended Range Twin Engined Operations.

The whole success of the 831 and other long range twin engined aircraft, like the Boeing 777, Boeing 787 and the Airbus A330, relied on ETOPS and being permitted to operate a relatively long way away from diversion airfields. I had explained that the concept was that modern engines were so reliable that even if one engine had to be shut down, the aircraft could continue flying safely for hours at a time on the other one. As far as the current rules were concerned, this meant that the 831 was allowed to fly for three hours and twenty seven minutes on one engine and this distance at the single engine speed was taken as 1,450 nautical miles. NWIA therefore, in planning their 831 route structure, always had to make sure that the aircraft when flying across an ocean or across a continent was always within 1,450 nautical miles of an airfield on which it could land safely. In fact, with this distance it was possible for example for NWIA to use the 831 on their non-stop Los Angles/Sydney route using Honolulu and Nandi as the intermediate ETOPS airfields.

I had seen that the pilots in my class, like the BBC's interviewer, were a bit surprised that aircraft were allowed to fly for such a long time on one engine but I had decided that I didn't really want to spend the rest of the time talking about ETOPS. We were meant to be discussing, amongst other things, how the ITAC 831 flight deck displays ensured that, whatever the emergency, the information on the displays indicated to the pilots what had to be done. The aircraft had an 'electronic flight bag' with all the necessary operating and emergency information being displayed on screens so that there was no need for the pilot to carry with him out to the aircraft the heavy manuals telling him or her what to do. The paper manuals were still kept on the aircraft but, hopefully, would never need to be used. My worry, as always, was the possibility of an emergency no-one had thought of.

The point I hadn't made to the NWIA pilots was that the ETOPS concept only worked providing all the systems of the aircraft, like the electrics, the hydraulics and the fuel supplies were as reliable as the engines. Twin engined aircraft had to be very carefully designed if the ETOPS distances that the airlines required for economic operation were going to be permitted; the European and United States certification agencies, EASA and FAA, had to be convinced that the whole aircraft, systems as well as the engines, met their safety requirements.

I switched on my computer and looked at the various airline schedules; it seemed that the quickest way to St Antony was via Los Angeles and Miami. It was going to take about twenty six hours actually travelling, but St Antony was thirteen hours behind so that if I was able to get a seat on the NWIA 8 pm from Sydney the following night I could be there about midday on Friday. I decided to call NWIA rather than book on line as I needed to cancel my Europe flights. I managed to get through without having too long a wait and the agent who answered me was very good. He managed to book me right through to Miami and, after some persuasion, found a suitable flight from there to St Antony with Caribbean Airways and I was all set.

Before going to sleep I sent a text message to John Southern telling him my ETA St Antony and reminding him to make sure Worldwide and AAIB knew I was on my way.

DAY 2

In the morning I decided to ring up Frank Westbourne, the boss of West Atlantic Airways in St Antony, who I knew as a result of finding out what had happened to one of his aircraft which had disappeared flying into Bermuda[3]. Luckily he was at home.

"Frank, Peter Talbert here. How's things?"

"Peter, I was thinking of you when I heard of the ITAC 831 ditching. I suppose that's why you're phoning?"

"How did you guess? I wondered if you had heard anything or had spoken to someone. It's a weird business."

"Well by chance I saw Tim Hardcastle, you remember, head of Air Traffic, as I was going to my office. He was just going to the TV studios to make a statement with the St Antony PM, after being in the tower all night dealing with the emergency. He told me that he had been called in, of course, by the duty controller when Nelson air traffic had been alerted by Miami that an aircraft had had an engine failure and had lost satellite contact with the air traffic system. Miami had received a couple of relayed VHF reports from other aircraft that Worldwide 442 was heading for St Antony. Apparently the Captain said they were trying to land but that they might have to ditch.

"Tim had alerted the coastguard main office in Cape Harbour and then, just as the aircraft was getting close to the airfield, it sent out a MAYDAY call saying it was ditching. The next thing he heard of the actual ditching was from the coastguard office. Fishing boats from Paradise Harbour had already been alerted by the coastguard and one of them had reported hearing an aircraft noise, seeing a landing light just above the water and then a loud noise, presumably the aircraft hitting the water. Apparently about ten minutes later two lots of emergency flares were seen and two fishing boats went towards the lights where they saw life rafts in the water with people in them and some more survivors in the water holding on to them. The boats rescued the survivors as best they could and went back to the harbour. They then went out again with another boat searching for more survivors and bodies. In fact there were emergency location transmitters, ELTs, on the rafts which

---

[3] *The Final Flight* by the same author

31

alerted the air traffic system. Of course the fishing boats didn't need to use the equipment to help in finding the rafts again since they had recorded the life rafts' GPS positions. They managed to get a coastguard helicopter airborne but it couldn't really help until it was light."

"Do you know what's happening now?"

"Not really. The survivors have been taken to St Mary's hospital in Cape Harbour and the radio said that there were not enough beds. Luckily, it seems that there were two nursing homes that they've been able to use for the survivors who were not too badly injured." He paused. "When are you coming out?"

"I'm planning to be with you Friday at midday coming in on a Caribbean Airways flight. Could you ask Susan to book me in the *New Anchorage* if she can and rent a car as well? I'll call you again nearer the time. I need to talk to the airline and hear what communication passed between them and the aircraft. Also between air traffic and the aircraft. Not certain how I'm going to do that. Anyway, remember me to the others and I expect I'll see you all soon. By the way, please don't bother to meet me. It's not as if I haven't been to the island before."

It was too late to call anyone in England so I checked out and got on the road to Sydney and the airport. The trip from Sydney to Thredbo on the way out had not been particularly interesting. I had felt a bit guilty not stopping in Canberra to see my contacts in the Australian air safety authority, CASA, and in the air traffic system, Airservices Australia, but had planned to do so on the way back. However, there was now no time to stop in Canberra and the trip back was even less interesting than going out. I decided that John Southern was definitely going to pay for my abortive visit to Thredbo, not to mention everything else. I felt particularly disappointed at not visiting Airservices Australia because of the work they were doing on aircraft automatically reporting their own GPS positions to air traffic instead of air traffic having to use expensive radars. It seemed to me that they were currently world leaders in using the technology.

At the airport, after checking in, I went up to the NWIA business class lounge. I consulted my watch for the umpteenth time; it was still too early to call the UK offices. On an impulse I called my home but nobody picked up to answer and my answering machine cut in.

"Mandy, if you're listening, why don't you pick up the phone?"

To my surprise she did.

"Because I don't want to talk to you. I suppose you're off to St Antony?"

"How did you know?"

"Because John Southern has been trying to contact you."

"Mandy, I need to talk to you."

"Why? You obviously got my letter."

"I think we should discuss things."

"Well we can never discuss anything these days as you are rarely at home."

"I'll call you when I'm in St Antony."

"You needn't bother. I'm thinking of taking a long holiday."

"You can start at St Antony."

"That would be my last port of call."

"Good. I'll wait for you to arrive." There was an indescribably rude noise and the phone went dead.

I felt very frustrated but there was nothing more I could do. The ABC news announced that there was a total of sixty nine survivors from the ditching with some on the danger list out of 245 passengers and crew. I felt very sad as I finally retired for the night.

DAY 3

The NWIA flight left on time and I managed to get some sleep on the 14 hour flight. At Los Angeles it was still 1600 on Thursday. I had plenty of time to change to the American Airlines terminal and then go to their Admirals Club lounge to wait for the red eye special overnight flight to Miami. In the event the in-bound plane was forty five minutes late arriving so we left about an hour late. We arrived at 0730 on Friday leaving me only just enough time to change fingers at the terminal and catch the Caribbean Airlines flight to St Antony. I sent a text message to Frank and hoped for the best. I was almost past caring but was fairly confident I would never see my bag again.

Five hours later I finally arrived at St Antony and made my way to customs and immigration. It was slow going as both a British Airways and a Lufthansa flight had landed just ahead of us but it finally became my turn. The immigration officer looked at my passport and smiled.

"I see you've been here before, Mr Talbert. Haven't we met?"

We'd met alright but I wasn't going to enlighten him. He was the one who only gave me three days to stay last time I was out and we had had to argue like mad to get extra time.

"Possibly. I was in and out a lot when I was here last."

"I see you've put business as the purpose of your visit. What do you do?"

"I'm an insurance assessor and I've come here because of the accident to the Worldwide Airways aircraft the other night. Can you give me two weeks?"

He looked at me again and I think he must have remembered our previous meeting. He glanced again at my passport which showed that on the last occasion I had been given unlimited access, endorsed by the head of the immigration service. I was amused to see that when he gave me my passport back he had given me a month. I've always felt it is who you know that counts.

To my amazement my bag was waiting for me and customs let me through without my having to open it. Even better, Frank Westbourne was waiting for me which was a delightful surprise. He was still very thin but his hair was now completely grey though he still had a small dark moustache. It was impossible to miss him as he was wearing a suit and a tie while the rest of the world seemed to be on holiday.

"Frank, I thought we agreed you weren't going to meet me?"

"My friend, there was no way I was going to let you land here without welcoming you after all you did for us. Everything is fine now and the airline is finally making money."

"I'm so glad you're here. I feel like a limp rag. I've been travelling for over twenty four hours. How's the accident investigation? Have you heard anything?"

"Well the divers who are going to collect the crash recorders are now coming to-morrow according to the local TV and CNN. Because of the delay, *Island Flights* started advertising trips round the wreck which was a great success, but the police stopped them doing it to-day for some reason."

"Round the wreck? Is it that close to the surface? If it's that shallow surely they ought to have got the recorders off by now?"

"Actually, the radio says the aircraft is about 35 metres down but the water is so clear they reckon it is very easy to see."

"But why haven't they got the recorders off?"

"Not sure. Apparently the racking where the recorders were kept was badly bent and they need expert divers who have done this sort of work before. There were no people suitable in St Antony. By the way there's been a development; apparently Jacko," I was paying Frank my full attention, "you know the drug baron, was on board the aircraft with some of his henchmen. There's a rumour flying around that there may have been some shooting on board. The police at Barbados were already lined up to meet them."

"Where did you get that from?"

"The *Announcer* has it all over its front page to-day."

"It must be true then." I smiled with the disbelief showing on my face.

"It's alright for you to sneer but there seems to be a very close link between Ben Master's office and the newspaper. Anyway they may have got the information from Barbados."

Ben Masters was the chief of police who again I had got to know very well when an aircraft from Frank Westbourne's airline disappeared flying into Bermuda.

"By the way, I did manage to get Susan to book you a car with Hertz as well as making a reservation at the *New Anchorage*. Can you remember your way?" I nodded. "Well, when you've settled down give me a call, you must come over to the house for a meal. I know Pamela is looking forward to seeing you again."

We separated and I made my way to the Hertz car rental desk, completed the formalities, took a map and wheeled my bags to the rental car lot. I chose a small Honda four door and the guard at the exit gate marked up my rental form. The roads hadn't improved much but the hotel was still there, looking just as idyllic as ever with the palm trees swaying in the breeze and the blue sea breaking gently on the white sand. I parked in the front and checked in.

"Mr Talbert," the girl looked at the reservation "you've been here before?" I didn't argue "There is a message for you." She gave it to me. "Would you like a room overlooking the pool?"

"No thank you. I'm working this time." I was last time but it brought back memories I didn't really need. "On the second floor overlooking the sea would be great."

"Of course. No problem." She looked at her screen. "Room 237. Do you need a hand with your bag?" I shook my head, went to the elevator, went up a floor and found my room at the end of a long corridor. I put my bags on the bed, turned the air conditioning down to avoid freezing and sat down to read my message. It was from the AAIB inspector, Tom Falconbury, who was in charge of the investigation in St Antony. He suggested I called him when I got in. He was also staying in the *New Anchorage,* room 156, but he had had the forethought to give me his mobile number. I dialled his room without success so I tried his mobile. A voice answered and we introduced ourselves. Tom was in the bar and I said I would be right down after a shower.

I unpacked my bag, sorted my things out and then had a shower and a shave. With some clean clothes I almost felt human again. I moved my car close to my room and then wandered along to the bar. A medium height, slightly blonde haired man came towards me; he was wearing a white shirt and long blue trousers, no tie.

"Peter Talbert?" I nodded assent. "I thought I recognised you from the pictures I saw in the papers during the enquiry into the loss of the ITAC 798 aircraft at Heathrow."

We got four beers and went back to his table at the back of the bar area. Tom introduced me to Stanley Carstairs from AAIB, a specialist in dealing with crash recorders, and also to Ian Stapleton, the United States National Transportation Safety Board Accredited Representative.

"Tom, how long have you been out here?"

"Well the accident occurred on Tuesday night and we managed to get here late Wednesday night via Miami."

"That's pretty good going."

"I'm sure you know we have to keep an emergency bag ready to go anywhere at anytime, but it was a wild rush because I had to bring a locator beacon receiver for finding the crash recorders with me. We went out first thing the next morning to the place where the aircraft had ditched and we've heard both recorders loud and clear. We had two local scuba divers with us and they dived down but reported that the aircraft had broken into two pieces and the part where the recorders were located was badly damaged. They could see what they thought was the rack with the two recorders coloured bright orange, but the rack was distorted and they couldn't get the boxes out. I decided that we needed some divers who had been trained in sorting these problems out and we're expecting them to-morrow from Miami."

"Sounds as if you've got everything under control. Who did you use to take you out to the aircraft?"

"*Emerald Diving*. Why do you ask?"

"Just force of habit, Tom. Where are they based?"

"Cape Harbour. Bob warned me you were very inquisitive."

"That's not very polite! When did he tell you that?"

"Yesterday when he found out you were coming here representing the insurance company, but he also told me that you were always very helpful."

"When you do get the recorders, what happens then? I believe St Antony want you do the investigation out here."

"I know they do but there is no way we can analyse the recorders out here. Their Ministry of Transport man, Joseph Benjamin, appreciates this and so all he wants from me are regular reports on how we are getting on, to give to his boss at the Ministry. As I'm sure you know, we have very special equipment which cost a fortune installed in our labs at Aldershot, so we will send the recorders straight back to England for analysis."

"Won't that delay things?"

"Shouldn't do if the memory modules are not damaged. The lab at Farnborough is very quick at getting a preliminary look at the data. They have duplicate aircraft recorders for virtually every UK registered aircraft flying and they just take the memory modules from the crashed aircraft's recorder and plug it in to the recorder type matching the one in the aircraft and then download the data."

Ian Stapleton, who had been listening attentively, cut in. "Have you been to the AAIB labs at Aldershot, Peter?" I shook my head. "You really should go there. It's a fantastic set up. We have something similar in DC but not quite as up to date, I'm afraid."

"Ian, are ITAC here yet?"

"Yes. They decided to send out Harry Markov as their representative here and he's setting up office in the *Golden Beach*. I'm from our Seattle office and we travelled out together last night."

"Are you staying here?"

"No. I'm in the *Admiral Nelson*."

"Tom," I decided it was time to try to get AAIB's current view, "What do you think happened? Why did he have to ditch?"

"Pass. It's all very odd. For some reason they lost their satellite radio shortly after they started the single engine cruise and so there was no further direct contact at all with either air traffic or Worldwide. There were a couple of relayed messages to Miami using VHF and then the next thing that happened was that the aircraft contacted St Antony on the approach VHF channel and sent out a PAN call. The airport radar could see the aircraft from about fifty miles lining up with runway 24. However, the Captain warned they might have to ditch and he confirmed it with a MAYDAY call just before they actually did it."

"Did the Captain say what the problem was? Were there any clues?"

"Absolutely nothing apparently. I haven't heard the tape from the tower yet but that was what the controller told me. There was no explanation at all."

"The 831's controls are electrically driven, aren't they, not hydraulic like the older aircraft? Couldn't that be a reason for the accident?"

"The aircraft has been fully certificated and flown for millions of miles. I would have thought that that was most unlikely to have suddenly got a fault, though I suppose it could happen."

"Well, might it have been fuel starvation of some type, either directly to the engines or perhaps to the digital engine controllers? Didn't the British Airways Boeing 777 aircraft that had that miraculous escape landing at Heathrow have fuel problems?"

"Hang on a moment, Peter. It's not certain that that 777 crash was due to fuel, though it might well have been."

"Where was the cross feed cock on that aircraft?"

"I've no idea. It wasn't my accident. Clearly, in our case the Captain knew there was a problem of some type but we don't know what it was due to. With the Heathrow accident remember, the pilots had no idea there was a problem until both the engines ran down."

"Well with Alpha Delta couldn't it have been simply a shortage of fuel?"

"But they should have had plenty of fuel. Losing an engine wouldn't make the fuel reserve critical. It's a complete mystery."

"Well there's got to be a reason. Why did the Captain say they might have to ditch?"

"Peter, it's got to be either fuel or control problems. The sooner we see and hear the crash recorder data the better. To be honest, we're wasting our time speculating when we'll know for sure in a couple of days."

"What's happened to the passengers? Have you spoken to any of them?"

"Yes, I managed to find two. For the record there were actually 245 people on the aircraft when it took off and there are 69 survivors though a lot of them are still in the two hospitals or in nursing homes of some type or another, but 30 people have been released. They are all trying to get away from here as fast as they can but I think it is taking time for them to get organised and of course most of them have no passports, money or clothes. Desperate. Worldwide seems to be doing a good job looking after them, though it is clearly very difficult. The two I saw were in the Central Hotel in Cape Harbour. Apparently the captain only made one announcement saying that he had had to shut down an engine. Then about ten minutes later the oxygen masks dropped down. The two I spoke to seemed a bit confused about what happened after that but shortly before they ditched the cabin attendants went round telling them all to put their lifejackets on and prepare for ditching."

"Frank Westbourne, the boss of West Atlantic Airways, told me that there's some story going around about Jacko, Jackson Turner, the drug baron, being on the aircraft and that some fighting may have taken place."

"Yes, the situation is complicated because one of the survivors I spoke to saw what he thought was a fight in the business class and heard some bangs. There was something odd happening up front but we don't know what. Of course, the only survivors we have are from the back of the aircraft so there is no one we can ask. Apparently the Barbados Government didn't want Jacko or any of his mob in Barbados and it was their intention somehow to send them elsewhere if they could. When they learnt that the aircraft was going to come here they must have been over the moon. Barbados immigration told the St Antony police and immigration here immediately about Jacko when they heard that the aircraft was going there."

"Did Jacko or any of his cronies survive?"

"Good question. Immigration have given Ben Masters a list of survivors and Ben is getting the UK Police to check them all. Jackson was flying business class and Ben tells me the other three were in the back."

"How many crew survived?"

"Only the two cabin attendants in the rear of the aircraft."

"Have you managed to speak to either of them yet?"

"No. One is still in hospital and the other is recovering somewhere and doesn't want to talk to anyone."

"How about the ditching itself? What did the survivors say?"

"Well there was a small shudder first, then an enormous bang and the passengers were thrown onto their straps in the brace position. The floor started to rotate down and they could see the water rapidly filling the front of the aircraft." Tom half choked as he was telling me the story. "It sounded terrible, Peter. They both told me they could hear screaming as the aircraft sank. The two cabin attendants opened the rear doors very quickly by all accounts and they shouted for everybody to get out. Apparently one of the girls had a megaphone. One of the survivors I spoke to was right at the back and the cabin attendant helped her out of the door but she just missed the life raft and fell into the water. Luckily for her she remembered to inflate her life jacket and grab hold of one of the ropes on the side of the life raft. She thought she was going to die but two passengers managed to help her climb into the life raft."

"It sounds desperate."

"I haven't finished yet. The other person, a man," Tom looked at his notes "Charles Prentice, was ten rows further forward and his feet were already in the water. He scrambled upwards towards the doors by pulling himself up, grabbing seat after seat, with the water creeping up behind him. Of course there were all the other passengers trying to get out at the same time so it was a nightmare journey to the rear door. By the time he reached the door he reckoned he was about the last to leave. People were fighting like mad to get out. Let's face it, Peter. It was survival of the fittest. There was very little of the cabin not under water, the floor seemed nearly vertical. The cabin attendant helped him clamber over the side of the door and he had to almost climb up to get into the life raft."

"What about the cabin attendants?"

"Prentice said the girl on his side followed him. Probably because there was nothing more she could do. As I told you there's one girl in hospital and I'm trying to find out about the other. It sounds, listening to Prentice, as if she might be alright. Flares were fired from his raft almost immediately so it was probably her. Later he saw flares from somewhere near which were almost certainly from the other life raft."

Tom stopped, looking shattered. He still had his notes out.

"Do you know the name of the other passenger you spoke to?"

"Margaret Proudfoot."

"Do you know where they are?"

"Worldwide has put all the rescued passengers up in hotels."

"What are Worldwide doing?"

"Well David Winston, their deputy chief pilot, came out Wednesday with two engineers on the same plane as we did and we've been keeping him in the picture."

"Does he have any ideas of what might have happened?"

"If he has, he hasn't told me. He is particularly puzzled as he was on twenty four stand-by duty all day Tuesday and got the initial call from Alpha Delta about the engine problem."

"What are their engineers here for?"

"I think in case I need any help. One is mechanical and the other is an electronics specialist."

"I would have thought they would be wasting their time at this stage. You could always telephone the airline at Gatwick if you had a problem."

"I know. But Winston seemed very keen to help."

"Have you heard the Worldwide operations tape?"

"They don't record all their communications with the aircraft. They don't need to as far as we're concerned as we can hear the conversations on the cockpit voice recorder. In fact I think they do record some of their in-flight communication but I'm not sure."

"Who's looking after the UK end for you?"

"Graham Prince. He's checking with Worldwide about the recording. I must also talk to him and find out if the aircraft was fully serviceable or was carrying any Acceptable Deferred Defects, ADDs."

I looked at my watch. It was only seven but I was beginning to feel very tired.

"Tom, you've been very helpful. Obviously the key thing is to get hold of the recorders. Maybe when you've got them and know a bit more we could talk again."

I went up to my room and slept right through until six o'clock. I looked out at the ocean; it was still dark and all was quiet and peaceful. I could hear the sea breaking gently on the shore but I could not put out of my mind the horrifying vision of Alpha Delta diving into the sea four nights earlier. The sooner we found out what had happened the better.

DAY 4

Dawn was just breaking as I went down to the pool. The attendant had just come on duty and gave me a bright blue towel, though it was difficult to tell the colour under the artificial light. I was first there and though the sun had not yet appeared the temperature was definitely very warm by UK standards.

After six lengths I was struggling due to lack of fitness. I put on a short sleeved shirt and no tie but before going down I called Air Traffic to find out if Tim Hardcastle was going to be in.

"Hold on, Mr Talbert, I'll call his home on our direct line." I could hear some discussion and then the person I was talking to in the tower came back on. "Absolutely no problem. He's looking forward to seeing you again. He suggests 0930."

No sooner had I put my phone down than it rang again.

"Peter, David Winston here. I'm deputy chief pilot for Worldwide. Charles Hendrick, my boss, told me you are acting for Hull Claims. I thought we should meet up."

"I'd like that very much. How about for a drink about six this evening? Where are you staying?

"Why don't we meet at the Astoria Beach? Let me give you my mobile number in case anything crops up."

We agreed, but I got the impression he would have liked to meet earlier. I made a note of his number, collected my computer and some papers and had a quick breakfast overlooking the Caribbean. Then I went to the car and managed to find my way back to the airport and park. In the terminal I went to the information desk and asked for Air Traffic. Tim in fact answered the phone and explained that with the strict security existing at the airport he would have to send someone over to the information desk to collect me.

I wandered over to the news stand and was examining the local papers to choose one for the best coverage when I was tapped on the shoulder.

"Hello Mr Talbert, fancy meeting you here."

I turned round and my heart didn't exactly sink but it was in two minds. Cindy Smart, the clever hard working local girl from the St Antony *Announcer* put out her hand. I didn't fancy her or meeting her for that matter but there was no choice. We greeted

43

each other and then she bent forward and picked up a copy of her paper.

"I suppose you're here because of the aircraft ditching." She didn't wait for an answer but showed me the front page of the *Announcer,* full of all the news they could manage to find with pictures of some of the passengers who were not in hospital with their stories of the rescue. She thrust the paper into my hand. "You've got to read it. I've been working on nothing else. Apparently there might even have been some shooting on the aircraft." She stopped and looked at me. "It's my lucky day. Can I have an interview?"

"Cindy, I don't know if this is your lucky day or not but I've got an appointment right now." I looked over at the information desk and could see a girl who looked as if she was looking for me.

Cindy followed my gaze. "Alright you're going to Air Traffic. How about later on? Where are you staying? At the *New Anchorage* again? I'll call you."

I gave no affirmatives to any of her questions but that didn't stop her. Perhaps that was why she was so good. There was no malice, just keenness in her voice. "Don't you think you'd better pay for the paper?" was my parting shot as I went over to a girl who confirmed that she was from Air Traffic. Her name was Lorna and she was Tim Hardcastle's secretary.

Lorna took me to one of the airside exit gates of the terminal and punched some numbers into a keypad. We were then able to walk about 100 yards to the tower by which time I was getting quite warm despite my lightweight clothes. Lorna punched some more numbers in to get into the building and it felt like going into an ice box. I never could get used to the hot/cold of the air conditioned tropical latitudes.

We went up one floor in the elevator and I noticed that St Antony air traffic still followed the British tradition of calling it the first floor unlike my hotel. She showed me straight in to Tim's office.

"It's great to see you again, Peter. I've never forgotten that you really saved my life last time you were out." [4]

---

[4] *The Final Flight* by the same author

"Tim, its good to see you as well. Particularly good as I'm trying to find out why on earth Alpha Delta ditched on Tuesday night."

"Well there's not a lot I can help you with. It was all very sudden. Would you like to hear the tape?"

"You bet. Have you still got it?"

"Yes and no. I learnt something from you. I got an instant copy made so that when the AAIB asked me for the tape I was ready for them."

"Do they know you have a copy? Not that it matters but they often like to keep everything as secret as possible in the early stages of an investigation."

"I wasn't there when they collected the tape and I have no idea what they said to my deputy, Larry James. I didn't tell any of the controllers that I had asked our chief technician to copy the tape and I told Vincent on pain of being sacked to keep his mouth shut."

I couldn't help smiling. Tim really had learnt from my last visit, when there was a lot of dissembling going on. We went back down to the ground floor into the engineering area and Tim introduced me to Vincent Greene and asked him to play the tape. We grabbed a couple of chairs, I got my notepad out and then Vincent started the recording straightaway.

"PAN PAN, PAN PAN , PAN PAN, Nelson approach, this is Worldwide 442. We are 85 miles to the north east of you at Flight Level 190. Making straight in approach runway 24. We may have to ditch. Advise when you have us on radar."

"Worldwide 442 this is Nelson approach. Your PAN call copied. Will advise radar contact. Cleared for straight in approach runway 24."

There was about five minutes quiet before the next exchange.

"Worldwide 442 we see you on our radar at 50 miles approaching centre line. You are cleared for a straight in approach on runway 24. Surface wind 150 degrees five knots."

"442, Roger. We have started our descent."

There was a pause.

"Nelson Approach, this is Air France 591 maintaining 15,000 ft."

"Air France 591 we have an emergency and the airfield is closed. What will be your intentions?"

"591 to Nelson Approach, we would like to go to Antigua."

"Diversion to Antigua approved. Maintain heading and altitude change to Antigua approach and stand by for clearance."

"Nelson, 591 copied. What is the problem? Can we help?"

"591 negative. Please change to Antigua approach for clearance. They are expecting you, cleared down to 8,000 ft."

A very brief pause and then

"Lufthansa 334 to Nelson Approach, on frequency request ILS clearance for 24."

"Lufthansa 334 please clear this frequency and call Antigua. We have an emergency and the airport is closed."

"Lufthansa 334 roger."

"MAYDAY, MAYDAY, MAYDAY, Worldwide 442. we can't make the Nelson runway. We're going to have to ditch. Will be turning on to 150° just before ditching. Anticipate we will be ditching four miles short of St Antony, just to the south of centre line."

Tim turned to me "That's it, I'm afraid."

"Did you hear the first officer's voice. She was as calm as anything. Magnificent." I felt a lump in my throat. "What an example of how to behave. So terribly sad."

We were all very quiet for a bit. Tim broke the silence.

"They didn't say anything about why they were ditching and the controller quite rightly didn't like to ask."

"Yes, they obviously had their hands full flying the aircraft. Luckily the flight data recorders should show exactly what went wrong."

"They are diving for them to-day, aren't they?"

"That's what I understand from AAIB."

"I'm not sure whether they will be able to get the recorders. It may be too deep. Here, I'll show you."

We went up into Tim's office and he produced a half million scale aeronautical chart of St Antony and the surrounding islands. Tim had marked on the chart where the aircraft had ditched, to the left of the extended runway centre line about four miles off shore. I made a note of the latitude and longitude.

"It ditched quite close to the entrance of Paradise Harbour, Tim."

"Yes, about five miles. That's why the fishing boats could get the survivors back so quickly."

There was not much more I could do. I made a note of the exact time of the various transmissions and Lorna took me back to the terminal. I went over to the Worldwide check-in desks and asked to see the manager. The man at the counter took my card, disappeared and then returned accompanied by a short, rather plump lady who I guessed was brought up in the Caribbean. She was wearing a smart grey trouser suit, unlike the rest of the staff who were all dressed in uniform.

"Mr Talbert, my name is Becky Samuels. I'm the manager here. How can I help you? I see you are an insurance investigator."

I explained my connection with Worldwide.

"How are you managing? It must be a nightmare keeping track of the rescued passengers, getting them home when they are well enough and running the airline station here."

She nodded. "You're so right. What we've done is to get a specialist firm, *Caribbean Airline Services,* to do the majority of the work and look after everybody, including financial support. Presumably in the end your firm will pick up the tab?" I made no comment. "They're having to arrange clothes, accommodation and even give the survivors money until they can get themselves organised. It's costing us a bomb and I keep having to ring London to get more funds transferred out here."

"I don't know the arrangement with Hull Claims. I'm happy to say that it's not in my remit. My job is to look after Hull Claims' interests and to try to find out exactly what happened, then let other people decide liabilities."

"I thought our government had asked the UK for AAIB to find out what happened?"

"You're quite right. But I do like to understand the issues. In fact I am only a consultant; I don't work for Hull Claims directly." I decided it was time to ask the question. "Is it possible to talk to the cabin attendant who is recovering out of hospital? I need to try to understand why the aircraft ditched."

"Peter," she did not waste time on ceremony, "you seem very well informed. In fact Helen Partridge is in what we call the Caribbean Airlines house, recovering. She told me just now that she was thinking of taking a cab and going down to Cape Harbour. I think she is getting a bit fed up staying by herself in the Caribbean Airlines place and needs to do some shopping. On the other hand she doesn't want to talk to anyone about the ditching."

"Becky, if you give me the address of the place I'll drive over now and take her down instead of a taxi. Do you think she'd like that?"

Becky smiled. "You really want to see her don't you?"

"We must find out exactly what happened. It must never happen again. Why don't you call her?"

She didn't say anything, indicated for me stay where I was and went back into the offices behind the counter. She was soon back.

"You're in luck. I told her you were a nice man and she agreed with your suggestion." I smiled my thanks. "I said you would be there within the hour." She gave me her card and written on the back was the address of the Caribbean Airlines house. As I turned to leave she added "You do know that no-one has spoken to her yet, not even your accident investigation people?"

I grinned. "I'll try to get over it."

Looking at the address Becky had given me, the house was between the airport and Cape Harbour, and I managed to find it with the aid of the rental map and my car satellite navigator. The building was a large, old colonial type of house, superbly located looking out to sea and surrounded by palm trees. It had been owned by British West Indian Airlines and Caribbean Airlines had taken it over when they bought BWIA. The drive up to the house was about two hundred yards long and needed some maintenance but the building itself looked in good condition, always difficult to do with tropical heat continually bearing down on the structure interspersed with tropical downpours and the occasional near miss from a hurricane. I parked in the front and as I got out of the car a woman appeared through the front door wearing a well worn polo shirt and ill fitting trousers. She had brown hair which looked as if it also could do with some maintenance.

"Peter Talbert?" I nodded "I'm Helen Partridge. Excuse the get up. It's all borrowed and I feel a wreck." I opened the car door for her and looked at her. There was no make up, she looked as if she had been crying and she also looked very tired. I guessed she was in her mid to late twenties. "What would you like to do? Do you want to go anywhere special?"

She hesitated. "I don't know. I keep on thinking of all the things I need to do but feel completely shattered so I don't do anything."

"Tell you what. I'll take you for a coffee at the hotel overlooking Paradise Harbour and then you can decide what to do next."

"But I look an absolute wreck."

"Come off it." I couldn't help smiling. "You're fine. I've seen a lot worse."

Helen looked as if she was considering a riposte which I felt was a good sign and then she slowly nodded agreement. We went to the aptly named *Paradise Hotel* on the hill above the harbour and sat down on the veranda, in the shade looking down at the yachts below.

We were the only people on the veranda and I could see Helen beginning to relax in the atmosphere. The hibiscus and bougainvillea bushes were magnificent, rippling in the breeze. The buzz of insects could be clearly heard but somehow the noise didn't obtrude but provided a perfect background ambiance.

"Peter, this is great. Just what I wanted. Such a relief to get away from the Caribbean Airlines house though they have been incredibly kind." She was obviously still in shock. "I can't believe what happened and somehow I don't really want to think about it. I just want to forget. I'm alive and I left all those people behind. I feel terrible. But everybody wants to talk to me about it and I know it's got to be done. I expect you're just the same?"

"Helen. Sometime yes, but it can wait." I paused. "Do you have a family? You've spoken to them?" She nodded. "They must have been relieved."

"I only managed a brief word with my parents yesterday. Worldwide had phoned them to say I was alright. I really ought to talk to them again. And I ought to talk to my boy friend." I must have looked surprised. "I know I should have done but somehow I didn't feel like it."

I offered her my phone. "You can do it now if you like."

She shook her head. "Thanks but I can't remember his number. It was on my phone and of course I never looked at it when I dialled." She stopped. "I keep thinking of all those people who were drowned. And of the people fighting their way out of the door as

49

the aircraft sank. It was a nightmare; I keep hoping I'm going to wake up."

"You did a wonderful job getting as many out as you did. You had so little time."

She looked at me more carefully. "Yes, you're right there. We didn't have any time. It all seemed so sudden." She was reliving the escape.

I prompted her. "You certainly must have done a superb job remembering all your drills. How on earth did you manage to get the survival gear and the locator beacon out?" She nodded. "Amazing. And as for the flares. What can I say? Your training really worked."

"Yes, I was lucky. I did remember where to find things. Just as well as the aircraft started to sink and pull the life raft down. Horrifying."

"Lucky? Hardly lucky, brilliant. What did you do? You couldn't have had a knife?"

She looked at me. "There was one fixed to the raft by the rope." Helen smiled at me. "By the way it wasn't quite as easy to fire the flares as it was sitting in the pool British Airways use for training --- not that we fired them there but we went through the motions. Thank God the boat arrived very quickly. Just as well, as there were some people in the water holding on to the life raft rope and the water didn't feel all that warm. They looked terrible, as if they couldn't last much longer." I could see she was remembering the whole thing again and I tried to lead the conversation away but she was still reliving every moment. "There didn't seem to be any room in our life raft and anyway they weren't strong enough to climb up and we weren't strong enough to pull them in. Some of them looked as if they were about to let go. Still I managed to make them all inflate their life vests."

I pushed the coffee she had ordered and some sugar towards her. She added a generous helping of sugar to her cup and took a long drink. I thought she ought to stop talking for a bit. "Come on, let's go and look down at the harbour."

She put the cup down with a sigh and I pulled her up. As I hoped, she started to enjoy the walk in the sunshine; certainly the weather was not unpleasantly warm and there was a cooling onshore breeze which made a rustling in the palm trees and waves in the bougainvillea bushes. She kept staring down at the harbour.

"Can we get down to the boats? It looks an amazing spot. I used to sail in the Channel quite a bit from Portsmouth."

"I'd have thought that you would have been there already."

"I've only been with Worldwide about six months and up to now I always seem to have ended up in LA or Barbados."

I paid for our coffee and we drove down to the harbour and marina below. It was an incredible place, rather like English Harbour in Antigua, though perhaps not quite as well protected, so that a breakwater had been built to narrow the opening to the Ocean. The harbour had a hill about seven hundred feet high behind it on the shore side and looking up from the car park we could only just see the roof of the *Paradise Hotel*. There were fishing boats on one side of the basin with supporting trucks and sheds surrounded by the characteristic smell of fish, even though every effort was clearly being made to keep the place spotless, judging by some modern sweepers and vacuum cleaners that I could see parked in the corner of the large car park. On the other side of the harbour a very modern marina had been constructed with excellent facilities on the shore adjacent to the floating arms going out to the boats. Both sides of the harbour seemed very busy with trucks coming in and out all the time.

Helen wandered over to the marina from the car park and looked at the boats. We couldn't go on to the fingers to get really close as there was a locked protected gate for each one with its own keypad.

"How about lunch? When did you last have a decent meal?" Her eyes suddenly lit up.

"Great idea. I haven't eaten a decent meal for days. By the time we had fed the passengers the food on the aircraft was cold and the microwave heaters had stopped working so we only grazed on the plane. After that I haven't fancied much at all."

We wandered over to the restaurant near the yacht marina and sat outside, under an umbrella. There was less wind than at the hotel so it felt quite warm but not warm enough to go inside and freeze in air conditioned discomfort. She ordered fried fish and french fries and I chose a shrimp salad.

Some of the motor yachts were enormous and there was a range of sailing yachts from about a hundred feet down to some day boats. There was not a lot of activity with the boats in the marina but a few small fishing boats were going in and out followed by the gulls, the boats' engines thumping away disturbing the peace, though their noise was matched by quite a lot of engine noise coming from the larger yachts in the marina using their air conditioning.

"There seemed to be so little time." I knew she was back thinking of the crash. "The aircraft hit the water gently at first and then there was a terrific bang and jerk to the right. It then started to tilt downwards, quite slowly at first. I opened my door and the slideraft inflated and fell onto the water which was some way below the door sill at first. I operated the manual inflation as well, just to be on the safe side. Linda had the megaphone and yelled for everybody to get out and after a pause there was a stampede to get out of the door. Linda had opened the door on her side as well." She hesitated. Presumably Linda was the other flight attendant at the back of the aircraft on the other side. "It was terrible. I helped everybody as much as I could but the floor was gradually getting steeper, the life raft was starting to block the door as the water level rose and looking behind me I could see the forward cabins were full of water. Then water started coming over the side of the door which was almost horizontal by now. I was having to stand on the side of the rear seat. I think Linda's side was a bit lower than mine but I didn't have time to look at what was happening."

I encouraged her to eat something and she stopped talking. In fact, once she started eating she did quite well and so I didn't say anything but ordered some ice cream.

"I never eat ice cream, though it does look rather good. Ah well." I couldn't hear the rest as the pineapple and ginger flavoured ice cream clearly met with her approbation.

From our position we could see the fishing boats quite clearly since they were not crowded on top of themselves as were the yachts in the marina. There were some buildings on the fishing quay, presumably to support the working boats. One of the buildings had *Discover St Antony* in large letters above the doorway, presumably a firm operating a boat or boats to take people round the island. Finally, there was a diving school, *Dark*

Blue Diving, though I only discovered the name later when walking by.

"Helen, would you mind if I left you here for a bit while I go over to the fishing boats?"

She looked at me and I could see her thinking. "Yes, I would mind very much. I want to come too."

Despite the ordeal she had been through and her earlier diffidence, she now exuded determination in her whole body and so together we walked over to the working side of the harbour. We passed *Dark Blue Diving* which seemed to be completely closed and went to what appeared to be just an office marked *St Antony Fish Sales.* There was a tough looking guy behind the counter, with a pointed black beard and half glasses, almost certainly from St Antony. I decided there was no point in dissembling; apart from anything else, having Helen with me could mean she might be recognised, though there was probably a world of difference between the way she looked now and the way she must have looked in the life raft.

"I'm involved with the terrible accident on Tuesday night. I'd like to talk to any of the captains who were out that night and rescued the passengers."

The guy looked me up and down, clearly deciding what to say, and then seeing Helen probably changed his mind. "You're the third guy who has come down asking that." He looked at a large blue 40 ft fishing boat moored alongside the quay. "Joel Davis might be able to help you, over there."

We wandered over to the boat and saw a man cleaning the decks. "Is Joel Davis there?"

"He certainly is. I seem to be the most popular guy in St Antony at the moment. Welcome aboard," and the speaker emerged from down below. As he said this a voice called out "Joel, don't let anyone else on board." Joel was about six feet tall and looked every inch a fisherman. He was clearly a local but one got the feeling he would have been that colour even if he had been a white Caucasian. He was wearing a multicoloured short sleeved shirt and blue shorts. His left hand had the second and third fingers cut short, probably a result of some fishing incident in the past. He looked at me.

"Don't mean to be rude but I've got someone with me at the moment." He looked at Helen, took another look, creased his brow and then recognition had clearly taken place. He smiled in a protective way. "Hello again. We've met before I think. How are you? Feeling better?" He came over to us, climbed ashore, ignored me and held out his hand to Helen. "I'm Joel. You did a great job, really great, looking after all those people."

Helen looked embarrassed but very pleased. "So did you. Thank goodness you came so quickly. I thought we were going to lose a lot of the passengers. You saved all our lives." Joel didn't look embarrassed but was clearly delighted.

While we were talking a man I recognised as a policeman working for Ben Masters, the chief of police, appeared from below where Joel had come from. He looked at me and half smiled. "I might have known it."

Joel looked at me and then Rick. "Do you know this guy?"

"Oh yes. He was involved in that aircraft disappearance a few years ago. Why don't you let them on board, Joel, and we'd better start all over again?"

Joel helped us climb aboard and then he led the way down into a small saloon area with a couple of benches and we all sat down. Rick turned to me.

"Joel had just started to tell me about the rescue Tuesday night. Mind you I've seen him on television telling the story. I feel I almost know it off by heart. He's our local hero."

"He deserves to be." Helen chipped in. "He saved all our lives, on our raft anyway."

"Rick," I joined in. "I want to hear the story as well. You know as well as I do that the TV people either miss out the most important bits or get it all wrong. Anyway that's my experience."

Joel started to tell his story. The coastguard had called him and warned him that an aircraft might be going to ditch and told him roughly where it was going to be. By chance his boat, *Blue Lobster*, was only about four miles away and so Joel immediately started pulling in the nets. Just as the nets were clear he saw what he thought was an aircraft flying very low in a south easterly direction with a light on. There was no engine noise. The aircraft hit the water though they could not see what happened exactly as they were too far away. They heard a loud noise a few seconds later and nothing else. Joel pointed the boat at the area where he thought the aircraft had crashed and opened the throttles fully so they were going about ten knots, the best they could do. After a few minutes they saw a red flare go up and they steered towards it. As they did so, another flare went up from a different direction but he decided not to alter course. Luckily, a second flare went up from the place where the first flare had been seen. Then a light flashed ahead. They could see what they took to be a life raft, quite close. He shone his searchlight towards the raft and saw things which he realised were people in the water. He throttled the boat right back and told his look-out to use his pole to point which way the boat had to go to avoid running over anyone in the water.

He had two other crewmen on his boat. He told them to put some steps down the side of the boat and then he manoeuvred as best he could to try to pull the people out of the water. It was very difficult work because they were very heavy, completely water sodden and almost exhausted though they had only been in the water for a little while. After they had rescued two women, a man and a teenager they came alongside the raft. He managed after a struggle to lash the life raft alongside with the help of a woman, he now knew to be Helen, who seemed be in charge. She helped secure the ropes to some canvas grab handles. It was particularly difficult as there were still people in the water holding on to the raft and they had to be moved sideways. They put some steps down and one of his crew got into the life raft and helped the people up into the trawler. Then his crew managed to get more people out of the water. He had about forty people by this time and he realised looking at the state of the passengers that if he didn't get them back to St Antony very quickly some of them might die.

He told the Coastguard station at Cape Harbour of the situation and estimated he would be back in Paradise Harbour within the hour. They told him another fishing boat, *Red Snapper,* was approaching what was presumably another life raft. He checked as best he could that there were no other survivors close by, noted his GPS position, undid the raft and headed for the shore but leaving the raft behind in case there were more survivors he had not found. They got as many blankets and towels as they could find from the boat's store but they weren't nearly enough. There wasn't room for all the survivors down below and Helen had organised the worst cases to have the blankets and go inside. The rest she had tried to huddle together to keep warm. Joel radioed the coastguards to make sure that all the ambulances had blankets and towels and warm clothing and he asked for extra blankets, clothing and towels for the boat as he intended to go out and continue searching. Finally, after what seemed like hours, he entered the harbour and came alongside. He was relieved to see two ambulances and two coaches on the quay with people to assist. They helped the survivors ashore though, by now, many had to be carried off being too weak to walk. The last survivor to leave was Helen who was completely exhausted.

Helen had been listening to Joel's account without saying a word. She was white and I suggested she had better go back to the Caribbean Airlines house, but she just shook her head. Maybe hearing it all was a form of therapy, I certainly didn't know.

Joel carried on telling his story. They had managed to find some blankets, towels and clothes for him and he took the boat back to where the raft had been, using the GPS position he had taken. It hadn't moved far and he cruised around using his floodlight. He found three floating bodies and one survivor, a young lad who somehow had kept himself alive and was clinging to the life raft. They dried the lad off, gave him some dry clothes and a hot sweet drink. He was obviously going to be alright so Joel stayed out all night until it began to get light but only managed to find one more body. The coastguard told him two helicopters were going to start searching and he came home.

Rick had had his recorder on all the time Joel was telling his story and there wasn't a lot more to be said. I asked Joel whether he saw anything of the aircraft at all after it had hit the water but he said not. I thought it was time to take Helen away but very understandably she wouldn't leave without thanking Joel again and again but he kept on saying, "The survivors should be thanking you, my dear. Without you they would all be dead. You ought to get a medal," expressing a sentiment with which I totally agreed. Helen made sure she knew how to contact Joel and we left.

"But what about *Red Snapper*?" I began to realise how determined Helen was and how lucky it was for the people who were rescued.

"Don't you think you've done enough for to-day?" but she shook her head. Luckily Rick was listening to our conversation.

"Eldine Roach was the skipper of *Red Snapper* and he's away in Barbados having a rest. May be back in a day or so."

I said good bye to Rick who was driving a plain blue Toyota Corolla and we got into our car. I turned the air conditioning full on and looked at Helen. "Where now?"

"Can you bear it? I need some clothes, underwear that sort of thing. If you could take me to Cape Harbour I could take a taxi back."

"We'll see. Have you any money?" a thought occurred to me. "Have you cancelled your cards?"

"Worldwide have given me quite a bit of cash. I reckon no-one is going to get at my cards so I only need replacements. I must talk to the providers sometime, but it is too difficult to do anything useful from here with the incredibly long queuing times to get anyone to answer and then the convoluted procedures people have to use when you have actually managed to get someone to talk to. BT must be making a fortune."

"Put cancellation near the top of the list when you get home, my dear. People don't have to have your cards to use them. Meanwhile I'll let you use my cards if you need to. You look like the sort of girl who will pay me back."

"You're very kind." She squeezed my arm. "Hopefully I won't have to take you up on the offer."

We arrived in Cape Harbour but though I had driven around the town some years ago I had never had to do any serious shopping. I stopped in a parking area and called Frank. Susan answered the phone and I asked for her advice for a name and location of a suitable store. WalMart was her recommendation and she told me how to find it, luckily on the edge of the town. Helen went off by herself and we agreed to meet in the coffee shop. I went to the news stand, bought a selection of papers and then went to order a coffee.

Cindy Smart had done herself proud. Her article was all over the front of the *Announcer* and then on to pages four and five. Quite a few of the passengers had caught flights the previous night to the UK and the USA. One or two had even carried on with the holidays they had booked. There were still twenty people in the hospital; the rest had left the hospitals and nursing homes to recover in hotels before carrying on with their travels or going home. Two of the twenty were on the critical list and were giving great cause for concern.

Cindy had clearly spoken to Joel since there was an account of his rescue efforts. Also she had spoken to the coastguards in Cape Harbour and the helicopter pilot. The article finished by speculating on the reason for the ditching. Jackson Turner had been on the aircraft with some of his associates and some of the passengers thought they had heard shots in the business class cabin. Jackson had not survived. She said that the most likely cause was that the shooting had damaged the aircraft since it had depressurised. I wasn't convinced by Cindy's article and particularly her remarks on the shooting, since it was most unlikely that any guns could have been brought on board the aircraft. Obviously more investigation was required. The crash recorders were clearly key.

My phone rang, it was Ben Masters. He must have kept my number on his phone list, but then he was a policeman.

"Where are you? Everybody's been looking for you."

"Why? What's the problem?"

"Rick tells me that you've got the cabin stewardess that saved all those lives with you and people have been looking for her, a Miss Partridge."

"Why? I still don't see the problem."

"Peter, you obviously haven't changed since we met last. It does not seem to have occurred to you that the accident investigators need to talk to her and you seem to have stolen a march on them. They couldn't find her in the Caribbean Airlines place and they called the police. Luckily Rick knew where she was because you were together in the harbour."

"Ben, have you told the accident people where Ms Partridge is?"

"I don't know where she is. I take it you do?"

"She is doing some shopping to get some much needed clothes. She is still very disturbed and I don't think she wants to be formally interrogated. It was pure luck she agreed to come with me."

"Peter, I know all about your luck. You're a smart operator and understand what makes people tick, and talk for that matter. What am I going to tell the accident people?"

"Tell them that you've found her, safe and sound, and she hopes to be back with Caribbean Airlines in an hour. Of course, I can't answer for her and she is still shopping. She may not want to go back and speak to people."

"Alright, I'll go along with what you want. I shouldn't really but you seem to know what you're doing."

"And Ben."

"Yes, Peter?"

"It's great to talk to you again."

Helen finally emerged from WalMart after about an hour. I only just recognised here. She was clearly already wearing some of the clothes she had bought and they did her no harm. I hadn't realised that not only was she a very determined lady but she could also be a very attractive one. She was carrying a smart, medium size red roll bag which would probably just fit in the overhead locker. I got out of the car to meet her.

"You look really great."

She looked at me thoughtfully. "Thank you. Am I glad that's over."

"You haven't bought a lot."

"You try carrying this bag. Hope nobody weighs it when I go on board."

I took the bag and I had to agree with her as I put it in the car. She certainly had bought some stuff.

"Told you it weighed a ton. Now I must arrange my flight. I'm not a hundred per cent but I'm sure I'm fit enough to travel."

"Well, one if not both of us is in trouble here in St Antony. I gather you haven't spoken to the accident people yet and they want to talk to you. I don't think they anticipated that you would be going out already and with a strange man."

"Well, I think you're rather nice and very understanding." She smiled in a rather relaxing way and kissed me on the cheek. "I don't want to sit down and talk to a lot of strangers about what happened."

"Well Helen, I'm afraid you're going to have to sometime. Certainly before you go back to the UK. Put yourself in their position. They are desperate to find out why the aircraft crashed."

"It's obvious why it crashed. The aircraft ditched and modern aircraft don't ditch safely. I think the right engine went into the water first and that was why the aircraft swerved to the right. Something must have broken near the flight deck and the water poured in. The fuselage went down and it was just a mad scramble to get out at the back as the aircraft sank."

"But Helen, why did the aircraft ditch?"

"I don't know. The right engine had to be shut down because it had some sort of fault and the aircraft depressurised. Apparently the rules permit us to plan to fly for hours on one engine."

"Nearly three and half hours actually."

"Well that seems far too long. I know these aircraft and engines are very reliable but I was much happier when I was flying in 747's with four engines."

I didn't feel it was the right time to enter into a discussion of safety, risks and certification rules but I found her comments very interesting.

"Well, Helen, what are we going to do now? Shall I take you back?"

"I know you're right and that sometime I will have to talk to all those people but if you take me back now they will expect me talk to them straightaway. Can't we go to a pub or hotel for a bit and then you can take me home when it will be too late for anybody to talk to me?"

"Fine by me, but you'll need to talk to Becky Samuels and tell her how you feel and what you are prepared to do. You can book your flight at the same time," I added to sweeten the pill. "and you might ask how your colleague is and where she is staying." I got out Becky's card and some paper and a pen. "Shall I dial the number?"

Helen looked at me. "You're quite an operator aren't you? What else do you want to know? OK, dial it."

The phone rang and I gave it to Helen with the pen and paper and got out of the car. I didn't want her to feel I was crowding her but I wanted to talk to the other cabin attendant. I wandered up and down the street keeping an occasional eye on her to see when she had finished. The call took a long time but finally it was over.

"She says the *Admiral Nelson* is a good place for a meal."

I tried not to look surprised. I was already beginning to realise that Helen was a force to be reckoned with, which of course was why she had saved so many passengers.

"Fine. Have you made the reservation?"

She suddenly grinned. "I'm beginning to like you. No. I've left something for you to do. She became serious. "You know, I would like to talk to Linda and see how she is."

"Where is it?"

"I'm not sure. It's in the town here somewhere. Here's the address Becky gave me." We both looked at the address. "Would you like to go to the Skyways nursing home to talk to Linda as well?"

"Helen, if you mean would I like to take you over to the nursing home to talk to her, I'd be delighted."

She smiled and passed the paper over to me with the address, her flight details back to UK on Sunday night, and Tom Falconbury's name with 10 o'clock next to it. I called Ben again but Jearl Sobers, his secretary, answered. Ben was out. I explained that Helen had spoken to Worldwide and that an appointment had been made for ten o'clock in the morning with the accident investigators. I asked Jearl to call Tom Falconbury and ask him to call Becky to get confirmation of the timing. Before ringing off I got Jearl to tell me where the nursing home was.

Helen had been listening and I realised she wasn't missing anything. I gave her back the paper and after some false moves I managed to find the place. A modern building in a new part of the town.

"You don't want me around, Helen. Off you go and I'll book a table for seven."

Helen looked grateful and went into the building. I phoned the *Astoria Reef* Hotel and asked for Winston. It took sometime before they found him in the bar. I made my apologies without telling him I had found a better offer.

"Peter, We really must try and make it to-morrow as I'm going back Monday."

"Shouldn't be a problem. The difficulty I had to-day won't happen again. Shall we keep to the same arrangement? I'll come round to you at about 1800." Understandably, he didn't sound too pleased at my not dropping everything and rushing round to see him.

To my surprise Helen came out after about ten minutes. "Linda says she doesn't mind your coming in. She's ready for some new faces."

We went into the building and took an elevator to the first floor. Like all elevators that have to take wheel chairs it seemed to take for ever. Helen led the way into a room with just one bed and Linda Sutcliffe was sitting in a chair. Her arm was in a sling, she had dressings all down the side of her face and her left leg had clearly been damaged. She was dark skinned, probably afro-asian. I got the impression she was a bit older than Helen.

"You've been in the wars. How do you feel?"

"I'm getting better, thank you, Peter, but it is all rather uncomfortable."

"You did a wonderful job getting all those people out and onto the life raft."

She nodded but clearly didn't like the memory. "It was terrible. People were fighting to get out. That's how my leg got fractured. I just managed to get out and into the life raft." She shuddered. "There were people drowning as the plane sank."

"But you managed to take the survival kit with you in spite of the chaos. That couldn't have been easy with your leg broken."

"How did you know?"

"I didn't," Helen looked at me curiously. "But there were some flares and they are not kept in the escape rafts."

"You're right. But I'd never have managed it by myself with my leg broken. Luckily there was a man who helped me into the raft and I told him where to look in the pack and what to do."

"In the dark?"

"There was a torch in the pack. Just as well as we had to cut the life raft adrift from the plane as it sank! He was very good. He seemed to take charge helping people. I must have passed out after a bit and then came to as the fishing boat arrived. It was agonising, but there were people who were much worse off than me."

"Do you know what happened to the man who helped you?"

"His name was Michael. That's all I know."

"Was he hurt at all?"

"I don't think so but I don't know."

We talked for a little bit longer but Linda was obviously getting tired. We made our farewells and went back to the car and I drove out to the *Admiral Nelson* which was clearly marked on my map. It turned out to be a typical tourist hotel overlooking the sea. We sat down at the outside bar and Helen just wanted a tropical fruit juice. I ordered a small beer and we looked at the water and the setting sun.

"It's difficult to believe what really happened. I know it sounds trite but it's like a bad dream. This island setting is so wonderful and what happened so awful."

"Well, you're going back to-morrow night and you can try to sort things out. It may not be all that easy trying to decide what to do next."

"Has anybody told you you're nice?"

"My girl friend used to."

"Used to?"

"Helen, I don't think I should burden you with my love life."

She looked at me carefully.

"I'm not at all sure about that."

I began to think that it was just as well she was going back to-morrow night. Maybe she was thinking the same thing.

"I really ought to call my boy friend, Peter. I haven't spoken to him yet."

"Won't your parents have told him."

"I expect so. Somehow I feel I want to think about everything."

I didn't comment. If I had been her Peter, I would have been on the phone to St Antony and it wouldn't have taken me long to find out how to talk to Helen. It occurred to me that either consciously or unconsciously Helen had come to the same conclusion and wasn't too impressed by her Peter's determination. The more I saw of Helen the more impressed I was with her. She was a lovely girl and obviously a born doer. Any partner of hers would have to be on his toes. We went in to the restaurant and had a meal though neither of us ate very much.

"You know I'm very curious about something. Do you mind if I ask you a question?"

"Try me."

"Well after the announcement of the engine failure and then the depressurisation, what were you told?"

Helen thought for a little before replying. "Very little. Gretchen, the girl looking after the whole of the economy section told me we were descending after the masks dropped down but she wasn't clear why. She said there was a lot of activity in the business section. After about half an hour we started climbing again. Then Gretchen came back later and said we might have to ditch."

"Didn't you wonder what was going on?"

"Of course, but we had our hands full looking after the passengers and trying to reassure them. As you can imagine they didn't know what was happening and they were very frightened."

I decided I had probed enough. I took her straight back to the Caribbean Airlines house. I gave her my card, told her I was in the *New Anchorage* and she gave me the airline phone number in case I wanted to contact her.

"Thank you Peter for looking after me to-day. You've been really kind, preparing me for returning to the real world."

"It's been a great pleasure. You know you did a wonderful job." She didn't say anything. "By the way, look out for Cindy Smart of the *Announcer*. She may try to interview you. She's OK but she's very persistent. Oh, and one final thing, it's not important, but there's no need for the accident people you're seeing to-morrow to know that I've already spoken to you."

Helen grinned and gave me a hug and then suddenly a kiss, which I think lasted a bit longer than either of us had intended. She drew back, squeezed my hand and I watched her disappear into the building. Back at the hotel there was a message from Tom Falconbury. I called him but there was no reply. I left a message and then managed to find him in the bar. He looked worried.

"Tom, what's wrong?"

"Is it that obvious? The divers could only find the flight data crash recorder. The cockpit voice crash recorder was missing."

"Missing?"

"Yes, missing. It looked as if someone had been there first."

"But you heard signals from both recorders?"

"Yes we did on Thursday. To-day the divers were briefed where to look and they found the FDR straight away but not the CVR. So we turned on the locator beacon receiver and we couldn't hear anything."

"Tom, I'm not clear how the recorders are arranged on the ITAC 831s. Do they have a separate cockpit voice recorder and flight data recorder or do they both record everything?"

"The two recorders are identical on the 831 but they are not 'dual redundant' at the moment. They actually record different parameters. It is easier to think of them by their function, that is a flight data recorder, FDR, and a cockpit voice recorder, CVR, though of course the cockpit voice recorder has a lot of other data on it, mainly stuff the pilots use like navigation information. Oh and by the way, there is a Quick Access Recorder on the flight deck which is used by maintenance for checking key parameters and whether there had been any unusual happenings like a heavy landing, not that the QAR will be any use after being underwater I imagine."

"What are you going to do about the missing recorder?"

"Good question. I don't know what to do. It's quite outside our experience. I've told the chief of police, not that he can do anything. Actually he was very sympathetic and asked me a lot of details."

I didn't make a comment but I wasn't surprised Ben showed some interest.

"Peter, how did you get on to-day?"

I told him of my visit to air traffic and also about the trip to the harbour. However there seemed no need to mention that Helen had been with me.

"Oh, I didn't realise that Air Traffic had a copy of the tape. Not that it matters. It didn't help much."

I nodded agreement. "When are you going to be able to get any details off the recorder and analyse the records?"

"Well the FDR is going back to our lab in Aldershot to-night on a BA aircraft. They should be able to look at it to-morrow providing water hasn't got into the memory module. Possibly I'll know something to-morrow night. Not that I'm permitted to tell you too much at this stage as you know. Of course whether they'll look at the memory module first thing, to-morrow morning their time, depends on what priority they give the job in the labs and whether the memory module is dry and can be plugged straight into a duplicate recorder."

"Don't you need the help of ITAC?"

"Not at this stage. We may need their help later when we've got the data and then we pass the relevant bits on to them, for analysis of performance for example. Of course we need the help of the flight data recorder manufacturer to know how the data is stored."

"Sounds very efficient. Are you going to lift the aircraft?"

"Depends what we find from the recorder. It would be very expensive and though your firm will have to pay for the hull, I can't see them paying for lifting the aircraft. St Antony won't want to find the money and neither will the UK Government." He paused. "I had hoped to talk to the cabin attendant to-day who was uninjured but apparently she had gone on walkabout. Luckily she checked in with the airline later on and we're seeing her to-morrow."

We chatted a bit and then I went up to my room.

DAY 5

I got up, had a swim and sat down to breakfast overlooking the sea. If there had to be an accident, then there could be worse places than St Antony with its cloudless sky, light sea breezes and bright blue water. But somehow I knew it was all too good to be true. To my horror Brian Matthews of the Daily Mail appeared in his long sleeved thick shirt, floppy collar undone, baggy grey trousers and plimsolls, not an appetising site to behold at any time but particularly at breakfast.

"Peter, great to see you again! Thought you'd be here. You can tell me everything that's going on. I haven't had time to get briefed. The Editor read about the ditching and decided to send me out. May I join you."

He sat down, uninvited. I tried hard to be charitable. Perhaps his newspaper found Matthews useful but for me he was just a nuisance, interfering if he could and shouting his mouth off. He also always seemed to be in the bar which made it difficult to talk to anyone else there privately.

"Brian, I know no more than you do." My papaya arrived together with my coffee and I ostentatiously surrounded myself with the *Announcer* which luckily was still a broadsheet.

"I see Cindy says one of the recorders has been lost." Brian was reading the back of the paper. "She's a smart girl, that one."

I lowered the paper briefly. "She's your best bet, Brian, if you want to know what's going on. Why don't you go and see her in Cape Harbour?"

"Peter, judging by last time, you were the only one who knew what was going on. And you didn't tell me."

"This is entirely different, Brian. I'm out here because of the ditching."

"Don't give me that. The cockpit voice recorder is missing. And Jacko and his team were in the aircraft. The whole thing looks very suspicious if you ask me."

"I'm sure that's just a coincidence," and I certainly wasn't proposing to ask him.

Brian didn't look convinced. I raised the paper again, gulped my coffee, and then went up to my room to read Cindy's piece. She said that Jacko wasn't on the survivors list. There was not much more I could do for the moment until the first data had been extracted from the flight data recorder so I decided to go back to Paradise Harbour. I sat down at the same place where I had been with Helen. The tables were full of people from the yachts but I managed to find a table at the front so that I could watch the commercial side of the harbour with a small set of viewing glasses I always carried with me. There was some activity at the fishing quay and at *Discover St Antony* but again *Dark Blue Diving* seemed to be closed.

"Found out anything yet?" Rick was in plain clothes carrying a cup of coffee. He sat down at my table as if our meeting had been arranged. He looked at my glasses. "Are those one of ours?"

"I'm not sure if they're the ones Ben lent me or my own. They're very similar. However, I think they must be Ben's as nothing seems to be happening." I grinned at Rick. "What brings you down here?"

"I was going to ask you that."

"That's easy. I can't do much until the data starts coming off the recorder and this is a super spot."

"Maybe. But it's also a good place to watch what's going on, Mr Talbert."

"Have you bugged my car as you did last time?"

"Certainly not. We know you'd find out if we did."

"Well you found me."

"Wrong. I came down here I suspect for the same reason as you did. We were curious to know what *Dark Blue Diving* was up to."

"Why on earth would I want to watch *Dark Blue Diving?*"

"You tell me, Peter."

"Well I did wonder why they always seemed to be closed. You don't make much money that way and I expect Paradise Harbour charge quite a bit of rent."

I didn't tell Rick that I was curious as to why Tom Falconbury decided to use *Emerald Diving* from Cape Harbour to help get the recorders and not *Dark Blue Diving*, who were much much closer. Presumably *Dark Blue Diving* weren't interested for some reason which was strange since it would probably be a big contract. I made a note to ask Tom sometime.

"Rick, what's special about *Dark Blue?*"

"I told you. We like to know what people are up to."

I made no comment but I did wonder why Rick found *Dark Blue Diving* so interesting. I made a resolve to come back later or possibly first thing in the morning. We started chatting and then my phone rang. I looked at it and saw it was Tom Falconbury.

"Where are you? We've got a problem."

For some reason, perhaps because I didn't like sharing too much information until I knew it's value, I decided not to discuss anything in front of Rick. "I'll come over. Where are you?"

"I'm with ITAC at the *Golden Beach*.

I made my excuses, thinking that Ben had a good man in Rick since he looked as if he didn't have the slightest interest in knowing who had called me. Of course he could follow me but I wasn't that important. However, I was sure he had come to Paradise Harbour for a definite reason. Perhaps they had another reason to suspect *Dark Blue Diving* which I knew nothing about.

I started the engine to get cool and got my map out. I hadn't been to the *Golden Beach* before and found it was on the western shore in the middle of White Coral Bay. It took me about forty minutes to get there, even with the help of my GPS, as the roads were narrow going across the island and there seemed to be trucks everywhere going about their business. When I finally got there I could see that the hotel was considerably bigger than the *New Anchorage* with three floors and some extra buildings not attached to the hotel. I managed to find a slot near the main entrance and got out of the cool car into the warm sunshine to walk across into the cold hotel. To my surprise I didn't have to go searching for the ITAC rooms as Tom Falconbury was obviously waiting for me and we sat down at the side of the lobby.

"Tom, you look concerned."

"I am very concerned and I wanted to discuss the problem with someone. I know I can trust you not to talk to anyone. Bob Furness tells me the trouble with you is that you won't talk." I ignored his little dig. "Incredibly the lab has had a quick look at the data in the memory module and there is something wrong with it."

"I thought there was a warning to the pilots if there was something wrong with the recorder to prevent the aircraft flying."

"'Fraid not. There isn't any warning if the crash recorders are not working but in fact that isn't the problem. The labs told me that there was the routine data at the beginning of the flight but shortly after the engine failed the data started to go wrong. Almost immediately most of the data was missing. I've never heard anything like it."

"Well what data have they got? Surely there must be enough to help."

"You would think so but fate seems to be against us. Apparently the navigation lateral position data is there but not much else."

"Altitude, speed?"

"No they're missing. We've got some fuel tank readings but not even all of them."

"But that's impossible isn't it? The whole point of having crash recorders is to ensure that they store all the data immaculately."

"Absolutely. But they tell me the data just isn't there. It's solid state of course so nothing actually moves. The timer has its own battery in the recorder so they could see when the aircraft crashed but there was no useful data as far as they could see." Tom consulted his notes. "Oh, I've misled you. All the right engine readings were there which was a fat lot of help. Nothing from the left engine, nothing."

"That's terrible. What are you going to do? Any news of the Cockpit Voice Recorder?"

"No. Ben Masters says he is doing what he can but so far without success."

"Won't this mean you'll definitely have to try to raise the aircraft to see if there was any structural damage?"

"Yes, Peter. I think we'll have to try to get the aircraft on dry land but it's going to cost a lot of money. However, to-morrow I'm getting the divers to have a really serious look for the CVR. It's got to be there somewhere."

"What about the bodies in the wreckage? Shouldn't you be getting them up?"

"Yes, you're right. But we also want to see how the bodies are located in the wreckage. I've spoken to Bob and he is approaching the UK Minister of Transport to get authorisation for spending the money to lift the aircraft. Unfortunately it's Sunday to-day which always delays things but hopefully we'll get agreement to-morrow. Of course, even if permission is given it will take Fugro several days to find a suitable salvage vessel with a remote observation vehicle and the necessary lifting gear and divers." Tom could see I needed more explanation. "We use Fugro to advise us and they are trying to locate a vessel with an ROV right now. There may be one free in Wilmington. Problem is that most of these vessels are on contract to the US Navy and agreement has to be obtained to release one. If we can get an ROV soon then we may start trying to get the bodies up once we have seen them and located them in the wreckage."

"What do ITAC suggest. They must be very worried."

"Yes they certainly are. The problem is being discussed in Seattle. The firm can't afford to have an unexplained accident like this. Boeing have made a spectacular sales comeback and ITAC are fighting for their life, trying to get orders against them and Airbus."

"Tom, I shouldn't say this but I've always been worried about the length of time an aircraft is allowed to fly on one engine over the sea, and at night. This accident underlines the problem."

"I know what you mean but statistically it's difficult to argue with the certification people. The FAA and the EASA agree that it's quite OK to fly for hours at a time on one engine and if the Europeans agree with the FAA then it must be OK." Tom looked at me. "Anyway that's not my problem. At this stage all I have to do is to find out why the aircraft ditched."

"You must be joking, Tom. You'll have a lot more to do than that. This is the first ditching at night. Surely you'll have to examine exactly what happened when the aircraft hit the water, and how the escape provisions worked. After all only about a quarter of the people survived."

"You're quite right but that's secondary at the moment. Anyway, the brutal fact is that whatever we recommend in our accident findings, this sort of happening is so rare that any loss of life from a ditching, particularly at night, will be accepted."

There was not much more to be said. Tom had been an inspector long enough to know that quite a few of the recommendations in accident reports never got embodied in the certification requirements. The brutal fact was that, as I had reminded John Southern, safety cost money and if an aircraft was 'safe enough' to meet the probability requirements for accidents then nobody was prepared to make the aircraft 'safer' and hence more expensive to buy and operate.

The decisions were now being made in London and possibly in Seattle, certainly not in St Antony. Tom went back to the ITAC facility in the hotel and I drove back to the *New Anchorage*. It was time I got ready to see David Winston. After a shower and a quick change I set off to find the *Astoria Reef*. Reception had pointed it out to me on their map and in fact it was not far from the *Golden Beach*.

As I asked for Captain Winston in the lobby a very tall man, about 6ft 3 in, with brown wavy hair got up from a chair, put his newspaper down and came over. He introduced himself and we decided to talk at the outside bar. I asked for iced tea and David got a beer.

"Well Peter, how are things going? Any ideas?"

"None at all at the moment. I gather you were on duty when the aircraft left so I was hoping you might know something. What happened after the ditching was horrendous but probably predictable. What is inexplicable is why the aircraft had to ditch."

"You're absolutely right. The first I knew that anything was wrong on the flight was when Jim called me to tell me about the engine. But we lost contact shortly afterwards."

"Was the aircraft fully serviceable when it left?"

"I think so. It had just come off maintenance so it should have been perfect. Anyway Peter, we'll soon know when the crash recorders are decoded."

"Presumably you've heard the cockpit voice recorder has disappeared." David look puzzled. "And has Tom Falconbury told you there is no data on the other recorder?"

David look amazed. "No data. How can that be? And where's the other recorder?"

"No idea. It was there on Thursday but it had disappeared by Saturday. Didn't you know?"

"Falconbury never told me anything about the missing recorder, or about the problem on the recorder they have for that matter. When did they find that out?"

"This afternoon."

"That's terrible." He paused. "That cockpit voice recorder must be there somewhere. It's not as if anyone would take it. If I were in charge I would get the divers to have a good search."

"You must be clairvoyant, David. That's just what Tom is going to do."

"None of this will help your firm. They are going to have to pay up whatever happens."

"I tend to agree with you though I haven't read the contract. By the way it's not my firm. They've just engaged me as a consultant to represent their interests. Have you spoken to any of the survivors?"

He looked uncomfortable. "No. I discussed it with the girl at the airport, Rebecca something. We agreed it would not help. I'm sure they don't want to talk about it more than they have to." I was not convinced about that but decided it was better not to challenge David. I certainly wanted to talk to some of them. It was my first job in the morning.

He went on. "This Jacko business could be very relevant. Perhaps the aircraft was damaged or they made the Captain do something which went wrong. However, we'll have to have data to find out. Unless some of Jacko's team survived to tell the story."

"David, that's the problem. Jacko was in business class I understand and as far as we know only the people in the very back of the aircraft escaped. Whether any of the survivors were with Jacko I don't know but I certainly would like to find out. The thing is a complete mess."

We went on to talk about other aviation matters. He asked me to stay for a meal but I wanted to collect my thoughts and plan the next few days. So much depended on the recorders it was going to be very difficult if vital data was missing. I drove back to the hotel and had a small meal in the coffee shop before going to bed.

DAY 6

In the morning I went back to the airport to talk to Becky Samuels.

"You caused a lot of trouble the other day going off with Helen. Where did you get to?"

"Oh we just wandered around. The police knew where we were."

"I gather you took my advice and ate in the *Admiral Nelson*."

"How did you know?"

"There's very few secrets on this island and don't you forget it." She added looking at me, "Anyway you didn't come here to chat me up."

"Do you have a passenger list I can have?"

"Of course I've got a list but I'm not sure I ought to give you a copy. Your job surely is to find out all about the accident. Not do a Cindy Smart and try to make a news story. What do you want to know?"

"Everything. In my experience everything is relevant. But never mind for the moment. I won't press you but I would like to talk to someone called Michael."

"Oh, the one that helped Linda in the boat?"

"Yes, I really need to talk to him."

"I've got bad news for you. He went back to UK on our flight last night. However I've got his details."

She went back in to her office and came out with a list which she gave me. "I think I can trust you to keep the information to yourself."

I looked at it. It was the complete passenger list showing survivors with their contact details and their current location dated yesterday. Michael Longshaw's address was in London in Earls Court and it showed that he had been staying in the *New Anchorage*, room 230 just down the corridor from my room, and had been booked for last night's flight. A near miss but that was life. Hopefully I would catch up with him sometime later.

I took another glance at the list. It showed several passengers staying in the *New Anchorage*. One, Jeremy Brock, was scheduled to go out this evening which told me he must be reasonably fit. I decided to try to talk to him. A young sounding voice answered the phone. He agreed to see me and I said I'd call him when I got to the hotel. I bought a newspaper and went out to my car.

We met in the hotel lobby. Jeremy was six feet tall, slim, about twenty years of age with dark brown hair. He was wearing a light blue long sleeved shirt and grey trousers; the clothes seemed very new which did not surprise me. I explained my position and we went outside and sat in the shade of an umbrella looking at the calm blue sea.

"I was coming out on holiday with a couple of friends. We were all sitting about twelve rows from the back near the front of our cabin. I was in the aisle seat. The cabin attendant told us we might have to ditch, to put on our life jackets but not to inflate them. The girls shouted out to brace and there was a bang and then the aircraft seemed to swerve to the right and start to pitch nose down. The cabin girls shouted to come back to the rear doors and I could see water rising in the cabin ahead as the aircraft pitched down. We left our seats and tried to get out but it meant clambering uphill with the water right behind us and rising fast." He hesitated visualising the scene. "It was a mad scramble with everybody trying to get out. My friends were right behind me when we started but we got separated. By the time I reached the door the water was up to my waist. The cabin attendant pushed me out and yelled at me to inflate my life jacket. The water felt very cold but somehow I managed to scramble up into the life raft. The plane disappeared shortly afterwards. Someone fired a couple of flares and later a fishing boat arrived."

"What happened to your friends?"

"I don't know. I think they must have drowned. They are not on the survivors list. I was incredibly lucky."

"Yes, Jeremy, you certainly were. Were you hurt at all?"

"My left arm was badly bruised and scarred a bit." He pulled up his sleeve and showed me his arm which was bandaged below the elbow and the top of his arm was covered with strapping. "I was in hospital for the first night and then they let me come here. I'm going back to-night."

I nodded. "What was the first part of the flight like? Anything unusual?"

"Well yes. The Captain announced after about four hours that he had had to shut an engine down. I think the aircraft started to descend. Then after a bit I could feel my ears popping and the oxygen masks dropped down from the roof. The girls came round making sure we had all put them on."

"What happened next?"

Jeremy thought for a bit. "I felt pressure on my ears as if we were getting ready to land. We must have descended some more."

"You seem very knowledgeable."

"My father was in the army and spent some time in Washington, DC. I went to boarding school in England and travelled to the States in the holidays." He carried on. "After what seemed some time we started to climb again as I could feel my ears popping and the cabin girls made sure we had our masks on. However we stayed at altitude then until we started to descend to land and then, shortly afterwards, we ditched."

"How long were you at the low altitude before you started to climb again?"

"I'm not sure. Not more than about three quarters of a hour, possibly less."

I digested what he was telling me. It all sounded very odd.

"Did they feed you at all?"

"We had a normal meal fairly soon after take-off but we did not get anything else. I think the girls were too busy dealing with problems. As you can imagine we were all very nervous and some of the passengers were hysterical."

"Anything else?"

"Not really. There seemed to be lot of activity at the front of the aircraft while we were low down but I couldn't really see. There were a lot of economy seats ahead of us in another section and of course the curtains were drawn shutting off the business section ahead of them. Sorry I can't be of more help."

"You've been a tremendous help. Hope you have a good flight back and your arm gets better."

We went back inside and Jeremy disappeared up to his room. I was left wondering about his story. It all seemed very clear but incomprehensible.

I picked up The *Announcer* which I had bought at the airport. Cindy had my full attention. She'd got hold of a story about one of Alpha Delta's survivors having been shot and killed in Cape Harbour. Another story which caught my eye was that a fishing boat had reported seeing lights underwater round the wreck of Alpha Delta.

I decided to go to the High Commission and sign in. I remembered that last time I was out in St Antony Lawrence Darling, the commercial attaché at the time, said that they liked people who were working on the island to make their presence known as it helped the local people in the Commission to know what was going on. In fact it was only part of the UK Caribbean High Commission based in Barbados but it was a bit larger than a normal consulate. The girl at the desk looked very surprised when I asked for the UK visitors book but she did manage to find it after searching through all the shelves. The last signature had only been ten days previously, so it shouldn't have been so hard to find. I entered my name and put Hull Claims Insurance as my firm. While I was looking through some of the glossy literature on a nearby display the girl called me over and gave me the phone.

"Peter Talbert?" I grunted an agreement. "I'm Reggie Pendlebury, I'm the senior service liaison officer out here and I also advise on aerospace matters. Anne has just phoned me because she thought I might be interested in meeting you. Are you involved with this terrible accident?"

I looked at Anne who smiled, looking rather pleased with herself.

"Yes, I'm afraid I am. I represent the firm that insured the hull."

"Rather you than me. That's going to cost your firm a bomb." He hesitated. "Have you got time for a coffee, or a sandwich?"

Reggie duly appeared. He was clean shaven, brown hair, short, probably five foot seven inches and about thirty five years of age. He led me to what turned out to be the Commission's restaurant. We both chose a local fish sandwich with some coffee and then we sat down overlooking the harbour entrance on our right and the Caribbean on our left. I reflected there must be worse overseas postings than St Antony.

"Tell me, how are thing going? The *Announcer* keeps finding stories. Did you see the one about a survivor being shot? And also about Jackson Turner being on the aircraft?"

I nodded. "I'm not the right person for you to ask how things are going. Our AAIB is out here helping St Antony find the cause of the accident and so I only know what they tell me."

"Well the *Announcer* says that one of the crash recorders has been lost and that the other one is not working properly. Is that true? It sounds a terrible state of affairs."

"So I understand, but they are getting a salvage vessel here with a remote observation vessel so maybe they will be able to find out why the aircraft had to ditch."

"But ditching an aircraft shouldn't kill everybody in it, should it?"

"Well everybody wasn't killed, but I know what you mean. The hard facts are that the chance of an aircraft having to ditch is so slight that it is accepted that it may not land cleanly, safely, whatever word you care to choose, on the water and that lives may be lost."

"That sounds very callous."

"Well safety is all a matter of probability as you know and, in fact, I believe this is the first night ditching of a two engined aircraft."

"Well let's hope there won't be another one. Poor Dorothy Henshaw in the consulate has been working incredibly hard looking after the British survivors. Money, passports, airline tickets, you name it."

"How does she check who people are?"

Reggie looked surprised. "That's a strange question. I don't know. I would have thought she would just ask them. I'll go and find out. She's over there having lunch."

Reggie got up and starting talking to a smartly dressed lady in her fifties who looked at me, I thought with some concern, as they were talking.

"She says it's no problem. She just checks against the passenger list from Worldwide."

We talked about the ditching a little bit more and then talked about other things, mostly aviation. I made my farewells, left my car in the car park and walked down to the harbour. After a bit I saw two rigid inflatable boats, RIBs, come in; they were painted bright orange and both had *Emerald Diving* painted in black letters on the sides. They tied up by the *Emerald Diving* building on the quay. There were about ten people in the boats and through my glasses I thought I recognised Tom Falconbury and Stanley Carstairs; however, I decided I would not try to talk to them but hopefully chat later in the hotel.

I made my way back to the High Commission, drove over to Paradise Harbour and then went over to the *Dark Blue Diving* facility. To my surprise the place was open. The man behind the counter looked as if he had been diving all his life. He was a local man, I guessed, dark as much from exposure as from skin colour. He was just under six foot and wearing a singlet so that his bulging muscles were clearly visible.

I explained I was staying locally and wanted to learn scuba diving again since I had only done it once before and it was a long time ago.

"No problem. We cater for all levels of experience. When did you want to start?"

"How about to-morrow morning?"

The man, Alvin Goddard, got a reservation book and looked at it. "I've got a beginner's class starting eight o'clock. Is that OK? It's a bit early but we like to finish before the sun is too hot."

"That's fine. Give me a card so that if anything prevents me coming I'll let you know." I paused. "There is one thing we haven't discussed. How much is it going to cost?"

"Well it depends on what you want to do. First of all you must buy your own basic gear, mask, snorkel, fins and you need some form of buoyancy. Luckily round here the water is warm and providing you are not going very deep you won't need a wet suit, but if you want to go down and stay in the water for a reasonable length of time you definitely will need one, though it will be much thinner than the one you would need in Europe. I would recommend you have one anyway as it gives protection from any jellyfish.

"With regard to the lessons we charge you basically by the hour."

"Can I buy the kit now?"

"'Fraid not. We'll do it in the morning. Here's a list of the gear you'll need with approximate prices. However, before you go we want you to fill in this form. It will save time in the morning. It's a bit long but we need to know if you have any medical history, next-of-kin, and all that sort of stuff."

I sat down on the only bench and started trying to answer all the questions. Until very recently I would have put Mandy as my next of kin but that no longer seemed appropriate so I put my father's name, though if anybody called him and told him I had passed away in the Caribbean doing scuba diving I did wonder whether he might immediately pass on as well.

Alvin left me filling in the form and I looked round the room. There were two internal doors, one seeming to go into a general office where Alvin had gone. The other was marked 'Managing Director' and the door was closed. When I had finished filling in the form I knocked on the door and a voice answered 'Come In'.

"Excuse me, I've finished filling in this form and I wondered where Alvin is?"

There was a man sitting at quite a large desk with a large flat panel computer display taking up a significant amount of room. He was smartly attired in casual clothes and a jacket was hanging up on a hook behind him. He looked very Anglo-Saxon and not at all brown, with a large amount of completely blonde hair. He either covered himself with sunscreen oil with an SPF rating of 100 or he never went outside and certainly never went diving.

"No worries. I'll find him."

The man left through another door and shortly afterwards Alvin reappeared behind the counter. I gave in my form, went back to the hotel and called Tom, who was in his room.

"How did you get on? I saw you come back in the RIBs."

"No luck at all. They did a really thorough search."

"What about the Quick Access Recorder?"

"The divers are going to try and get that out to-morrow. It needs some cutting work to get at it. Not that I'm expecting it to be much use."

"Have you had a chance to talk to Graham Prince?"

"Yes. I've just spoken to him. He's been to Swanwick and listened to the air traffic communication tapes. To be frank, they sounded as if they were no use at all."

"Was the aircraft carrying any defects?"

"Graham said he hasn't had a chance to look at the log yet but as a result of a conversation he had with the chief engineer, Stan Bellow, he thinks the aircraft was clean."

"The whole thing's a mystery. Are you having anything to eat?"

We agreed to meet in the bar and then eat in about an hour. I got ready to have a shower when the phone rang.

"Peter Talbert?" I nodded in spite of myself. "We haven't met. My name's Charles Hendrick. I'm Worldwide's Chief Pilot and I'm in my office at Gatwick.

"I was on holiday when this terrible accident occurred. Obviously I've rushed back and I'm trying to sort things out. David Winston of course handled everything and he tells me you've met up out there. Thank goodness he'll be back to-morrow. He's a real expert on the latest avionics.

"Peter, obviously your name is well known to me as a result of the Heathrow accident and that aircraft that disappeared near Bermuda. Clearly Hull Claims are completely liable but I know your reputation for finding out what happened regardless of who is to blame. We are desperate to find out what went wrong to avoid any possibility of a repeat."

"Charles, AAIB are sure to find out. You know it's not my job to second guess them. However I well understand your concern. Have you caught up with the fact that one of the crash recorders didn't work properly?"

"Yes, I know. It's a really worrying situation as I understand that the other crash recorder has disappeared. David mentioned that the divers are searching for it now."

"Well the bad news is that they still haven't found it. It must be down there somewhere. As you know this guy Jacko was on the aircraft with his entourage which is confusing the whole thing. I feel there's something going on we don't understand."

"Well, let me know straightaway if anything develops."

I rang off and went down to join Tom and Stan. It was a quiet meal. I think we were all feeling the strain.

DAY 7

I rang *Dark Blue Diving* at exactly eight o'clock. Alvin answered the phone and I apologised and said I could not make the course after all. He didn't sound too pleased and I rang off. However, I put on a bathing costume, long trousers, shirt with long sleeves, packed a small bag, drove to Paradise Harbour and parked the car. There was some activity at *Dark Blue Diving* and I kept as far away as I could from them as I made my way to the *Discover St Antony* building.

Inside the building was a very big room with pictures of boats all over the walls. There was a large chart of St Antony and a very detailed chart of Paradise Harbour itself. A girl came over to me and asked what I was looking for.

"Do you rent out boats?"

"We most certainly do," was the answer. "what were you looking for?"

"I'd like to rent a RIB for a couple of hours if the weather is going to be OK."

"Have you driven one before?"

I reassured the girl, Beverley, that I had had the necessary experience in England and we agreed a price. After completing all the necessary formalities she took me to the quayside and we walked along a pontoon to a RIB with large orange inflatable tubes. Beverley briefed me on the gear, life jacket, radio, charts and engine. I asked her to come with me while I tried the boat out, a request with which she clearly thoroughly approved. I started the engine, cast off the ropes and steered the boat slowly out of the harbour. Outside I opened the throttle fully and we leapt out of the water and probably reached 30 knots with spray streaming out on both sides. I throttled back a little and turned the boat back to the harbour. At five knots I nosed the boat back from where we had left and came alongside to drop the girl off. Beverley leapt out, pushed me off and I was on my way again.

Outside the harbour I pointed the boat towards the spot where Alpha Delta had ditched and as I came close I could see some yellow buoys marking an obstruction. I stopped the RIB by one of the buoys and the water was so clear I could just make out what I was pretty sure was the aircraft. I saw a boat with COASTGUARD on the side coming towards me so I decided to move away and go round the outside of all the yellow buoys. However, the boat turned round to meet me as I completed my circuit; it clearly wanted me to stop and so I went alongside. There were two people on board and the guy not driving the boat took all my details down and I was told in no uncertain terms to move off and keep away from the wreck. I drove the RIB around for a bit enjoying the thrill of its speed, before returning to the harbour and *Discover St Antony*. Beverley had seen me coming in and took the mooring lines.

"There's a message for you. Would you ring this number."

"How did anyone know I'm here?"

"Don't ask me." She grinned. "That's your problem. But the voice sounded very formal."

The penny dropped. I rang the number and Jearl answered. Would I like to come over and see Ben? I left Beverley and walked slowly back to the car, keeping well clear of *Dark Blue Diving*. For once there was room in the police parking lot and I went inside to the desk. A lady, who turned out to be Jearl, came down and escorted me up to Ben's office.

"Peter, we meet again!"

"Ben, good to see you but you must be very busy. How can I help you?"

"Do you want the straight answer?" He didn't wait for my reply. "Keep away. You're starting to interfere in things that don't concern you."

"I don't understand you."

"Why were you out at the spot where the aircraft crashed?"

"There's no law against me having a look, is there? I didn't go inside the buoys. Anyway it does concern me. You seem very sensitive."

"Too right I'm very sensitive. First of all they lose a crash recorder and then a survivor gets killed. And Jackson Turner was in the aircraft with a load of mobsters." I nodded. "The guy was absolutely ruthless. Your police must have been out of their minds letting him out and then not putting him away again for something else."

"I thought they did catch him and put him away."

"You're right, but he got parole and by all accounts started again."

"What happened then?"

"Nothing apparently. They couldn't make anything stick. And so they let him loose to run around the Caribbean."

"Ben, that's not fair. From what you've just told me they couldn't prevent him leaving. Anyway he wasn't a survivor. He was in business class."

"So I understand, but I won't be happy until they get the body up from the wreckage and we can get a positive identification."

"Ben, who was the guy that was killed?"

"That's one of your typical questions, Peter. Why does it matter to you who the guy was?"

"It could be relevant. We just don't know what happened on the aircraft. Is there something you haven't told me?"

Ben looked at me thoughtfully. "I'm sure you know the Caribbean islands are ideal places for drug runners." I nodded. I remembered Ben telling me that before, trying to explain why St Antony had spent so much time and money installing very sophisticated electronics on the island. "Well we were tipped off that Jackson Turner was on his way to Barbados on Alpha Delta and that he'd just managed to buy an almost priceless cut diamond in Amsterdam with money which we believe must have been laundered drug money."

"But surely there was nothing the UK police could have done, Ben? Anyway I thought there were rules about laundering money. The Dutch should have prevented it happening."

"Problem was that he had a lot of money in his Dutch bank account but apparently he could justify it from selling stocks and shares."

"How much did he pay for the diamond?"

"Not certain. Rumour is over $50m. It may be worth a lot more, depends on the colour."

"Well, these days that's not priceless and owning a diamond is not a crime." I looked at Ben. "Anyway, while this is all very interesting why are you concerned?"

"The plane is in shallow water. Would you believe at about eight o'clock on the Thursday night, two nights following the ditching, lights were seen in the water by the submerged aircraft?"

"How do you know?"

"A fishing boat saw the lights."

"Shouldn't you have a guard on the aircraft?"

"Ideally yes, but the Coastguard doesn't have enough boats and people to keep a twenty four hour watch. As you now know, the aircraft is well marked and we normally have a boat there during the day keeping people like you away. We believe that someone was looking for the diamond."

"What's your theory on the murdered survivor?"

"We don't have a theory. His name was Toby Makepeace. We are assuming he was tied up with Jacko but we don't know."

"Cindy said he was shot. Have you got a weapon or bullet?"

"Well Cindy was wrong for once. He had a broken neck. Done by an expert according to our doctor. Perhaps he'd already found the diamond."

"Unlikely. Ben, how on earth would you find a diamond in the water?" I thought for a moment. "Do you know the names of Jacko's people in the aircraft? How many there were?"

" You're at it again. What's it to you?"

"It might be relevant to the cause of the ditching."

"Maybe." He went on. "We're not sure who Jacko had with him and the UK police apparently weren't sure either, which personally I think seems very unlikely. However, they had heard through their sources that Jacko had at least two of his gang with him. So we got Worldwide in the UK to show the police the passenger list and they told us that Thomas Smith and Geoffrey Hudson were definitely his people."

"But not Makepeace?"

"They didn't mention him."

"Could you give me a picture of Jacko?"

"Why on earth do you want that? Are you going to volunteer to help in identifying the bodies?"

"If necessary."

Ben called Jearl and asked her to organise the photos.

"Can't do that, Mr Masters, the copying machine has run out of toner and the people we rent it from don't have any."

"That's crazy. Tell them we'll cancel the contract."

"I've done that already but they didn't seem too worried. Next week was their promise. I could probably find another one on the next floor but it's overloaded because ours is down."

Ben shrugged and gave up.

"Peter, we'll send some photos round when we can."

"Thanks a lot."

I went back to the hotel and did some office work on my computer. Tom rang at about five o'clock. "They've looked again. Still can't find the recorder."

"What about the Quick Access Recorder?"

"We've got it out but they are still deciding what to do to try to find out if it has any data. It has a PCMCIA laptop card but the sea water may have prevented the data being recoverable. We'll send it back to our people at Aldershot for a start and let them decide."

I put the phone down and reviewed the situation. The phone rang.

"Peter, it's Helen here."

"Where are you calling from?"

"The Caribbean Airlines house. I didn't get away after all. The flight was full and there were quite a few survivors needing seats. I volunteered to stay until the next flight to-morrow."

"You sound very brave. It must have been a great disappointment not getting home."

"Yes, it was. But I did manage to get my first good night's sleep. Anyway that wasn't why I called. What are you doing this evening?"

"Taking you out to dinner downtown."

"You obviously include mind reading in your accomplishments."

"Where are we going?"

"I haven't the faintest idea. See you at seven."

I went down to the lobby and asked the bell captain for a recommendation.

"Why don't you try to get in at Moby Dick's? It's a really local place and not frequented by tourists. Would you like me to ring them for you?"

I nodded, knowing full well that there was probably an arrangement between them. I indicated that the table was for two and the deal was struck for 7.15pm. The bell captain tried to explain where the place was situated. Back in my room I showered and changed and then drove round to the Caribbean Airlines house.

Helen appeared wearing a close fitting top with a very smart pair of trousers. I looked at her, showing appreciation.

"Well I had to do something to-day."

"With great success."

"You really know how to be nice."

She held my hand as we went out to the car and I helped her in. I started off towards Cape Harbour not feeling very confident navigationally.

"Where are we going?"

"I'm not sure. The place is called Moby Dick's."

"Oh, that's easy. I saw it to-day near Arthur's where I bought this outfit."

"You can navigate me then."

Between the instructions the bellman had given me, the GPS navigator and Helen saying 'this way' right at the last moment at each junction, we found the place. It didn't have its own car park and the building didn't look all that smart. I managed to find a parking space not too far down the street. Despite its unattractive appearance, the restaurant's menu outside seemed to cater for all tastes. We went in and immediately I recognised from the look of the tables, tablecloths, napkins, cutlery, glasses and the smells that perhaps everything was going to be alright. We were shown into a small room with only two other tables, both empty.

"Drinks?"

"Why not? I'll have a Chardonnay"

I ordered two glasses but the waiter tried to persuade me that it would be more sensible to have a bottle. Helen thought about it.

"For a variety of reasons I think we should stick to glasses."

"Like we might want to change to red?"

"I'll let you think of the reasons."

I confirmed our order for two glasses and, looking at her delightful figure, decided it might be better not to think of the reasons.

The menus arrived with the drinks. The wine tasted good. Helen chose an 8 oz filet steak medium well done and I followed suit though specifying 10 oz and medium rare.

The major domo appeared and showed a couple to one of the tables. They seemed to be locals and knew the waiter well. Our food arrived as the major domo appeared, yet again, this time with two men both very smartly dressed. However, one of them looked a bit shaky on his feet and had to be helped by the other.

"Have you photographed them yet"

"What do you mean?"

"Peter, you're a lovely man but I can see why you are a very successful investigator."

"I don't know what you mean."

"You've been very attentive and appreciative but you've also been staring at the other tables and watching them like hawks."

"I suppose it's just force of habit."

"Is that what upset your girl friend?"

I looked at Helen who stared back.

"I thought we'd agreed we weren't discussing my love life."

"I didn't agree. I like to know all about the men I'm dining with."

" .with whom I am dining."

"No, with whom I'm dining."

She grinned and I thought it was just as well she was staying in the Caribbean Airlines house. Particularly as she squeezed my hand, very softly.

"You didn't have a starter. Would you like a dessert?"

"The steak was super. I don't really need anything else."

"We're not talking of needs."

"Pity. I'll have a ginger ice cream then."

To my surprise they had ginger ice cream and so I had one too.

"They say that ginger is in the same category as oysters."

I looked at her.

"I'm not sure that at the moment either of us needs oysters, or ginger for that matter."

Helen grinned again. "I think you're right. I must be getting better. Perhaps it's just as well I'm going home to-morrow."

The coffee arrived which I thought was well timed. The other two tables were both having conversations in low voices so I could not hear what they were saying.

Helen kicked me under the table. "It's no good. They're talking too softly. Even a hearing aid won't help you. I'm nearer them than you are and I can't hear either. Anyway, why do you want to hear. You don't know any of the people on either table."

"I like to know what the locals are saying."

"If those two on the table nearest us are locals then my ... let me rephrase that, then I must be the Prime Minister and you are head of the Secret Service."

I couldn't help laughing. There was something about Helen that I found almost irresistible. She was clearly a brilliant leader, very intelligent, though I hadn't discovered anything about her education except that she was as sharp as a tack.

Luckily the two men left just before we did and the face of the one who was unsteady reminded me of Mike Mansell. The other man I had already recognised as the one behind the desk in *Dark Blue Diving* but I didn't feel it was necessary to share the information. Unfortunately, I was pretty confident he had recognised me.

We drove back to the Caribbean Airlines house very slowly and stopped outside. Helen leant over and kissed me but this time there was no doubt what we both wanted.

"Are you coming in?"

"It's a lovely idea but I don't think it would be sensible. We hardly know one another."

"It's that time in the month. I don't feel sensible."

"I agree. You feel absolutely gorgeous. However..."

Helen sat up. "You're quite right as usual. To be on the safe side don't get out of the car."

I watched Helen going into the house and wondered if I would ever have a straightforward accident investigation.

DAY 8

Tom called me after breakfast. "There's going to be a delay on getting the salvage ship out. Fugro can't get one for ten days."

"Fugro?"

"They're the people I told you about. They support us if we have work overseas, finding aircraft, getting crash recorders and lifting aircraft."

"What about the QAR?"

"Our lab people have recommended that the memory card goes back to the manufacturer for analysis. It is definitely mechanically broken from the impact quite apart from being immersed in sea water. However they might get something from the storage chip if it isn't completely broken."

"Can't your specialist divers help while you're waiting?"

"Yes, you're right. I'm going to get them to have a good look around. So far they've only concentrated on the recorders. There may be something else we've missed."

"Tom, in view of the delay I think I'll go back to the UK for a few days. I haven't been home for weeks."

I didn't think it would help if I told him I wanted to check on a few things. Unlike Tom, I could decide where and what I wanted to investigate since John Southern never questioned my movements.

I would have liked to use Lufthansa, avoiding Gatwick and going to Southampton but a quick look showed that there wasn't a flight that night. It wasn't worth going to Barbados to catch a Lufthansa flight and I knew there was a Worldwide flight that night because Helen was scheduled to go on it so I called the airline to see what was available. There was room in business class and I got myself a window seat at the back of the business class section.

I called John Southern and explained the situation. "I'd be wasting my time here and I need to visit the airline. I'm sure we're missing something. And I need to talk to AAIB and the flight data recorder people if they'll talk to me."

"You may be right but it's not going to help Hull Claims."

"Can't help it, John. We must find the truth if we can. By the way, can you let me have a copy of the agreement between you and Worldwide?"

"Be delighted. Don't forget to read the caveats we built in."

"Will I need a magnifying glass for the small print?"

"Don't think so. We're a very straightforward firm."

"Good. Perhaps you could send it by courier to my office in Farringdon Street. I'll probably try to get some sleep on the plane and go in there first before going home."

My next move was to call Charles Hendrick but he was out and I spoke to David Winston. He knew about the delay to the salvage vessel.

"Could I visit you on Friday?"

"Of course you can. What time suits you?"

"How about 10.00?"

There was a pause. "Oh, I'm sorry I won't be available. I'm unexpectedly scheduled for simulator training on Friday."

"Will Charles be there?"

"Not sure, I'll ring you back."

Feeling a bit frustrated I wondered whether to ring Bob at the AAIB or his inspector Graham Prince but decided all I would hear from him was what I knew already. However, I did ring Farringdon Street to warn them I was coming in.

I was in two minds what to do for the rest of the day but elected to have another ride in a RIB with *Discover St Antony*. In fact it wasn't the ride I really wanted, but to chat up Beverley since I reckoned she knew everything that was going on. I parked the car and kept well away from *Dark Blue Diving* where the class I didn't join were making there way onto a covered thirty foot launch towing a RIB. My luck was in as Beverley was behind the counter.

"Did Ben tell you off?"

"Is nothing secret on this island?"

"Absolutely not. We make our living by being fully informed."

"Is there a RIB free?"

"Depends where you're going. I got told off for not warning you to keep clear."

"I'm not really going anywhere. I've got a couple of hours to kill before I catch a flight…"

"…to UK."

"Is it that obvious?"

"Yes it is. Particularly as I've discovered you're an insurance investigator."

"I give up. OK then, why didn't I join the *Dark Blue* scuba diving course?"

I could see that I had touched a raw nerve. She looked at me and then her face showed understanding. "Oh, so that's why you've come in, isn't it?" I tried not to show that she'd guessed correctly. "You wanted me to tell you about them."

She turned her head and shouted "Vivian, can you look after the desk for half an hour."

Vivian duly appeared and we wandered over to the other side of the harbour and ordered some coffee.

"Beverley, tell me about *Dark Blue*, what does it do? In the modern vernacular, what's its mission?"

"It teaches scuba diving and, perhaps more important, it also organises diving parties. Why do you ask?"

"For the same reason that you looked concerned when I asked. From the moment I looked at it from this coffee shop I felt there wasn't enough activity. So I went there to sign on for a course. Who runs the place?"

"Philip Smithson. You should know, he's a Brit."

"Does he have blonde hair?"

"Oh yes. Lots of it. You've met him?"

I nodded. "How many people work there?"

"Not sure. I try not to notice. The only one I've met is Alvin Goddard. He seems to run all the courses. But there are others, at least two more. They seem to work early in the morning and after we finish." She looked at me. "I feel uncomfortable having them near me but to be honest they've not done anything wrong as far as I'm concerned."

"They don't seem to have a regular work pattern."

"You're right there. The last two days they've done virtually nothing."

"How many boats do they have?"

"That's a good question, Peter. I'm not sure. They've got a small and a large scuba diving boat but I've also seen quite a large motor boat as well, not to mention at least two RIBs. But they are not always in the harbour."

She looked at her watch. "I'd better get back. Do you really want to rent a RIB?"

"I think I'd better in case anyone has been watching."

"I hope you're joking. They're not that bad."

I didn't comment but I thought I'd better ask Ben about *Dark Blue Diving*, particularly as Rick had been down watching as well. Beverley sent me off in the RIB and this time I kept well clear of Alpha Delta. In fact I could see activity inside the buoys which I guessed were Tom's scuba divers. I also saw what I guessed to be the *Dark Blue Diving* training course with its boat and RIB. I was back in an hour, said goodbye to Beverley and went back to the hotel.

It didn't take me long to pack up and be on my way to the airport. I looked at the Arrivals board and saw to my relief that the Worldwide aircraft was on time. I checked in and waited in the business class lounge until the flight was called. We took-off on time and for once there was no-one next to me. I was just settling down, avoiding the evening meal, when I felt a tap on my shoulder.

"You didn't tell me you were going to be on the flight."

Helen was wearing some shapeless outfit which I assumed was her sleeping gear. "I didn't know. I only made my mind up this morning when I found that there was going to be a delay to the salvage vehicle."

I decided to be sociable even though I preferred to get as much sleep as possible. "How did you know I was here?"

"Becky told me. She thinks you've got a soft spot for me."

"That's an oxymoron."

She smiled. "You'd better be careful. I've got an honours degree in English Literature and I don't think that's an oxymoron. However I don't think we should discuss the matter any further."

"Alright then. You can sit and tell me where you got your degree. This seat appears to be free."

"It's a lovely idea but I've been upgraded and am travelling first class."

"I'm offended and it's not fair. They should upgrade the fare paying passengers."

"No, it doesn't work like that."

However I quickly changed my tone. "I apologise."

"What for?"

"For a moment I forgot. If I was Worldwide I'd put you first class all the time."

She leaned forward in a rather noticeable way and kissed me. "You're a love. In fact they're going to. They are making me a first class purser. Off you go to sleep. I expect you're stupid enough to be working to-morrow. I'm on holiday recovering"

I watched her go forward and then settled down. It occurred to me that I didn't actually know if I would be working in the morning as David Winston hadn't called me back

My breakfast arrived at the same time as Helen and I wasn't at all sure that I was ready for the double event. However, I pulled myself together rapidly as I detected a note of urgency in her voice.

"Peter, Worldwide have got some publicity stunt going. They've told the press what I did and they think it's newsworthy. They've told me to get off the plane first and they are taking me to the interview room. Normally I'm decisive but now I definitely don't know what to do."

"Helen. You're recovering from an unforgettable and terrible experience. I'm not at all surprised you're not sure. Do you want some advice?" She nodded. "Don't agree to do it. You're on sick leave anyway. The airline is getting criticised and it is affecting its business so it is trying to show that it did everything that could be done and you are the typical example of what their training produces. I don't blame them for that but they've jumped the gun and haven't thought things through."

"But I can't just say no?"

"Of course you can. They are very lucky to have such a loyal employee but they mustn't try to take advantage. They've probably asked some publicity firm to advise them without thinking of the human dimension. Just tell them the truth, and it is the truth Helen," I emphasised what I was saying, "you're not yet strong enough. Tell them you'll do it later, in a few days time." I changed my tone. "But only if you let me give you some more advice."

Helen started to look less strained. I pressed the call button and then when the steward appeared I asked that she might be served breakfast next to me and never mind the full first class treatment.

"You're not short of confidence are you? Sorry, I didn't mean to be rude. I really am grateful."

"Who told you all about this press conference?"

"The message came through the Captain and the Chief Steward."

"Well call him over and tell him that you are not going to do it as you don't feel up to it."

Helen's breakfast had arrived so she couldn't get up to impart the news but the Chief Steward came over and she told him sitting down.

"Helen," he obviously knew her, "they are going to be very unhappy if you don't agree."

"It is not a matter of disagreeing or agreeing. I am just not well enough. Please pass my decision on." As the steward left she added "Tell them in a few days it should be OK."

She turned to me. "OK?"

"Very good but then that's what I'm beginning to expect from you. But don't think for a moment that they've given up." She looked surprised. "They've got a fleet of reporters corralled up in some room at Gatwick, maybe a VIP enclosure, and their star performer isn't going to be there. They will try and get you to change your mind."

She studied my face carefully.

"OK, I'm beginning to understand you." She smiled. "If you're right, what's your plan? Well?"

"Make your way to the back of the aircraft. Do you know any of the cabin attendants?" She nodded. "Well explain the situation and sit there for landing. The flight isn't full, is it?"

"No, there are quite a few seats at the back but what then?"

"I'll wait for you and we'll leave together as a couple. Try to get some covering for your hair, it's always a give away."

"You seem to have thought of everything."

"And try to make sure the cabin attendants don't say 'Goodbye Helen' as we leave the plane."

Helen got up, returning shortly with her bags and sat down next to me. She had had to check her new red bag and she gave me the claim tag. About an hour out from landing she left me to look after her gear and went to the back of the aircraft. The Chief Steward came over, looking concerned.

"Do you know where she is? I'm beginning feel like the meat in the sandwich."

I shook my head and the steward was starting on his way to the rear to look when the Captain summoned him on the Public Address system. By this time we were descending for landing and the cabin attendants were fully occupied going through the formalities.

There were no delays and the aircraft landed at Gatwick on time. We taxied to the North Terminal onto a finger and as the doors were opened there was an immediate announcement asking

Helen Partridge to contact the ground staff on disembarking as there was an important message for her.

About halfway through disembarkation Helen appeared with a baseball cap with 'Mets' written on it, which did nothing for her but did cover her hair. She had put on her jacket so that the collar covered her face almost completely. We left together carrying our bags and as we filed up the aisle she kept on talking to me about the flight, the English weather, then started asking me where I lived and what I was going to do to-day. I responded trying to find out where she lived, not that she told me, or what she was going to do. It all seemed to take a long time so that we managed to get past the ground staff without being stopped. It was with a sigh of relief that we reached the concourse on the way to customs and immigration.

"Thank God that's over. I don't know why I felt guilty."

"Because one of the nice things about you is that you have a great sense of responsibility. That's why you did so brilliantly during the ditching."

We made our way slowly to immigration and then down to customs. Once we had our bags we fought our way out of the customs area through the multitude of unnecessary shops and went towards the station and the direct link to Victoria.

"What now?"

"Why not come to my office? There is a shower there and then you can decide what to do."

"I thought you had an appointment?"

"I do, with either David Winston or Charles Hendrick."

"But that's here."

"I know but it's still early and I've got work to do in the office. Anyway I need a shower as well."

Everything worked and we arrived at Farringdon Street at 9.15, shortly after the office opened. Jill looked surprised as I arrived with Helen but rallied round to help. She showed her the shower area and changing room. I tried to sort myself out and find some clothes to wear. Helen was incredibly quick in my view, but then she didn't have to shave. She had found a suit I hadn't seen before which presumably she must have bought in St Antony. I left her in my office while I showered and changed but when I got back she was sitting in the waiting room watching the TV.

"Any news?"

"I had a look at Sky. Apparently there was a statement from Worldwide." Helen looked at me. "You were quite right. I couldn't have done it. I'm not really fully fit. I still go in fits and starts, one moment I'm fine and then a moment later I'm a wet week." She paused again. "You'd better be careful. You seem to know what I need," and she squeezed my hand, probably to reassure herself.

I wondered what to say and settled for "Why don't I give you a quick breakfast somewhere and then I'd better go back to Gatwick."

"No. You're very kind but I must get on with my life and you must get on with yours." I must have looked a bit surprised. "I know how to contact you if I need you."

"But how do I contact you? Anyway I wanted to make a suggestion about dealing with Worldwide and the media. I'm not sure I'm ready for you to disappear."

"Tell you what, I promise to call you before I agree to anything. Give me your mobile number."

I gave her my card and we went down to the street. A cab appeared and we kissed goodbye but without commitment. I went back upstairs feeling rather desolate. Maybe Helen was beginning to mean more to me than I had realised.

Jill had a sheaf of correspondence waiting for me but first I rang Charles Hendrick. He was in and invited me to meet him and have lunch at Gatwick. There was nothing particularly urgent in the mail. However I read the Hull Claims insurance agreement with Worldwide, which had arrived from John Southern, before I started to deal with the more pressing items. To my unpractised eye it looked straightforward but the agreement made it clear that the aircraft had to be operated and maintained within the rules and requirements of the certification and operating authority, EASA. Failure to do that could render the entire insurance void. No wonder John Southern wanted me to check on everything. All AAIB wanted was to find the cause of the accident and associated matters like how the aircraft ditched. AAIB had no mandate to decide as a result of an accident who picked up the tab, always assuming the aircraft was insured.

Later, as I caught the tube to Victoria I suddenly realised that I hadn't thought of phoning Mandy.

Charles was free when I arrived and Mary Turner, his secretary, showed me straight in. He got up to greet me and then we sat on a sofa. He was wearing a dark pin striped suit with a plain blue tie and looked very fit, dark brown hair, neat hair cut, about 5ft 10in.

"Well this is a fine mess, Peter. To be honest we are no nearer a solution than we were when the accident happened over a week ago. Any ideas as a result of your trip?"

"Not really. The nub of the matter in my opinion is why did he have to ditch and that seems impossible to find out. It might have been a sophisticated aircraft fault or I suppose it could have been Jackson Turner and his two friends having some form of fracas, but most unlikely I would have thought. There appears to have been very little communication with the airline or with air traffic apart from the initial engine failure. Is there any record of the conversation with Alpha Delta and your Operations discussing the engine failure?"

"Yes in fact there is. We don't have to record our conversations with our aircraft but we do record the airborne ops channel though not the ground one. The AAIB are not normally interested since they can hear the conversations on the cockpit voice recorder."

"Can I hear it?"

"Of course. I'm afraid it won't help. Let's do that on the way to lunch." He called Mary and asked her to arrange the play back in the operations room. "I think I told you. I was away when the ditching took place. I arrived back the next morning and I agreed with Winston that he'd better go straight out."

"Was the aircraft carrying any faults, ADDs?"

"None that I'm aware of. It had only just come off maintenance and should have been clean."

"Can I speak to the dispatcher who released the aircraft?"

"I don't see why not. I will need to find out who it was first and then we can find out where he or she is. I'll ask David." He dialled a number and then turned to me. "I've just remembered, David had to do a simulator session at short notice to-day. I'll get Mary to investigate while we're having lunch and when we get back you may be able to talk to the dispatcher."

"How about maintenance. Can I talk to some one?"

"You seem very keen on seeing if the aircraft was serviceable."

"Yes, I am. On an ETOPS aircraft it's absolutely crucial. It's no good having perfect engines if the systems can't support the aircraft for over three hours."

We went over to the operations room and then into a small room leading off it. We sat down and the technician started the tape.

"Worldwide Ops. This is 442. We have a problem with No. 2 engine and we're going to have to shut it down. We're past Bermuda as a diversion so we're carrying on to Barbados. Awaiting clearance from Miami."

"Worldwide Ops to 442. Copied your engine shut down message. Stand by for duty operations officer."

There was a pause.

"Worldwide 442 from Operations. Jim, this is David Winston here. What's the problem?"

"Worldwide Ops from 442. David, we have a low oil pressure warning light on No. 2 engine and the oil gauge is pretty well out of sight. Also the engine sounds rough. We are going to have to close it down. Unfortunately we're having to head off 45° to the right to clear traffic on the direct route since we haven't got a clearance yet from Miami. Hopefully they are going to clear us direct shortly as there are some thunderstorms forecast to our right."

"Worldwide 442 from Ops. Jim, we've never had an engine problem before. I suppose it is a genuine failure?"

"Worldwide Ops from 442. David, I'm Captain of this aircraft and responsible for the safety of the passengers."

"Worldwide 442 from Ops. Jim, I wasn't questioning what you did. Call me when you've heard from Miami."

I looked at Charles. "Is that all. Wasn't there a call later?"

"No, Peter. Obviously the satellite communication failed but we don't know why. It was an absolutely first class crew, both very experienced on the 831. The Captain was Jim Scott and Jane Brown was the first officer."

"What about any earlier calls? On the ground before departure?"

"As I mentioned, we use a different frequency when the aircraft is on the ground. It's got no range and we don't record the conversation. If there was a real problem Jim would have spoken to David, who was the duty management pilot that day, as you know."

Charles led the way down to the self-service restaurant in the main concourse.

"I often eat here. It's quick and normally not too busy. OK for you?"

I nodded agreement and we both had fish and chips which were very good.

"Are you going to let AAIB have this clip? Bearing in mind that they are having trouble with the cockpit voice recorder they might be quite keen to hear it"

"They've heard it already. I spoke to the inspector in AAIB, Graham Prince and we sent him the recording over the internet."

"I'm looking forward to talking to the dispatcher."

"Let's go back and see if he's in or how can get hold of him."

We threaded our way back into Worldwide's offices and Mary Turner spoke to Charles.

"The dispatcher no longer works for us. He was an American and he joined American Airlines."

"I don't understand, Mary. What was his name?"

"Ricardo Gonzalez. You know him, he has or had an English wife. They had just split up, so the bush telegraph said. There was a problem in our San Francisco operation and he left to sort it out. They said he was quite keen to go."

"Who told you all this?"

"Janet Johnson."

"The girl who does the scheduling?"

"Yes."

"Charles," I felt I had to interrupt. "Who do the dispatchers work for?"

"They work for me, not directly of course. There is a senior dispatcher, Sandy Thomas."

"Would he be the one who sent Ricardo out to San Francisco."

"I imagine so."

I expect my frustration was starting to show. "We're not having much success with our investigation, Charles. How can I find out the loading details of the aircraft on departure? I was assuming the dispatcher would be able to tell me."

"Those are kept in the dispatch office filing system for six months. I'll get Sandy to let you have a copy if he made one. He

101

will have given the original to AAIB." He wrote a note which he gave to Mary Turner.

"Can I speak to your head of maintenance? Stan Bellow?"

"Yes, that's right. How do you know his name?"

"Tom Falconbury mentioned it when we were talking in St Antony. Apparently Graham Prince spoke to him."

We went into Charles' office and he telephoned Bellow who said he could see me in about half an hour. To fill in time Charles showed me round the operations room in more detail. The room we had been in was normally reserved for the duty management pilot.

Charles explained. "Not all airlines have a duty pilot. It is expensive. But for a small airline we like to monitor what is happening, particularly if a captain wants to make a diversion. Obviously, the captain of the aircraft has the last word but there may be choices, in which case the duty management can discuss the options with the captain."

I raised my eyebrows. "Just like Winston and Jim Scott?"

"Exactly."

Charles asked Mary to take me down to Stan Bellow. We went down a corridor past the operations room, down an elevator, past a room with a service hatch door which seemed to be full of electronic spares, then a library of maintenance manuals with a similar door and finally came to his office. He got up from his desk to greet me. He wasn't what I was expecting. He looked more like a business executive than an engineer, with heavy glasses and a smart dark suit.

"Peter, how can I help you. I've got another meeting in about twenty minutes but I didn't want to say no to our meeting. I know you're working for Hull Claims."

"I'm trying to find the maintenance state of Alpha Delta. Was it fully serviceable when it left?"

"As far as I know. It certainly should have been. It had just come off two weeks servicing."

"Can I look at the maintenance history sheets?"

"I'm afraid not. The AAIB took away all the papers."

"How about the QAR. I know you download the data automatically but it has a removable PCMCIA card. Do you ever take them out?"

"No. Not unless we didn't get the data when the aircraft was on the stand."

"What about during maintenance?"

"We just reformat the card so there's no data in it."

I looked at Stan. "We're in a real mess. Apparently, the one crash recorder we have doesn't have any meaningful data and the chances of getting anything from the QAR seem slight. There was no communication from the aircraft explaining the problem. All we know is that they were trying to land at Nelson but advising at the same time that they might have to ditch. There's got to be a clue somewhere."

"I wish I could help you but everything seems absolutely normal."

"Can I talk to the crew chief who dispatched the aircraft?"

"You don't give up, do you?"

"In my job that's what it is all about."

"Well I've no idea who it was."

"Can't you find out? I really would like to talk to him. He would know if there was any problem."

"I'll try and find out and see if we can't arrange for you to talk to him. Will that do?"

"Stan, that would be an enormous help. Thanks a lot."

There didn't seem any point in talking any more and I made my way back to Charles' office. However as I passed the operations room, on impulse I opened the door and asked for Sandy Thomas. A man sitting at a computer took his headset off and pointed at the room where we had been before. I knocked and went in.

David Winston was there talking to another man who I took to be Sandy Thomas. I introduced myself and started to explain that I was seeking information on Ricardo Gonzalez. However David got up and took me out into the corridor.

"Good to see you again, Peter. Excuse me for bundling you out but the ops room is meant to be secure and only for escorted visitors. I gather Charles brought you in earlier and of course that was fine. I'd get into trouble if our security bloke found you in here by yourself. Anyway, how can I help you? Let's go to my office. I'm sorry I wasn't in earlier but I've managed to escape from the simulator."

In his office I told him about my wanting to see Gonzalez.

"Sorry, I'm afraid I can't help you. Apparently there was a problem in San Francisco so he was sent out there. The annoying thing is that the moment he got there he resigned and left for American. Pity as he was very good."

"Have there been any developments in the last twenty four hours while I've been travelling?"

"I don't believe so. AAIB are still awaiting an ROV and a salvage boat."

The telephone rang. David listened for a moment and then put it down. He apologised and rushed out of the office. I looked around. There were the usual family pictures, a few taken on holiday in front of a large house on a beach, perhaps a Caribbean one, impossible to tell. The rest of the office was wall papered with bookshelves of Worldwide aircraft and certificates of a degree in computing and Fellowship of the Royal Aeronautical Society. I pulled down a manual on the 831 to check on some of the systems.

The aircraft was unique in a certain way as the power to drive the flying controls came from electrical alternators and not from high pressure hydraulic pumps. This meant that the flying control motors were not connected to hydraulic pipes running all over the aircraft but were operated by electrically driven motors, each flying control surface having its own electrically driven hydraulic motor. Almost every other commercial aircraft had several hydraulic systems and in the event of a failure the hydraulic pumps had to be switched from one system to another. ITAC had gone for this electrical solution as there was a significant saving in systems weight.

The 831 therefore relied completely on electrical supplies obtained from variable frequency alternators from the engines and from the two auxiliary power units, APUs. There were two alternators on each engine, each alternator driving an aileron, an elevator and half of one rudder flying control. The aircraft had four elevators, four ailerons and two rudder surfaces. In the event of a failure of an alternator the other engine alternator would automatically take over and then be driving half the aircraft's flying controls.

Besides the two alternators on each engine there was an alternator on each of the two standby jet engined APUs, so that in the event of an engine failure the alternators on either of the APUs would be able to drive half the flying controls with a back-up from the other APU. In the event of a failure of the electrical supply to a control surface or if the electrical motor itself went wrong, then the control would not move but would trail in the local airflow. The chances of this happening were statistically remote. The beauty of this system was that there was no need to run high pressure hydraulic pipes, with their propensity to leak, all over the aircraft, hence the saving in weight and it also gave greater reliability. The engine alternators could also act as starter motors, again to save weight.

Beside providing high voltage AC for the power controls, the alternators also provided 28 volt DC power for all the routine services like radio, avionics, control circuits etc through low voltage Transformer Rectifier Units, TRUs.

David Winston came back. "Sorry to keep you waiting. A rostering problem which needed sorting out. I see you managed to find something to read."

"Yes. I wanted to check on the 831's electrical system. I wondered if there might have been something wrong with it."

"But the aircraft can't fly if the electrical system doesn't work."

"I know, but there may have been a complicated fault. I may need to get properly briefed by ITAC."

"Surely AAIB are doing all the investigation. How do you fit in? Hull Claims will have to pay up."

"You're absolutely right but Hull Claims likes to know of any ideas I may have, ahead of AAIB determining what actually happened."

"Well, if I may say so, you could well be wasting your time."

I nodded agreement and David took me back to Charles' Office. However Charles wasn't there and Mary gave me a message, 'I'm afraid I can't help you with the loading details. As I feared, Sandy had to give the original to AAIB before he had time to make a copy.' I told Mary to tell him it wouldn't be a problem.

"I'm sure Tom Falconbury in St Antony must have a copy by now. Thank him for trying."

I made my farewells and headed back to Farringdon Street where I decided to call Graham Prince at AAIB. He wasn't in and I was beginning to feel almost desperate. I looked through my action list and tried to call the man who had helped Linda in the second life raft. I dialled the number on the passenger list and a woman's voice answered. Michael was out but would be back after six that evening. I gave up, collected some letters and publications that needed my attention and went home to Kingston.

As I opened the door I saw a ring with the two front door keys on the floor beneath the letter box, presumably the ones Mandy had been using. The house felt empty without her but I suddenly realised that everything seemed more relaxed, possibly because I was not wondering what she was up to. I looked around and she seemed to have done a very good job of emptying all her stuff. She must have brought her car up from Bournemouth.

I sorted out the clothes from my bag and put the washing machine on. Then I went through my papers and waded through my emails, some of which I had looked at in St Antony but not downloaded. When I had finished I rang Michael who this time was in. I explained who I was and how I had found him.

"Michael, by all accounts you did a superb job in the life raft cutting the raft adrift and finding the flares."

"The stewardess did a great job too but she was in great pain. She told me what to do."

"That's not the way I heard it. You took over and saved some lives pulling people out of the water."

"I did what I could."

"Wonderfully. Have you ever done anything like it before?"

"You're not a reporter are you?"

"No, I'm not a reporter. I told you I represent the insurance company that will have to pay Worldwide for the value of the hull."

"Well these days it is difficult to know who or what to believe. Who do you work for?"

"I work for Hull Claims, the insurance company. I'm not a full time employee. They use me to look after their interests."

"Do you mind if I ring them and check you out."

"Not a bit. Do you want me to give you the number and the man to talk to or will you find out yourself?"

"I'll find the number. Don't worry. I'll call you back."

After about five minutes the phone rang and it was Michael.

"Peter, sorry to be so suspicious but I don't want to find my words all over the papers."

"No problem. We are in a complete mess trying to find out why the aircraft had to ditch. I wanted to talk to you about the flight as well as the rescue."

"Fine by me. Go ahead."

"What do you remember happening?"

"Well there was an announcement on the public address system that an engine had to be shut down but that the aircraft would continue to Barbados."

"When did that happen?"

"Oh, after about four hours I would think. We had had our meal. Then I could feel my ears popping and all of a sudden the oxygen masks dropped down. The girls came round making sure we had strapped them on." Michael was trying to remember the sequence of events. "The next thing that happened was that we started to go down for some reason."

"How do you know? Was there an announcement?"

"No. Strangely the Captain did not tell us anything. But my ears felt as if we were going down. My guess is that we stayed down for about forty minutes and then we started climbing again judging by my ears and the engine noise which increased. I suppose we weren't using full power on the engine at the lower level. I didn't hear the engine being throttled but an hour or so later, just before the aircraft started to descend, the girls came round telling us to put our life jackets on and prepare for possible ditching. They told us to adopt the brace position and then there was a shudder as the aircraft hit the water, a bang and then the aircraft seemed to turn suddenly and start to go nose down. One of the girls yelled at us through a megaphone to get out and there was a desperate scramble to get to the rear doors."

"Where were you sitting?"

"I was right at the front of the rear compartment and I could see the water coming towards me as the aircraft seemed to nose down. Passengers were trying to get out of the compartment in front so that there were people behind me pushing as I tried to get to the door. I only just made it but I'm not sure if anyone behind me got out. I was able to help the stewardess with what I think was an emergency bag but nearly got drowned trying to do that and inflate my life jacket at the same time."

"Michael, that was very helpful. I managed to talk to someone who survived in the other life raft and your stories agree almost exactly. Do you fly regularly?"

"No, but I do have a private pilots licence."

"What is your job if I may ask?"

"I'm a civil servant working in Whitehall."

"That's a broad spectrum of jobs."

"Yes I know. There are a lot of us about."

"Michael, thanks so much. May I ring you again if I think of anything else to ask you? I'll give you my number in case you think of anything that might help."

I rang off and made some notes of the conversation. When I'd finished I turned on the television to see if there was anything worth watching. It was all pretty desperate, mindless stuff so I settled for a concert on BBC2 and, not altogether surprisingly, I dropped off to sleep half way through. When I woke Newsnight had started and I dragged myself off to bed.

DAY 10

In my dreams I heard the Lutine Bell ringing as they announced the loss of Golf Whiskey Whiskey Alpha Delta. I rushed around to Lloyds in Lime Street and saw it was Mandy operating the bell by knocking on it with one of my old deck shoes. I asked her to stop it but she carried on ringing the bell. The note sounded strange, more like a telephone and I was about to tell her to change the way it was ringing when I woke up with a start.

I found the phone and picked it up.

"Sorry, did I wake you?" It was Helen. "I thought you'd be up and away by now."

"What time is it?" I looked at my bedside clock, it showed quarter past eight. "Good Lord, I must have been tired."

"What time did you go to bed?"

"I've no idea, elevenish. Your first class seat cum bed obviously did you a power of good."

"Nonsense. The business class seat is almost the same as first class. What makes the difference is that I went to bed at about seven."

"Helen, I'm sure you didn't ring just to say 'good morning', delightful though it is to talk to you."

"You're right. Worldwide want me to go on the box to-morrow night. I seem to remember that you had some ideas."

"All I was going to suggest was that you wore a dark wig and got the make–up people to give you a pair of glasses to wear if you can't get hold of some plain glass spectacles. When they try to put make-up on you before you go on, they are bound to notice the wig but don't say anything. Let them takes lots of pictures."

"Why on earth would I want to do all that?"

"Well if by any chance you become a celebrity and all the networks want to interview you, then you might decide that you do not want to be recognised in the street."

"I think you're over dramatising the situation."

"Maybe. You're probably right. Anyway when I take you out next you can always wear the wig and the glasses so you won't be recognised."

"When that's going to be?"

"When are you free? Where do you live? It obviously can't be to-morrow night."

"I'm free tonight."

"OK. You're on. What would you like, show or meal?"

"Are they mutually exclusive?"

"Definitely not. Shall I decide?"

"Yes. I'm fed up making decisions."

"There's one thing I'll need to know. Shall we eat before or after the show and how are you getting home?"

"Let's eat after the show somewhere."

"OK. Why don't we meet at the Royal Air Force Club, Piccadilly for a drink at 1800 and then go to the theatre?"

"Done."

"How do I contact you if I need to?"

Helen gave me her mobile number. I realised I still hadn't found out where she lived. I got up and tried to decide what I needed to do. Clearly I had to sort out the evening with Helen. It didn't seem worth going out to buy a paper so I decided I would use the internet. The best deal seemed to be the people who sold packages. I settled for Guys and Dolls and Bertorellis in Convent Garden. On impulse I booked a room at the RAF Club as well, to save my having to drive home or catching a late train.

I decided to ring the AAIB flight data expert, George Sandford, who I knew from discussions we had had in the past and from attending meetings and conferences. George answered the phone.

"You know I'm not allowed to discuss current accidents with you, Peter."

"I'm not asking for any detail. Just one question on the crash recorder you've got."

"Go on then."

"Is the missing data compatible with a power failure?"

"Had the aircraft been on maintenance we would have been checking the power supplies." The phone went dead.

John Southern called. "How's it going?"

"Not well. The only consolation is that as far as I know the AAIB people are equally puzzled. As you know they're waiting for a salvage vessel with an ROV. I'm not sure how that is going to help. The aircraft needs beaching somewhere."

"What about Jacko and his lot?"

"Maybe that's the answer. But how are we going to prove it? Where does Hull Claims stand now?"

"We have given an interim payment to Worldwide."

"Is it an open claim?"

"Oh no. With Worldwide we are liable for the hull plus £75,000 per passenger. It's a hell of a lot but at least it's capped. When are you going back to St Antony?"

"If you want me to go back I will, but I'll wait until the salvage vessel is there otherwise I'll be wasting your money."

"Yes, Peter. We want you to go back. You must decide the best time to return."

We stopped talking and I spent most of the day doing my paperwork. At about 2pm I decided to look at the *Announcer* on the internet. Cindy was in full spate again. Another survivor had been killed and I wasn't entirely surprised to read it was Geoffrey Hudson. I had barely finished reading her piece in the paper when Frank Westbourne came on the phone and told me about the murder. I tried to settle down and do some work but I kept on wondering about what was happening in St Antony.

Eventually, I had a shower, got changed, caught the train to Waterloo, then to Green Park by underground and walked to the Club. After checking in I sat down in the lobby to wait for Helen who arrived nearly twenty minutes early, as I had expected, carrying a bag. We kissed perfunctorily.

"Have you been here before?"

"No, I haven't."

"Well you have to check your bag here, in the lobby with the porters."

"I gather you're staying here. I'd like to go up to your room and freshen up. Can't I take my bag up with me?"

"OK. But bring it back down. I'll be in the lounge bar on the first floor."

I gave her my key having established that a Pinot Grigio would be very welcome. I was drinking my beer slowly when she reappeared having changed, looking very smart indeed with a close fitting suit, blouse underneath the jacket and dark stockings underneath a short skirt.

"You look terrific."

She leant forward to be kissed and there was some perfume which definitely didn't go amiss. I was glad I'd shaved.

"Thank you. I've left my things in your room. Is that OK?"

"I keep meaning to ask you. Where do you live and how are you getting back to-night? I don't suppose we shall finish our meal until elevenish."

Helen looked steadily at me. "I live in Portsmouth still, but fortunately I see you've got two beds."

"That sounds very exciting. We'd better keep off the oysters and ginger ice cream."

"You can make your own arrangements. I'm going to have a good night's sleep."

We only had the one drink and then walked to the Haymarket. Helen hadn't see Guys and Dolls before but she knew the music.

"I really enjoyed that, Peter. Where now?"

"Covent Garden. Bertorellis."

"Great, I've been there once before and really liked it."

We walked across Leicester Square and then along Long Acre. The weather was fine and neither of us had coats. The table was along the side of the room as I had requested and I ordered a bottle of champagne.

"What are we celebrating, Peter?"

I thought of saying 'your wonderful performance on the aircraft', but realised it would only bring memories back which she was clearly trying to forget.

"Nothing special. It just seemed a good idea. We don't have to drive home."

"You're right. It's a lovely idea. I'm having a super evening."

We clinked glasses and then all of a sudden she stopped and her face went blank.

"Peter, I seem to be alright for a bit and then suddenly I start remembering and reliving the whole flight." I took her hand in mine and tried to reassure her. "It seems so wrong that we should be sitting here having a wonderful time," this time she clutched my hand, "when all those people were killed. I was the last to leave but I had to leave people behind me."

"I know it's easy to say this but that's the way life is. It's all very unfair. Just a matter of chance." I held her look. "Always remember that you did a really wonderful job saving so many lives.

You couldn't have done anything more. You should be very proud."

"You're lovely, Peter. But there's a void there. I think there always will be."

"Maybe. But I really believe that time does heal things."

I gave her the menu to decide.

"I'm not that hungry now. I'll have a prawn cocktail and maybe a dessert."

"I'm going to have a dover sole I think."

The waiter came over and poured out the champagne and took our order. Helen seemed to have lost all her earlier sparkle and lust for life. She only sipped from her glass and kept squeezing my hand.

"You're great, Peter. I hope you don't mind my unloading my problems on you."

"Not a bit. Forget it. Do you want to go home now? It's not too late is it?"

"That's the very last thing I want to do. I need looking after."

She held my hand very hard. "You're a great help."

For once I felt a bit inadequate. I wasn't sure I deserved her plaudits.

"You know, Peter, there was something you asked me about the flight. About announcements from the Captain. I've been thinking. He made one announcement telling us he was shutting the engine down and there were no more. But I think he tried at least twice more. There seemed to be a noise, a word and then another noise."

"In that case why didn't the cabin supervisor make an announcement. For example about the ditching?"

"Perhaps the PA wasn't working at all. She did come back and ask us to let her know if any of the oxygen masks didn't come down instead of using the crew intercom."

"And had they all come down?"

"Oh yes, no worries there."

For the first time, listening to Helen, I began to imagine at least some of things that might have gone wrong. Helen kicked me.

"Alright, I'm sorry I started talking about it. Let's enjoy the meal and the ambiance."

"But you must talk about it. It was a harrowing experience. It's bound to take you a long time to recover fully. Anyway, apart from getting it out of your system I need to know everything that happened, however trivial it might seem. Incidentally, are you sure you're going to be able to handle the TV to-morrow night?"

"I don't know. How about you coming with me?"

"Helen, it's very nice of you to ask me but it is you they are interviewing. If you want my advice I would put it off again for a week or two. Whose doing it anyway?"

"Panorama. It is only part of the programme."

"Are you sure? I hate TV. You never know what the agenda is. A lot of the questions are intended to support a case the producer has already decided. And interviewers are always trying to make names for themselves. I know Worldwide want to show they did everything correctly but I'm beginning to think the whole thing is more complicated than they realise. Take my advice and ask for a delay."

"Peter, funnily enough that's exactly the conclusion I was coming to. But it's a bit late to ring Worldwide now."

"Ring the BBC newsdesk. That way you won't have to argue with Worldwide."

I got my phone out and using directory enquiry I found the BBC number. I dialled it and asked for the Panorama newsdesk. I offered Helen the phone but she signed for me to talk. I sent a message saying that Helen Partridge would not be well enough to be interviewed for the Panorama programme the next night.

"You're super."

"Thank you. I just didn't want you to run into trouble."

" I know." She lifted her glass. "To us."

It seemed rude not to respond and I noticed she had a good drink for the first time.

"What happened to your Peter?"

"We decided that it was all over. What happened to your girl friend? What was she called?"

"Mandy. She decided that it was all over."

"Sorry?"

"I was for a bit but I'm beginning to see she was right."

Helen thought about that for a moment but didn't comment.

"Peter, what you have just done with the BBC has taken a great weight off my mind. I was really worried."

"Do you want a dessert? You've barely eaten anything"

"Do they have ginger ice cream? You know I rather like it."

We both had ginger ice cream. Helen had changed from squeezing my hand to fondling it in a way that I found rather disturbing. We walked back to the Club.

"I'd like a coffee. Can we have one in the lounge?" She disappeared, but up in the lounge I found the bar closed. I broke the bad news to Helen on her return. I hadn't given in my key so we went straight to the elevator.

" Did you ever bring Mandy here?"

"As it happens I didn't. We always went back to Kingston."

"This arrangement is much better. No driving or train journey."

In the room Helen took her jacket off and we kissed, gently at first and then more seriously.

She broke away. "We'd better get some sleep."

She went into the bathroom and returned wearing a thin nightdress that was not very long and her black bra and panties were clearly visible. She got into bed and I went into the bathroom. There was a bathrobe there which I decided to use since I never wore pyjamas.

"You may kiss me good night."

I obliged but she broke off a lot sooner than I expected. "Thank you for a lovely evening." She vanished under the bed clothes leaving me to switch the light out and get into the other bed feeling that I had missed something.

DAY 11

I woke up in the middle of the night. Helen was sleeping deeply in the other bed. My mind was wrestling with what Helen had told me and trying to make sense of what had happened. I realised I really didn't know enough detail about the 831's systems. I needed to talk to someone who did. It took ages before I drifted back to sleep again.

"What time is check out?"

Helen was leaning over me still wearing her nightdress and underclothes.

"What time is it now?"

"Half past six."

I shuddered. "Ten o'clock I think is check out."

"Good. I see that we can have breakfast sent up."

I forced myself to open my eyes and look at her.

"It's not breakfast that I was thinking of."

"Don't you mean 'I was thinking of something other than breakfast?'"

"That too."

She grinned.

"No, I don't think I'm quite ready for that, my love. But you can move over and hold me."

"Helen, be reasonable," but I didn't argue.

In fact we checked out at 0945 and, carrying our bags, we had breakfast in Henry's.

"Peter, thank you so much for everything."

"But I didn't do everything." I raised my eyebrows and she dug me in the ribs. "I meant cancelling the interview. And a lovely evening last night."

"When are you thinking of starting work again?"

"Don't know. Not for a bit. Then I'm due for a first class purser's course I believe. I won't be flying the line for ages."

"You need a holiday. Get away from it all."

"I'll think about it."

"You haven't told me where you live and how I contact you"

"I'm not sure I want you to know. You've got my mobile."

"Don't be silly. I want to see a lot more of you."

"You saw it all last night."

"No I didn't."

"Well you've got something to look forward to."

"Don't you mean 'to which you can look forward.'"

"I know what I mean."

"Helen, for God's sake give me your address."

"You've got my mobile number. I'm quite good at texting."

"I think I prefer the real thing."

We both went to Waterloo. She went to Portsmouth and I went to Kingston. Back at home I wondered whether I should have suggested to Helen she could stay with me but perhaps it was a bit early in our relationship. Certainly the house felt very empty.

I had bought the Times and Telegraph but there was not much aeronautical news and nothing about St Antony.

About one o'clock my phone rang. It was Helen. "Peter, thanks so much for the theatre and everything. I really enjoyed it. I'm still a bit shaky though. The accident has really upset me. Thank goodness you called the BBC. The PR man at Worldwide called me and didn't seem too pleased but I didn't react. He rang off in disgust. When are we going to meet again?"

"You shouldn't be saying that. That's my line."

"I know but it needed saying. You're very cautious."

"Well, you would be very welcome to stay here."

"Peter, it sounds a great idea but I think that might be rushing it. I've never moved in with a partner. I barely know you."

"In that case, you would always be welcome to visit."

"Have you got somewhere to park?"

"In the drive, if that's OK with you. Have you got a GPS navigator?" I gave her my address and postcode. "When had you in mind?"

"If I'm not interrupting you how about in a couple of hours? I'll bring something to eat."

She rang off before I could answer. I was beginning to realise that when Helen had thought something through, she didn't hang about. I tried to concentrate on my outstanding jobs but Helen's rapid forthcoming arrival had caught me by surprise. I decided I'd better get some milk and essentials in and went down to the shops. At 3.30pm two things happened. Helen arrived at the front door and my phone rang. I waved her in as I held the phone.

"Peter, Frank Westbourne here. Have you read the *Announcer* to-day? Cindy Smart has got hold of a story that there was some sort of fight on board the aircraft and that AAIB are beginning to think that the solution to the accident could be due to that."

"Is there anything else you've heard, Frank? Anything on the TV or Radio?"

"Nothing, but I've been working and may have missed something. You can read the *Announcer* on the web I believe."

"Good idea." I thought hard. "Frank, you'd better ask Susan to book me in to the *New Anchorage* to-morrow night and rent me a car again. See you to-morrow."

"That was a brief romance."

"Helen, that's my life, anyway just at the moment. Love me or leave me I think is the phrase."

"I might do both if you're not careful."

We sat down on the sofa and she looked at me. "It's stupid really but I like being with you and not having to think about what happened."

She leant forward and kissed me in a way which didn't help my concentration on the accident. We stopped for a moment.

"I definitely feel the same but at the moment I'm spending all my time trying to work out what happened. It doesn't make sense and it's not fair on you. Look, right now I've got to book my flights and read what Cindy put in the *Announcer*."

Helen released me and I went to my computer. The front page of the *Announcer* was completely filled with Cindy's article about the fight. She didn't disclose her source but I suspected the leak must have come from Ben's department; AAIB would never disclose anything at the current stage of the investigation. I was in two minds whether to ring Tom Falconbury and Ben Masters but decided it might be better to wait until I saw them.

I looked at the flights to St Antony. British Airways had a direct flight but Worldwide only had a flight to Barbados. Lufthansa had a direct flight from Frankfurt and I was tempted to go to Southampton and avoid Gatwick. However, I decided to travel by economy Worldwide as that way I might get to learn something about the safety drills.

Helen put her arms round me from behind so I had to stop. "Late lunch is ready, Sir."

We sat down at the dining room table which Helen had laid out with all the plates and cutlery. "This is great. I can't remember when I last had a meal on this table. How on earth did you find everything?"

"It wasn't very difficult." She produced a Chinese meal with dishes I didn't recognise but that tasted great.

"You're a wonderful cook."

"That's one of things they teach you when you are training to be a flight attendant."

"Like how to tell which are the best take-aways?"

We grinned. I had to admit that I rather enjoyed having her in the house though I wasn't sure it would accelerate my written output.

"Let's go to Kew Gardens. You can drive."

It was a lovely late summer afternoon and after walking around and looking at the Princess Diana house we sat down to drink some tea.

"I've just thought of something else." She had my full attention. "Jerry came back looking for a screwdriver in the rear toolkit just after we descended to low level."

"Who on earth is Jerry?"

"He was one of the business class cabin attendants." She hesitated remembering it all again.

"Did he find one?"

"Yes, I think he did."

"Did he tell you why he wanted a screwdriver."

"No. He seemed in too much of a rush."

"Did you tell all this to Tom Falconbury?"

"Who on earth is Tom Falconbury?"

"The AAIB man you spoke to."

"No. He seemed more interested in the mechanics of the ditching. Anyway I've only just remembered what I've told you. Oh, he did say he wanted to talk to me again when I felt better."

"You know what you've just told me is very interesting indeed." I grinned. "In future I'm going to get all my female witnesses to stay with me."

"Oh no you're not, my darling. Forget it. This is a one off."

I realised that I was rather glad she was being proprietorial. We made our way back to her car and back to the house. Helen brought her bag in with her this time but I made no comment.

"You had better do some more work and then we can have a drink at the Red Lion. We don't need another meal, do we?"

"You've clearly got the Good Pub Guide in your bag. It's a good choice. It is very pleasant there in the back bar and garden."

I went back on line, made my reservations, checked in for the flight and selected an aisle seat very near the emergency exits doors. A little later we walked to the Red Lion.

"We'd better get back early. You've got a long day to-morrow."

"But not a particularly early start."

Back home I carried Helen's bag upstairs and showed her her room. She seemed pleased and I left her to unpack while I got my bag out to pack. She came downstairs wearing the bathrobe hanging on the back of the door.

"I'm not sure I like wearing this bathrobe. I'm sure Mandy used it or one of your other girl friends."

"Actually she didn't but you can always take it off if you don't like it."

She came over and pressed her body very close to me. She was smelling of a different perfume from the one the night before but I didn't think that would matter.

"It's your robe, I'll let you take it off." It seemed rather rude to refuse. "Very slowly."

DAY 12

In the morning I woke up very early and tried to get up without disturbing Helen but I failed. "Could you bring me a cup of tea?"

I sat on the edge of the bed as she drank the tea. "My love, what are you going to do to-day?"

"I'm taking you to the airport and then I'm going back to Portsmouth"

We both got dressed and I had a breakfast of fruit and toast ready as Helen came down. As we went out to the car I realised she was only carrying a small bag. "Haven't you forgotten something?"

"Not really. I don't need all the other clothes I brought. I can collect the rest next time when you come back, my dear, if I need to that is."

"Great idea. I shall really look forward to it."

"And so will I."

We got into Helen's car and we were at Gatwick at 1030 for me to check-in. We kissed goodbye and I watched her drive off. There was the normal line for economy check-in and I wished I had booked business class. After about an hour my turn came, I checked in my bag and gave the girl at the counter the boarding card I had printed out the night before. She looked at my passport which was covered with immigration stamps from all over the world, spoke to her supervisor and I could see she was about to upgrade me to business class. She was very puzzled when I refused the upgrade, I suspected it had never happened before. After a bit she went back to her supervisor and had a conversation I was not allowed to hear and then she came over to the desk and indicated that I was to wait by the first class check-in. I managed not to get angry, didn't move and asked for the supervisor.

"Mr Talbert, we have to be very careful these days. I have asked our security to come over."

"Look Mr," I paused and then read the supervisor's badge. "Look Mr Standish, I know this all looks strange but I have a gold frequent flyer card with British Airways and also with Singapore Airlines. I normally travel business class but I've only travelled with Worldwide Airways once before. I'm travelling economy with your airline because I'm an insurance investigator and I want to travel in the back of the aircraft."

Standish looked very doubtful and then he was joined by a typical security man, nondescript, taciturn with a moustache and wearing a grey suit.

"If you don't believe me call your chief pilot, Captain Hendrick." I opened my carry-on roller bag, found my card carrier and fished out Hendrick's card. They began to look as if they thought I might actually be telling the truth. I got my mobile out from my pocket and started to dial Charles' number. They stopped me and looked at one another. The security man nodded and the supervisor led me to the first class check-in desk.

"Mr Standish I do understand you have to be careful. No hard feelings?" He nodded. "Now I want the seat I had booked right at the back." Standish looked puzzled again. "Please don't worry. There is a very good reason why I want to sit there. Are you sure you don't want to talk to Captain Hendrick's office?"

This time he decided he would take up my offer but he dialled the number and I couldn't hear what was said. However all of a sudden he handed the phone over to me. It was Charles himself.

"Peter, why didn't you tell me you were going to St Antony? We would have upgraded you to first class. By the way, I'm sorry I missed you yesterday when you left. Still I gather you saw David."

"No worries. I only decided to go St Antony late last night. I didn't want to bother you."

There was a pause. "But Standish tells me you are right at the back." Another pause. "You're going to be looking at the layout and the slideraft arrangements on the way, I suppose. Alright, I'm beginning to understand. They told me you were a smart operator. I'd better warn the cabin crew."

"Charles, that's really not necessary."

"I'd like to. It's important you see everything. I'll also tell Bill Dawson to expect you; he's our chief technical pilot and has taken over from David Winston in St Antony. Good luck."

I handed the phone back to Standish who looked very relieved. He checked me in, gave me my boarding pass and baggage tag. He also gave me a pass for the express security line which I appreciated, not that I reckoned it would help all that much as in my experience there was often no discipline so that everybody seemed to join the so called express line if there were long queues.

Sure enough there was an enormous security line in the express lane. It took me forty five minutes to get through and it was the normal zoo when I finally made it.

Because I had arrived early I still had over an hour to spare in spite of the delays so I went to the BA lounge, showed my card and got some coffee.

The Worldwide departure gate was a long way from the BA lounge which meant I had to leave in plenty of time. Worldwide loaded the passengers from the back which suited me and I found the aisle seat I had chosen close to the rear galley. There was an elderly couple in the window seat and the seat next to me and I helped them put their bags in the overhead lockers. The aircraft soon filled up and the back seemed completely full; no wonder the girl was suspicious when I wouldn't accept an upgrade.

We taxied out spot on time and for once I found myself listening to the safety briefing. Not that there was any hardship in watching the cabin attendant, since she was a tall slender rather attractive blonde. She seemed very young. I watched her demonstrating putting on the life jacket with some interest. Mae West had nothing on her. I was fairly sure that had Mandy been with me she would have been looking at me and digging me in the ribs and not looking at the girl. I wondered what Helen would have done. The demonstration finished by pointing out the escape route indicating the two rear doors. It was a very professional demonstration and infinitely better than the videos displayed on the passenger entertainment systems of some airlines. For a change, most of the passengers around me seemed to be watching but I couldn't decide whether that was due to the recent ditching or the cabin attendant or possibly both.

For once there was very little delay getting onto the runway and taking off and, despite the plane being full, the cabin service was very good. There were two girls looking after our section and the attendant who did the briefing was working on my side of the aircraft and seemed to spend a little longer with me than I would have expected. I waited until the meal had been cleared and went into the rear galley. The two girls were clearing everything away and the one I was beginning to recognise grinned.

"They told me you would be chatting us up."

"I'm definitely not chatting you up. I'm seeking information."

It was the turn of the other girl to grin.

"I've never heard it called that before."

"Alright. I don't know what they told you but I'm an aviation consultant retained by the insurance company that insures your aircraft. I'm trying to help establish what happened to Alpha Delta when it was lost the other night."

Immediately, I could sense the girls had turned on their full professional attention.

"As I understand it, only the rear of the aircraft was above water and that's why only two escape chutes were launched. I don't know in detail how the escape procedure and rear doors work so, as I had to come out to St Antony anyway, it seemed a good idea for me to see the arrangements in the rear cabin." I looked at the girls. "What exactly do you have to do if there is a ditching?"

The blonde girl responded. "Well the Captain alerts everyone to the situation. If there's time we would get all the passengers to get their life jackets on and particularly remind them not to inflate them in the aircraft. We would then get everybody to go to the brace position just before the actual ditching." She paused obviously remembering training. "After the impact we would get the doors open. The escape chutes, which act as life rafts then inflate automatically and we have to get the passengers out as quickly as possible." She paused again. "It would be a nightmare, I guess. It would all depend on where the water was. As you said, apparently with Alpha Delta only the rear of the aircraft was above the water. The aircraft was nose down and the front fuselage full of water." She shuddered.

"Yes, that's what I heard." I hesitated and looked at them both. "You didn't tell me your names. Mine's Peter."

The darker girl chipped in. "I'm Moira and she's Wendy. It really is awful about the aircraft. We don't know who was drowned. Have you seen a list yet?"

"Only of the survivors. I expect you already know that only two cabin crew survived, Helen Partridge and Linda Sutcliffe. Do you know either of them?"

"Don't know Linda, do you Wendy?" Wendy shook her head. "I think she is fairly new. We both know Helen. She's been with Worldwide a bit longer and is very good."

"Would you mind showing me the doors and indicators?"

124

Wendy nodded and we went to the door on my side.

"The doors are, of course, in automatic during the flight so that in an emergency if we open the doors the sliderafts extend immediately for the passengers to slide down. For ditching we still leave the doors in automatic, the escape sliderafts inflate automatically and act as life rafts. Then we pull a handle which partially releases the slideraft from the aircraft. Oh, we also have to manually inflate the slideraft as a back-up if we can." She thought some more. "Obviously we have to get the passengers out as quickly as we can before the aircraft starts to sink and we can use this megaphone." She pointed to a stowage in the luggage rack behind the right door. "As we leave, if there's time, we each take an emergency pack. For this door the pack is stowed here." She pointed to the luggage racks on each side ahead of the rear doors.

I grimaced. "Sounds alright but I don't expect any ditching would go to plan. And certainly not the one for Alpha Delta. Clearly the floor angle was pretty steep and it was dark. How anybody got out at all is a miracle. Helen and Linda did a wonderful job."

"They certainly did. Did you know that the training notes say that a ditching is catastrophic?" I looked surprised. "Really, several times. Doesn't fill us with much confidence. And you have to remember to cut the line which connects the life raft to the aircraft."

I thought about this. It sounded crazy, because then if the aircraft sank it would drag the life raft down with it.

"Is there a knife to cut the rope?"

"There's meant to be, though how you would find it in the dark goodness only knows. Amazingly, both Linda and Helen managed it."

"Wendy, what's in the survival pack?"

"You name it. Would you believe a survival booklet." She looked incredulous. "I can just imagine sitting in the life raft having survived and reading the booklet. Not very likely." I nodded agreement but I supposed if a miracle happened and it was a perfect ditching it might have some useful information. "I'm not sure the contents card would be much good either! Maybe we're meant to use our mobiles and report a deficiency! Insect repellent; that'll be handy. To be fair there are one or two things that were obviously absolutely vital; a mini flare pack and some day/night distress signals. First aid kit. A torch as well. That should have been useful."

"You're right. They used the mini flare packs, the distress signals and the torch. And by the way there must be an emergency beacon somewhere because Air Traffic at Swanwick were alerted."

"Sorry. I forgot to show you the ELT in the stowage here above the left door." Again she thought about the situation. "Those girls really did a fantastic job even to get the ELT beacon out as well. Yes. When everything settles down there must be a full de-briefing."

I thanked her and went back to my seat absentmindedly watching her delightful rear view disappearing into the galley. Three hours later we landed and made our way to Barbados immigration and customs. I went into the transit lounge and an hour later took a Caribbean Airlines flight to St Antony. Clearing customs and immigration was much quicker than usual. The immigration officer looked at my passport, saw the previous stamps and gave me a month.

Susan met me and explained that Frank was tied up in an important meeting. She went with me to Hertz, saw that all was in order and left me. I chose a Honda again and went to the hotel and got room 212 this time, but still in the same corridor overlooking the sea.

I rang Tom's mobile and got his answering machine. It was too early to go to bed even though it was eleven o'clock UK time so I went down to the bar. I chose a Budweiser and sat in the dark trying to read the *Announcer* which I found in the lobby. Cindy must have had a day off as there was no article following up her coup of the day before.

Tom appeared and suggested we went outside to avoid Brian Matthews who was lurking in the bar.

"What brought you back?"

"The *Announcer*."

"How did you hear?"

"Frank Westbourne called me and told me of the article. Is there anything in it?"

"Not sure. You remember the survivor that was shot?" I nodded though I remembered that Ben had told me Makepeace had had his neck broken and not shot as Cindy Smart had written in the

Announcer. "Well another survivor was found dead in Cape Harbour. Ben Masters, I think you know him, is wondering if something had happened on the aircraft. Apparently Jackson Turner was on the plane with a valuable diamond and he is investigating if there is any connection with the two survivors who have been killed. He's sure Jacko, I think he calls him, was involved. The coincidence is too great."

"But why are they fighting if Jacko is dead?"

"Maybe they've found the diamond."

"Underwater?"

"Well Masters told me that lights have been seen round the wreck in the middle of the night by the fishermen."

"I though the aircraft was being protected?"

"Apparently they can only do it during the day, Peter. They don't have enough coastguards for 24 hour surveillance."

"That's terrible for you. It's interfering with the evidence."

"Tell me about it."

DAY 13

After breakfast I rang Harry Markov, the head ITAC man, at the *Golden Beach.* He agreed to see me and I drove over straight away. He was five foot seven, grey hair, sixtyish and looked very experienced in aviation matters.

"Peter, what can I do for you? Our Roger O'Kane speaks very highly of you in connection with that terrible landing accident in freezing fog at Heathrow some time ago."

"I need some performance information Harry. Is it possible to get hold of a plot or tables of the fuel required flying on one engine for a given distance depending on departure weight? I should have looked at the manuals when I was at Gatwick with Worldwide."

"I'll try but why do you need it? Is fuel an issue? There should have been plenty on board."

"I suppose I'm like AAIB. I like to explore all the possible issues. There might have been a fuel leak. That would explain the ditching."

"Alright I'll ask. Shall I say you're asking on behalf of AAIB? Does Tom know you're asking for all this information?"

"Not yet. But when you get the answer please send AAIB a copy. I think AAIB are wondering whether foul play in the aircraft could be a possibility but these days I find that hard to believe with all the security checks. Nobody carries guns on aircraft except the marshals and their guns are very special ones, tasars mostly, which won't damage the aircraft if used sensibly. I thought of waiting for your answer before trying theories out on Tom."

"You've got theories? Wouldn't they like to know them?"

"I'm sure Tom has got all the possibilities listed. My ideas are just a few thoughts."

Harry looked at me. "I'm not sure I believe you. Anyway I should have the information you want by to-morrow if they'll release it to you."

I went back to the car and called Bill Dawson who was staying in the *Astoria Reef* where I had met David Winston. He said he would meet me at the *New Anchorage.*

Back in my room I called Ben to see if he had the pictures of Jacko yet.

"So you're back. What did you find out in England?"

"Nothing worthwhile. Nobody seems to know anything."

"My friend, that's par for the course. And would you believe we've only just got our copying machine working. I'll get Jearl to send them round."

"You can email them to me if you like."

"I'd rather not."

Bill Dawson arrived about half an hour later. He was a very thin, short man and I soon discovered he didn't have a sense of humour but lived for aircraft. We had coffee at the beach bar.

"Any ideas, Bill? "

"Not really. The problem with the crash recorder shows that AAIB are absolutely right demanding that ICAO should make serviceable crash recorders mandatory for flight."

"But they are, surely?"

"I mean that the recorders should give a warning to the pilots if they are not working properly and in that case the recorders have to be repaired before the aircraft can leave."

"Yes, I'm sure you're right but what about Alpha Delta? It's too late for that now."

"I think I favour a problem with Jacko and his people for some reason. The aircraft seems absolutely perfect from a design viewpoint."

"Possibly, but it is difficult to believe that there were weapons on board with all the present day security. I wondered if there was something wrong before the aircraft took-off."

"I can't believe that, Peter."

"Problem is I have not been able to talk to the dispatcher. I've got to try to locate him and have a chat. Charles told me he has left the company and is working for American in the States somewhere."

"Can't you phone him?"

"I'm going to try. Do you happen to know the number of your San Francisco office? They will be sure to know how to contact him."

Bill got out his phone and wrote down the number on a page of his notebook and gave it to me. I looked at my watch. It would be eight o'clock in the morning so it would be worth calling them. I dialled the number.

"Worldwide Operations, San Francisco."

The voice sounded very English. "My name is Peter Talbert, I am working for Hull Claims Insurance which insures all Worldwide's aircraft. I'm trying to contact Ricardo Gonzales who used to work for you and was in your office."

"Well Mr Talbert, you obviously know he has left us. I'm not sure that I can give you his number. If you give me your number I might be able to give it to him."

"Thanks very much. I'll pass on that for the moment. I'm thinking of coming out to the West Coast and I'll call if I may."

"Please do. I'm the manager here, Tony Suffolk."

I rang off and Bill passed me another piece of paper.

"This was Ricardo's UK mobile number if that helps."

I put the number Bill gave me in my wallet and went up to my room. When my laptop computer had finished the lengthy starting routine, characteristic of all computers running Microsoft operating systems, I opened Skype, added Ricardo's number and tried calling the number. I was connected to the answering service and left my mobile number without any details.

There was a message from reception; a package had arrived for me from the police and did I want it sent up. Mentally wishing that Jearl hadn't sent a police car round, I went down to collect the parcel and then went back up to my room to see what Ben had sent. There were four pictures, all significantly different but all labelled 'Jackson Turner'. One of the pictures reminded me of someone I had seen recently, but where kept escaping me.

There was nothing more I could do straightaway in the hotel so I called Becky Sharp and asked if she could spare the time for a short chat. She agreed and I drove to the airport and went up to the coffee bar in the viewing area. Becky appeared very promptly.

"Well Peter, how can I help you?"

"Becky do you think it possible that a survivor could have been rescued and given a false name?"

Becky looked at me in surprise. "You know I've had the police round asking me all sorts of questions about the survivors who were killed here but no-one has asked me that question. Maybe Cindy Smart was right about you. She said that I should watch you as you always knew a lot more than you let on and that you won't let the grass grow under our feet." She thought for a moment. "I don't see how it could be done but you clearly do."

"I just wondered when exactly the tie up was made between the survivors being rescued and the passenger list."

"Well, the priority was to give medical aid to everyone and some of the survivors could barely talk, so they were given temporary identification."

"Who had copies of the passenger list?"

"The police of course and we had to give a copy to the immigration department."

"Customs?"

"Yes, they did ask for a copy though I'm not sure why."

"Who authenticated that the survivors had given their correct names?"

Becky looked concerned. "Nobody. Why would anybody want to give a false name?" Her eyes lit up. "How would a survivor know the names of the passengers and be certain that the one he chose had not been rescued? Anyway the next of kin would know if that happened."

"I know, it does seem very unlikely. But for a start, airlines don't take the next of kin for passengers. Furthermore, not all passengers have next of kin as such. I'd like to know all the survivors who were given temporary identification numbers?"

"The hospital would know that. There were about thirty survivors who were in that category. As they recovered the hospital told us the names and we checked the names against our list."

"Did the hospital have a list?"

"Yes they did."

"One final question. Have you ever issued a list with the allocated seats?"

"No, what would be the point?"

"Is it possible to have such a list? Does the airline keep the seats allocated?"

"Well we don't here when we despatch a flight. I don't know what London do. Would you like me to ask them?"

"No, please don't bother. You've got quite enough on as it is. Thanks so much, Becky, for all your help. It has been extremely useful."

"If you say so Peter. It all seems very straightforward to me." Her phone rang. She looked at it and then her watch. "I'd better get back to work."

I went to the Cape Harbour General hospital and asked to see the person dealing with the survivors. A very efficient lady whose name was Debbie Braxton appeared and we sat down in reception. She was dressed in a working suit but was not wearing the jacket; I guessed she was about forty five years of age and perhaps not from St Antony. I introduced myself.

"I'm curious about the patients who were so badly hurt they were not able to identify themselves."

Debbie looked at me curiously. "Are you from the police?"

"Not at all. As I told you, I'm just retained by the airline's insurance company to advise them of what is happening. Do you have any patients left in the hospital?"

"Yes we do. Three survivors are in a very poor way."

"Do they know what occurred?"

"Oh yes. And their next of kin are on the phone every day. In fact one is coming out to-morrow."

I produced a complete survivors list. "Could you mark up the ones who are left and the ones who had temporary numbers until they recovered and the date on which they left."

"I suppose so, but why should you need to know this information if the police don't?"

"I'm not sure. The insurance company asked me to find out. I suppose they have to deal with individual claims."

Debbie seemed satisfied with my answer and she went back to her office to get the details I requested. She was soon back and I glanced at the list. There were four people, all men, who had been given numbers and the dates they left the hospital.

"Debbie, did any of these four get any visitors?"

"Yes, I know for sure that one of them did. He couldn't tell us his name at first but another survivor who wasn't hurt came to see him, I think his name was Hudson. He told us after a couple of visits that the man was called Thomas Smith."

"Debbie, when you found his name do you remember what you did?"

"I just called Worldwide to let them know. He seemed to recover very quickly as he was only with us for a few days."

I thanked her again and went to the girl in reception.

"Do you work here regularly? I'm trying to locate a friend of mine who was on the plane that ditched a week or so ago."

The girl nodded. "I sure do. I've been doing this job for fifteen years."

I smiled. "You don't look old enough." She returned the smile." Do you recognise any of these people?"

The girl looked at the four pictures of Jacko that I showed her. She picked out the clean shaven one. "That one looks familiar but its difficult to be sure because he was wearing dark glasses."

"Do you know his name?"

"No. He was in the hospital until about three days ago."

"Did he have any visitors?"

"You seem very inquisitive."

"I told you. He was a friend of mine."

"Well in fact he was very lucky as he had a friend who visited him frequently."

"Do you know the friend's name? Presumably they have to sign in?"

"No, I'm afraid I can't help. We don't keep the day's sign-in sheets. We give them to the administration and I think they are binned the next day unless a query occurs."

I showed her the passenger list. "Do you recognise any particular name?"

She looked and shook her head. "I can't recognise any particular name, I'm afraid. We get so many visitors."

Back in the car I looked at the four names and addresses. According to Becky's list they were all still on the island. Two had addresses on the outskirts of Cape Harbour, one was in the *Paradise Hotel* and the fourth, *Leewards,* seemed to be in an area near Frank Westbourne's house. I decided to go round to the *Paradise Hotel*; the receptionist dialled Jim Moorhouse and announced that she had a call. A female voice was on the line.

"I'm looking for Jim Moorhouse. I'm an aviation consultant representing Worldwide insurers."

"This is Mrs Moorhouse speaking. Jim is very tired and having a rest. Where are you?"

She agreed to come down and a lady of about seventy appeared. It transpired that she was Jim Moorhouse's mother. We discussed her son's state of health and I tried not to show that though I was very interested in her son's recovery, he was not at the top of my list of concerns. Mrs Moorhouse very understandably started talking about money and wanted to know how her son should claim for the pain and suffering he had had and was still enduring, not to mention the loss of earnings from his business. I explained that initially he should go through the airline and perhaps use a solicitor.

I returned to the *New Anchorage* and rang Frank and asked if he knew about the address given for the fourth survivor on my list.

"Not sure exactly where you mean. I think it might be one of the large houses in a fairly new development near here. Why do you want to know?" There was a pause. "Peter, you worry me. You always seem to be exploring things that should be done by the police or some other authority."

"Not really. I just like to understand all the issues in any accident."

"Alright, come round this evening but come early while it is still light so that we can find the house you want. Do you remember how to find us? I seem to remember Charlie was navigating last time."

I ignored his reference to the very smart female art insurance investigator who had helped me investigate the disappearance of one of Frank's aircraft. We agreed 5.30pm. There was about three hours before I had to be with Frank so I decided to get some exercise and go for a swim in the pool. It was almost empty which suited me since I was able to swim some lengths without interruption.

Back up in my room I lay on the bed and tried to guess what could have happened on the aircraft. For some reason it had depressurised after losing an engine, it then seemed to have gone to low level and then climbed again. The Captain knew that they might have to ditch but didn't say why. Was it a system problem? Were the pilots having difficulties controlling the aircraft or were they running out of fuel? There clearly had been a problem in the front passenger part of the aircraft. The whole thing was confused by having Jacko and two of his people on board the plane. Now two of the survivors had been killed in St Antony. Perhaps there was a connection but it was going to be difficult to find out exactly what had happened, particularly without the flight recorders. I had a feeling I had missed something obvious which I found very frustrating.

***

The weather was still warm with a cloudless sky as I made my way out to the car and drove off to Frank's. My timing was perfect as he was just ahead of me arriving at his house. He got out of his car, got into mine and we drove to a fairly new area not too far from his house, with some very expensive homes. I guessed the houses were four or five years old. We entered into what appeared to be a new private road and the house at the end had two very large gates and *Leewards* written on a board attached to one of the brick pillars supporting the gates. There were palm trees along the entrance drive and along the front of the plot so that the front of the house was completely obscured, though bits of the roof were still visible.

"I might have known it. Peter, you've chosen what must be one of the most expensive houses on the island."

"Do you know who lives here?"

"No idea. As you can see, whoever it is doesn't believe in open plan living. Those large palm trees have been planted there quite recently. What was the name of the survivor, the guy you think may be here?"

"Thomas Smith, not that that means very much." I looked carefully at the location of the house in relation to the sea. "Frank, have you got a chart or map of your house with latitude and longitude marked and also covering this place?"

"Yes I have as it happens, an Admiralty chart. I was thinking of having a boat dock and putting a few steps to get down to the water from the house. However, as bad luck would have it the water seemed very shallow in front of the house so we gave up. Why do you want it?"

"I was just curious to see the exact position of *Leewards* and its water frontage."

"Alright, I suppose I'd better let you look at it. If I don't you'll go and find it somewhere else for sure."

I was able to turn the car round by driving round the circle in front of the house and we drove back to Frank's. I parked behind Frank's car and we climbed up a couple of steps into the house. Pamela appeared to greet us and then disappeared into the kitchen. We sat down on the porch overlooking the water which seemed incredibly clear and blue with the white sand underneath showing up very clearly. Frank produced two gin and tonics and a glass of wine for Pamela who reappeared after a few minutes.

"Frank, fantastic. What an ideal spot. You're very lucky."

"You know, visitors like yourself always think that but one soon gets used to conditions here and then we complain about the things we haven't got like music, theatre, decent shops and the like. And of course we miss the rain most of all. There's either none at all or too much from storms and hurricanes."

"If you say so."

"The question you have to ask yourself is 'Why don't I, Peter Talbert, move to St Antony and work from there?'"

"In my case I need to be near the insurers and the UK airlines."

"Exactly. There are very few jobs here and it's not easy running firms since, very understandably, there is a requirement to employ as many local people as possible. The government doesn't shower out work permits like confetti. Problem is that we need top engineers to maintain our modern aircraft and there just aren't enough local qualified people, though the government is doing its very best to get people trained."

We sat down to a delightful meal which Pamela had prepared of grilled prawns followed by fresh fruit and, while we were having coffee, Frank went to find the chart of the local area. Pamela cleared the dining room table and we laid the chart out.

"Your place seems to be the only spot along this part of the island that shoals right out."

Frank nodded glumly. "I know. I wish we had thought of it before we built the house. We could have bought the land where *Leewards* is now. I think he has a pier or dock or something. Of course they dredged a ferry channel for all the other houses in the development that didn't have access to the sea." He changed the conversation. "Any news on the cause of the accident?"

I shook my head. "No. I think the salvage ship must be coming in soon. Presumably they will try and beach the aircraft somewhere but in this climate the whole thing could be very unpleasant with all the bodies entwined in the wreckage."

I made my farewells and drove back to the hotel. There was a message light on in my room. It was from Ricardo Gonzales.

"This is Ricardo Gonzales. My mobile number is 653 997 0100."

It was only 1930 on the West Coast so I decided to try calling the number but there was no reply. I decided not to leave a message.

DAY 14

After breakfast I went down to Paradise Harbour and rented a RIB from *Discover St Antony*. Beverley as usual was behind the desk.

"You know where you mustn't go?"

I nodded. "Can I borrow a GPS?"

"Whatever for?"

"So I don't get lost. I'd better have a chart of the Eastern shore. And some fishing gear, please."

Beverley looked through a pile of smallish waterproof charts and selected one.

"This should do you. There's a weighted fishing line in one of the side pockets in the rib. And here's a Garmin GPS. It will cost you 300 US dollars if you drop it over the side. It's waterproof within reason, if you're not going scuba diving. Tie this GPS lanyard here to the rib and you should be alright."

I did a quick check on the chart for the position of Frank's house and it looked fine. It took about 30 minutes to get there having to go past the wreck of Alpha Delta and the extended centre line of the main runway. Once opposite Frank's I extended the fishing line and went slowly past the end of a substantial pier which extended from the beach in front of *Leewards*. There were two covered vessels tied alongside a 100 ft pier, one about 40ft long or a bit less and the other a small vessel maybe 20ft, which I took to be a diving boat. I turned round to have another look and realised that I had caught a fish, conveniently near the pier. It was a small bonefish which I managed to get off the hook and threw straight back. The pier looked in very good condition, presumably having been built at the same time as the house and therefore only a few years old.

Leewards itself was a very substantial building with steps going down from the house to the pier. The other houses in the development only had access to the water through a canal which must have been made when the houses were being built. From an environmental viewpoint it was surprising that the dredging had been allowed but the tides here were less than two feet, even at springs, so that the houses were able to have small power boats at the bottom of their plots with access to the Caribbean.

I carried on 'fishing' until I was back in front of Frank's house and then pulled in the line and returned to Paradise Harbour. Beverley came down to meet me.

"You were away a long time." She was obviously curious where I had been. "Where's the fish?"

"I threw them back. It seemed a shame to keep them. They were only small bonefish."

"Where did you go?"

"Oh I just went north for a bit and tried my luck, just past the end of the runway."

"South would have been better under the cliffs." She examined me closely. "You didn't put enough sunscreen on. You look a bit red."

She was right but it was a bit late to do anything about it. However I did put on more protection when I got back to the car. In fact the skin didn't look too bad in the car mirror. I drove back to the hotel, rang the High Commission and asked for Dorothy Henshaw. I was in luck as she answered the phone. I asked if she could find time to see me for a few minutes. There was a long silence and she said she didn't have any time but we could talk over lunch if I came straight round. I had a very rapid shower, smartened myself up and drove round to the High Commission as fast as I could. The same girl was on duty and asked me if I wanted to see Reggie Pendlebury again and looked surprised when I asked for Dorothy Henshaw. She gave me a badge after checking my passport again and the lady I had seen at lunch the other day appeared. She suggested that we should go straight in and eat to save wasting time.

"How can I help you? Have they found out why the aircraft ditched yet?"

"Not yet. I believe they intend to salvage the aircraft."

"Isn't that going to be very difficult? Where are they going put the aircraft parts? There's nowhere on the island suitable."

"I can't answer that I'm afraid. Our AAIB are in charge of the investigation and they make that sort of decision."

"But I thought you were out here representing the insurance company? Surely AAIB lets you know what is happening?"

"Yes they do up to a point. I think the problem at the moment is that they don't know when the salvage vessel is going to be here.

They also don't know what size the aircraft pieces are going to be. And then of course there is the problem of the bodies that are trapped in the wreckage. It is all very difficult. As you probably know the real difficulty is that the crash recorders didn't work properly."

"I thought that there was a problem due to a person called Jackson Turner being on the aircraft."

"Yes, you're right. It's not clear yet whether Jacko and his people might have caused the accident." I tried to change the subject slightly. "I wanted to see you in connection with a Thomas Smith. He had a bad time in hospital and initially was given a number because he could not be identified."

Dorothy looked at me thoughtfully. "I thought you might be asking about him. His was a strange case. I'm not really sure I should be discussing it with you." Luckily she put her reservations aside. "We thought he was dead but it turned out that he was one of the survivors."

"That must have been awkward. Presumably you gave him a passport once you had all his details."

"Yes I did." Dorothy looked very uncomfortable. "I haven't told this to anyone else here yet but I wasn't sure about him. But he had all the right answers."

"Has anyone else asked you about him?"

"No, you're the only one."

"In this digital age can't the Passport Office send you the passport they have on record?"

"Apparently not. Only the very latest ones use digital photos and fingerprints."

"That's amazing when you think that DVLA at Swansea have been using digital photographs and signatures for years."

"You're absolutely right. The Passport Office had a problem to do with the identity card database which was being developed in parallel with the new passport system and the programme was too big for the programmers to handle."

"Dorothy, may I ask you a delicate question?" I didn't wait for an answer. "Did you send off Thomas Smith's photo to the UK?" Dorothy nodded looking rather disconsolate. "Have they replied yet."

"Yes, it came in this morning. They said the photo did not seem to match very well with the copy they used on Thomas Smith's passport. Anyway why are you asking?"

"Oh just to keep the records straight for the insurers I represent. Presumably you took passport photos, addresses and all that sort of thing."

Dorothy looked at me again, almost as if she felt I wasn't confiding in her fully. "I suppose you're now going to ask for a photo and all the details?"

"If you could."

"Well I don't know if I should but as it happens I'm very keen on aerospace matters and I'm aware of the various accidents you have been involved with, Mr Talbert. I will give you the details and photo you want but please remember, it will be unofficial." She smiled. "Good luck with your investigation and please let me know immediately if you have any new information on Mr Smith."

"Of course, but one other thing, Dorothy. Did the Passport Office ask you to do anything?"

Dorothy hesitated. "I'm not sure I should be telling you this. They told me to try to get Thomas Smith back here for another photo and try to recover the passport."

"And what have you done?"

"I haven't done anything as I don't know the telephone number of the place. Anyway if the person is not Thomas Smith then it is a police matter, way outside my remit. I told that to the Passport Office and that seemed to be the end of the matter as far as they were concerned. They haven't come back to me."

She changed the conversation to general aviation matters and discussed the revolution that was taking place in modern aircraft design and the ever increasing efficiency of the new aircraft. She was very knowledgeable and clearly realised that my interest in Thomas Smith was more than superficial. We finished our meal and went up to her office. There was a new double drawer filing cabinet in the room and she went to it, got some papers out and disappeared, I guessed to a copying machine. She was soon back, got an A4 envelope from her desk and put some papers and a photo inside. She didn't waste any time but gave me the envelope and took me downstairs to the lobby.

She smiled at me. "All the best Mr Talbert, I expect I shall hear what you are up to in due course."

I drove back to the hotel, opened the package. Inside there was another envelope labelled Thomas Smith. I opened it and looked at the photo of the man who was with Philip Smithson at Moby Dick's and who looked uncommonly like one of Ben's pictures of Jackson Turner.

***

The phone rang. It was Tom Falconbury in England. "Peter, I thought you might like to know that we have decided to salvage the aircraft and put it in a hangar."

"Isn't that going to be very difficult? Have you got a suitable hangar?"

"Yes and no. The airport has just finished laying a concrete base for parking aircraft on the far side of the airfield away from the terminal near the West Atlantic Airways hangar. The government has told the airport authority to make it available for us. They've found a firm in Michigan, *Immediate Construction Inc*, which specialises in building temporary hangars very quickly and they are chartering an Antonov 124 to fly the materials in."

"But that's going to cost a fortune. Who's going to pay for it?"

"Apparently the St Antony Government and the UK Government have done a deal and ITAC are going to contribute as well."

"It's going to need air conditioning, plumbing, drains the whole nine yards."

"Tell me about it. Luckily *Immediate* specialise in this sort of work."

"But how are you going to get the airframe pieces there?"

"Well the salvage vessel, *Deep Fathom Five,* is going to carry each piece to *Lovers Bay* beach which has an access road. We're going to have to improve the road to take the weight of the transportation trucks and also widen the roads all the way to the new hangar."

"Incredible. When does the salvage vessel arrive?"

"Not for a week but that's OK as it will take about ten days to get the hangar up."

"Tom, I'm very impressed. Well done. I don't know how you managed to persuade everybody."

"It wasn't quite like that Peter, though thanks. Bob Furness is determined that we will find out what really happened, as are ITAC and the St Antony Government and they have both been incredibly cooperative. As I told you, it was the Government who made the whole thing possible by organising a space for a temporary hangar."

"I assume because you're doing all this that you've made no further progress in the investigation."

"You're right. Hopefully, when we examine the structure on shore we will be able to see if, for example, there was any unusual damage to the fuselage. I'm still worried about Jackson Turner and his mob being on the aircraft and what was going on in the front cabin."

"Won't beaching the aircraft mean that you will have to deal with a lot of bodies?"

"Yes, you're absolutely right. And that's another reason for doing it. Naturally, the relatives are keen to get the bodies back for burial. We've decided to start bringing them up, after photographing them in the plane as best we can. We are taking them to the mortuary in Cape Harbour. We've got to try to arrange identification if we can and that is not going to be easy after some time in the water. Bob is trying to organise a couple of experts to come out and help the St Antony coroner and police. When the hangar is built we'll have a mortuary there."

"Presumably a lot of the bodies are not strapped in but near the two rear exit doors."

"Yes, the pictures the divers have taken are quite horrifying."

There was not much more I could say but I was conscious that I had not told Tom about my suspicions that Jackson Turner might be alive. However, I felt I needed time to think who to tell first. My inclination was to confide in Ben Masters, even if Tom would not be pleased when he found out I had been withholding information from him. While I was pondering Harry Markov came on the phone.

"Peter, I have those charts and tables you asked for."

"That's incredibly quick."

"Yes, it was quick bearing in mind all information on the accident, in and out, has to go through Ronald Raycroft, technical

143

support. He's been made the sole source of contact for all information. He's attached all the information to an email I've just got. Apparently it was agreed you could have the information because it is available in the public domain. In fact Ronald mentioned that you could have copied it all from the manuals I've got here in St Antony."

"I did think of doing that Harry but I wasn't convinced that they would have the single engined cruise performance. It isn't needed for a normal aircraft dispatch. Anyway thanks a lot. Can you forward the relevant part of the email to me?"

"No problem. Do you think Tom Falconbury would like a copy?"

"Not sure. Like you he's bound to have the manuals already in his office. Any chance of your printing the charts and tables for me? I don't have a convenient printer here."

"Yes, I'd be delighted to do that. I've got a printer here. I'll put the sheets in a large envelope and send them over with some stuff I got for Tom."

Harry's information would be very useful but I still needed to know the dispatch weight, fuel and cg. The conversations I had had with Jeremy Brock and Michael Longshaw indicated that the aircraft had been flying at low altitude for some time before climbing up again. The problem was trying to decide why the aircraft flew so low after the engine had failed. Not that I had much time to think about it as Rick Welcome came on the phone.

"The boss wants to see you."

"Any reason?"

"He thinks you might have some ideas that you haven't shared with him."

I didn't argue. There was no point as I was only on the island courtesy of Ben. I got into the car and went to his office in Cape Harbour.

"Peter, how are you getting on?"

"Not very well. The recorders were no use as you know so AAIB are going to salvage the aircraft. Let's hope they find something."

"That's not what I meant. You've been out three times in a RIB from *Discover St Antony* according to Beverley, the girl who looks

144

after the boats. Where did you go this morning?" I hesitated. "Beverley doesn't believe you went fishing and neither do I."

"Ben, I know you won't believe me but I was about to tell you where I went."

"Try me."

"Well one of the injured survivors, who was given a number initially, claimed to be Thomas Smith when he was able to remember."

"But Thomas Smith was one of Jacko's men."

"Exactly. In fact Thomas Smith was not on the survivors list until he remarkably survived."

"Well what's so remarkable about that?"

"Ben, I felt that something strange was going on so I checked with the High Commission and she gave me a passport picture of Thomas Smith." I handed a copy I had made to Ben.

Ben looked at me. "Jacko?"

I nodded. "Looks like it. It might explain at least one of the killings."

"Run it by me."

"Well we know that Thomas Smith was one of Jacko's mob. May not have been his real name but it was the one he had a passport for and the one the police told you he was using. I established that the guy in hospital had been having a regular visitor, presumably a survivor and I assumed Geoffrey Hudson who was on the survivors list."

"But how did Hudson know Jacko was in the hospital?"

"They must have been in the same life raft so Hudson went looking for him. I suppose he told Jacko that Smith was missing. Jacko saw this as a wonderful opportunity to disappear. He probably knew enough details of the real Smith to be able to convince Dorothy Henshaw that he was Thomas Smith."

"Peter, who on earth is Dorothy Henshaw?"

"The consular lady responsible at the UK High Commission for issuing passports and travel documents to all the survivors who had lost them."

"You get around. No wonder I have to be worried when you're on the island. Alright Sherlock, tell me about the two murders."

"Well I can only surmise the second murder. I've got no ideas on the first one. But for the second, you see Geoffrey Hudson knew that Jacko was alive and so he had to go. Jacko didn't want anyone to know he was alive. So Hudson was killed. You did tell me he was ruthless."

"How? Jacko didn't have a gun. And why would most of his clothes have been taken off the body? You've got to do better than that."

"That does sound a bit strange. However, I did have a stroke of luck." Ben shook his head, almost in despair. "I was having a meal in Cape Harbour when Philip Smithson, who I believe owns *Dark Blue Diving*, came in a with a friend who I did not recognise, though he looked familiar. I realised later that this friend was probably Thomas Smith alias Jacko. So then I had a theory. Thomas Smith was staying at *Leewards*. It would all make sense if Philip Smithson actually owned *Leewards*."

Ben nodded. "Well you're right there. Your man Smithson does own and live at *Leewards*. He knows everybody, very very influential." There was a very long pause while Ben looked at me. "I suppose I can trust you. What I'm going to tell you could get me into a lot of trouble because Smithson knows so many people. The thing is that we have reason to believe that he may be involved with drugs in a very big way. We can't prove anything and I'm sure he would try and get his ministerial friends to fire me if he thought we were after him. He seems to have a lot of money but it's not clear where he gets it from." He stopped for a moment. "So you think Smithson arranged for someone to knock off Hudson at Jacko's request so no-one would know Jacko was alive?"

I nodded. "Well it's a theory. You know more about Smithson than I do but I didn't like the look of *Dark Blue Diving* and I found it incredible that Smithson had no sunburn at all. Hardly a dedicated diver."

"But why would Smithson want to do Jacko a favour?"

"Probably Jacko could tell him a lot about the UK drug market, perhaps he was one of the people Smithson supplied in the UK or possibly Jacko offered him a huge amount of money. It would have to be huge, from what you say, to influence Smithson."

"Must be something like that. Jacko and Smithson, a match made in Hell. But what happens next?"

"I suggest you take photos of the two survivors who were killed and show them to the girl at the hospital reception. I think

146

you will find that one of them was the regular visitor to the guy who became Thomas Smith."

"Peter, I've got to hand it to you. You should have been a detective."

"Ben, I am a detective in a way, maybe not in the way you think of a detective. I have to investigate things just as you do in order to find out the reason for aircraft accidents. It's not my fault if things happen on the way."

"Alright then, have you got any leads on the first guy who was killed?"

"No. Nothing. On the second one obviously your people need to find the gun used to kill Hudson and find if Smithson is involved."

"Well as I told you Peter, we think Smithson is involved in the drug business on the island in a big way. We think *Dark Blue Diving* is more than just a teaching establishment. We believe it is involved with landing and delivering the stuff."

"Well Jacko is tarred with the same brush. Of course it is just possible he only wants to get out of the business. Perhaps he's made enough money to retire and now wants to enjoy it. Certainly he's taken great advantage of the situation, trying to disappear."

"More likely, he wants to disappear to prevent the UK police catching up with him. Anyway it's very frustrating, Peter. I can't very well arrest Jacko since, on this island, he's done nothing wrong."

"He's impersonating someone else."

"We can't prove that."

"You can take his finger prints and compare them with the UK records. I happen to know that the UK Passport Office is worried about the passport that Dorothy Henshaw issued to Thomas Smith."

I told Ben about my conversation with Dorothy Henshaw. "I expect the Passport Office or the UK police will be contacting you anyway."

"We are in St Antony. I can't arrest him and take his fingerprints. You can bet his lawyers would run rings round us."

"Maybe the UK police will try to extradite him?"

"But there is no Jacko any more and unless we can think of a reason, Thomas Smith will not give us the time of day. No, we're stuck. Thomas Smith is safe and we're going to have to put up with it. Anyway we can't be certain Smith is Jacko." He looked at me. "Peter, you should be finding out why the aircraft crashed, not getting involved with criminals."

"Ben, you called this meeting, not me. Anyway, I would like to know what happened in the front of the aircraft during the flight and if it affected the safety of the aircraft and made it ditch."

"You haven't told me yet what you were doing in the RIB."

"I was just looking at *Leewards* to see what it was like on the beach side."

"And what was it like, Peter?"

"You know perfectly well, Ben. Ideal for getting afloat at all stages of the small tide you have here. Just what is needed for landing and delivering drugs I should think."

Ben made no comment but it was inconceivable that he did not know what Philip Smithson was up to. Presumably he or the customs had never been able to catch his people red handed and tie it back to Smithson. He indicated that I could go so I went back to the hotel and reviewed time scales. Nothing was going to happen for some days and I realised that I needed to go out to California to talk to Ricardo Gonzales. This time there was an answer to his mobile.

"Ricardo Gonzales."

"My name is Peter Talbert. I believe you were the dispatcher of the Worldwide 831 aircraft which ditched near St Antony. I'm advising the insurance company and I would like to come and visit you."

There was a long pause and I wondered if I had lost Gonzales but luckily I could hear noises in the background.

"What do you want? What do you need to know?" The voice was not unfriendly but rather guarded.

"I'd rather not discuss things on the phone. Can I come and see you?"

"Where are you calling from?"

"I'm in St Antony at the moment but I could be in San Francisco to-morrow evening."

"I'm with American at the main airport. I finish my shift to-morrow at 1400. I have to go back home but I could meet you in Palo Alto later on. Let me know what time you can be there by text message."

I logged on, made reservations to Miami and onwards to San Francisco but left my return open as I needed to contact Roger O'Kane in Seattle to try to make an appointment to visit their systems specialist. I reckoned I should be in Palo Alto easily by 1900. The Cardinal seemed to be the only hotel in the place but I managed to reserve a room. I texted Ricardo and then I rang Roger. He answered his phone straightaway, which was a bonus.

"Roger, great to talk to you again. Can you help me? I'm working on the Alpha Delta ditching for Hull Claims who insured the plane. I need to talk to someone about the possible causes of the accident."

"It's good to hear from you Peter but I don't think I can help you directly. Everything has to go through Ronald Raycroft. I can put in a good word for you if you like."

"That would be very helpful. He might remember my name though as your man out here, Harry Markov, has already got some information I needed through Raycroft. I shall be in San Francisco to-morrow evening and plan to come to Seattle the day after to-morrow, Thursday, if someone will talk to me. Can you give me Raycroft's number and I'll call him to-morrow evening?"

There was not much more I could do. I emailed John Southern and went to bed.

DAY 15

I decided to start the day by ringing Helen.

"How are you doing, Peter? It is Peter, isn't it?"

"Alright, I'm in trouble."

"Actually I've been following your advice and resting and I'm beginning to feel better. I shall probably let you try to get back in my good books when you get back. Mind you, Worldwide want me to start my first class pursers course as soon as possible."

"Helen, please don't let them rush you. Once you start work they will almost certainly try to make a heroine of you to prove how good their training is." Helen tried to interrupt. "I know you really are something very special, not only to me, but please don't let them use you, my love."

"Actually Peter, I have to admit you're probably right. A guy from some TV outfit rang me yesterday asking me when I was starting work. He could only have got my number through Worldwide. You need to be here, to advise me. The closer the better, come to think of it."

"Sounds a really great idea."

"Well if it's that good an idea when are coming home to test it?"

"You know it's not that simple, darling. I have to go to San Francisco to-day, then Seattle and then back here."

"You need to think of a reason to come back here."

"I can think of a really super reason but I'm not sure I could convince Hull Claims."

"I'm a key witness. You need to interview me closely again."

"Can't wait. But there's a limit to what I can claim in expenses."

"Well you'll have to make your mind up. I don't like to admit this but I think I need you. That accident has unsettled me. I'm thinking seriously of coming out if you don't come back soon."

"Don't you think you'd better wait until I come back?"

"Don't see why, I'll stay in the Worldwide rooms which they rent full time in the *New Anchorage* for the Cabin crew."

"But that's where I'm staying."

"I know, my love. See you soon."

The phone went dead and I didn't know whether to believe her or not. I didn't have a lot of time to get to the airport. Luckily I had decided not to check out but I did have to check the car in. I just made it and reached San Francisco at 1630 on schedule. I hadn't checked any bags but there was a long line at the Hertz car rental. I finally got on the road at 1740 and my Garmin navigator got me to the hotel by 1830, not that there was anywhere to park and I had to drive to the city council underground parking lot in the next block.

As I checked in a dark complexioned man with a black moustache came up to me. Ricardo seemed very friendly and explained that we would have to go out for food and drink since the hotel had no facilities except for rooms. I went upstairs in a really antiquated elevator to get rid of my bag and then we wandered down the road a couple of blocks to a small Italian restaurant.

"Peter, I've been expecting someone to try and contact me. It seemed to me that Sandy Thomas did everything he could to make sure that I couldn't be found. He bundled me out here as fast as he could."

"Sandy Thomas, the Worldwide senior dispatcher?"

"Yes. He asked me to go to the office here. I went the following morning. Mind you there really was a problem here – the dispatchers kept on getting the loadings wrong."

"Why did you expect someone to come and see you?"

"Well, as you clearly know, I was the dispatcher of Alpha Delta. After clearing the aircraft and starting the engines Jim Scott, the Captain, had a problem with the serviceability of the aircraft so they told me when I got back to the Ops room; apparently there was something wrong that should have been fixed. He shut the engines down and spoke to the duty pilot in Flight Ops. The finger was not reconnected to the aircraft so I couldn't get back on board. There was quite a delay, maybe twenty minutes, and then Jim decided to take the aircraft. There was a further delay before air traffic gave start up clearance. Obviously, I wondered if the accident was anything to do with the problem Jim Scott had."

"Have you got any more details of the problem?"

"I'm afraid not. The problem occurred only after I had left the aircraft."

"When did Sandy Thomas ask you to come out here?"

"He called me at home the following morning and arranged for me to go straight out."

"So you didn't see or talk to anyone at Worldwide before you left?"

"That's right. Only a quick visit to the Ops room as I told you. To be honest I was quite glad to get away. My wife had just divorced me and I'd come to the conclusion I'd do better back home than there. We didn't have any kids. I knew American were looking for senior dispatchers so I left Worldwide the moment I arrived out here. I've been with American about a week, under training of course."

As we ate our meal I tried to get more details from Gonzales but he wasn't able to give me any more. I couldn't make up my mind if he was deliberately holding something back but I gave him the benefit of the doubt.

"Ricardo, you've been a great help. If you remember anything else please call or text me on my mobile or send me an email." I gave him one of my cards as we separated at the front of the hotel and then went up to my room having another tussle with the elevator which must have been fitted in the 'thirties, complete with manual folding gates on tracks.

DAY 16

In the morning I went to a French style café next to the hotel. At 0800 I called Ronald Raycroft and he answered immediately.

"Peter, I've arranged for you to talk to Jimmy Benson who is the electrical design engineer in charge of the 831. When can you get up here?"

"I suppose I might manage this afternoon if I rush but it would be more sensible 0800 to-morrow morning if Benson is free then."

"That's what he had anticipated. He works in our Bellevue design office. Do you need a room reservation?"

"Thanks for the offer but it might be easier if I do it from here. I'm shooting for the Red Lion in Bellevue as my first preference."

Back in my room using the internet I managed a room in the Red Lion and a car reservation with Hertz. My next call was to Michael Noble, Seattle Editor of Aviation Week. He wasn't committed for the evening and we agreed to met in the Red Lion at 1830. Then back to the laptop and I booked a 1330 departure to Seattle with Alaskan getting in at 1535. I looked at my watch and decided Helen might be at home.

"Two calls in two days. You must want something."

"Well yes that's true." I stopped before I gave myself away.

"I can't see you, Mr Talbert, but I suspect that you want to talk about Alpha Delta and not how lovely I am." There was a pause as I judged it was better not to say anything. "Go on, what's troubling you?"

"Well I just wondered how long you reckon the plane was at low level after the masks came down?"

"For about three quarters of an hour or so I think. We did climb up again. I'm sure I've told you that. What do you really want?"

"That seems to agree with what I heard from the passengers. The other point that interests me"

Helen interrupted. "Now we're coming down to it."

"You're very rude. I've nearly started so I'm going to carry on. The other point that interests me is about the fighting to get out of the aircraft? I think you said there was quite a bit. It clearly was a case of survival of the fittest and the aircraft was rotating nose down very quickly."

153

Helen's voice changed abruptly, to a very subdued tone. I almost wished I hadn't asked the question but I needed to know. "Peter, I knew you'd want more detail of this sometime but quite honestly I'm trying to forget the whole thing."

I interrupted her. "Sorry, I didn't want to remind you of the nightmare."

"No, I know you had to ask. It was all rather horrible with people fighting."

"Would you recognise any of them?"

"I might, but I hope I never have to see any of the survivors again. Some of the men were unbelievable, pushing women out of the way. And there was a fight right at the door which delayed the exit. It's the fighting aspect of the escape that has really upset me. Linda was telling me she had the same problem on her side."

"You've been talking to her? How is she?"

"Yes, we've been talking every day. She hopes to be coming home to-morrow."

"I'd better have another chat with her."

"Only if I'm there. I'm not as understanding as your Mandy."

"How do you know how understanding Mandy was?"

"I don't, but I think you find it difficult to resist temptation. In fact you'll be delighted to know that I arrive to-morrow in St Antony."

I think I sounded horrified. "But I won't be there. I'll still be in Seattle."

"Don't you worry your pretty little head about that. I told you Worldwide have regular rooms booked in the hotel for the cabin crew. And if they're full I'll stay in your room."

"But how do you know I didn't sign out?"

"Thank you for that. Just checking."

"Helen, you're too clever by half."

"Nice isn't it? You'd better get used to it."

The phone went dead. I wasn't used to being outwitted but, surprisingly, I realised I didn't mind too much. I put my few belongings together, checked out and drove to the airport. All went according to plan and I was in the Red Lion at 1630.

Michael Noble arrived on time, two hours later, and we went into the bar.

"Have you solved the ditching yet, Peter?"

154

"You know very well it's not my job to find out causes. That's up to the AAIB. I just watch on behalf of the insurance company, Hull Claims."

"Just like that accident at Heathrow?"

"Well that was different. The AAIB inspector was leaking all sorts of stories to the press. I was sure he was on the wrong track. The inspector on this case is first class but he is having real problems."

"So I understand. The crash recorders weren't working. Didn't I read somewhere that there was a well known criminal suspected of being in the drug trade on board?"

"Yes, that's right. Probably a coincidence."

"But I thought he had some associates with him?"

"So I understand, Michael."

"Were any of the gang saved?"

"That's a very interesting question and I'm not sure what the situation is."

"You mean you won't tell me, Peter." I smiled and didn't respond so Noble carried on. "In that case why are you visiting ITAC?"

"Off or on the record?"

"Off, but I want you to tell me when I can use what you are about to tell me."

"I'm not sure what I am going to tell you is worth anything to you, Michael, or anyone else."

"Well I'll risk it."

"I want to understand the flying control systems. The 831 is very modern in its design. The flying controls are driven by electrically powered hydraulic motors. I'm wondering if there was something wrong with the design or with the aircraft when it took off."

"I'm sure there's nothing wrong with the design. FAA and EASA will have been through it with a fine tooth comb and there's not even been an incident up to now. If there was something wrong when it took off that should be easy enough to find out." He paused. "But there are no records from the crash recorder?" I nodded. "Peter, you've got a problem."

"AAIB have a problem."

"Come off it, Peter. They're not here, you are."

155

We had an interesting evening discussing the aerospace industry. Michael was incredibly well informed and realised how vital it was for ITAC to solve the problem. I told him about how AAIB were going to lift the wreckage and put it into a hangar. He had not heard of that development so he was very pleased and I gave him Tom Falconbury's name and the hotel number.

"Keep in touch, Peter. I know this is not your investigation but you always seem to know what's going on. Av Week ought to pay you a retainer except that I know you wouldn't take it. You like to be completely free." I nodded. "Well good luck anyway. ITAC and the relatives need to know what happened."

I went straight up to my room after Michael had gone and slept very well despite the traffic on the freeway close by.

DAY 17

I woke early and used my laptop to book a red eye special back to Miami and then an early flight to St Antony. At 0800 exactly I was at the ITAC design office signing in to see Jimmy Benson. He came down from his office almost immediately; He was quite tall, six foot one at a guess, very thin with very black hair. I guessed he was about forty. He led me up to his office and introduced me to a short, fat bald man, aged fiftyish. I must have looked surprised to find he was Ronald Raycroft.

"Peter, this accident is almost life and death to ITAC. I've come along to this meeting not to listen to what Jimmy says but to hear your views. I know this is AAIB's investigation but you are involved and seem to be very close to the action."

"I wish there was some action, Ronald. I've come to learn, not theorise." I looked at Jimmy Benson. "As you know the crash recorder doesn't have any data on it after the engine was stopped, so it is proving very difficult for AAIB to find out what actually happened on the aircraft. The only thing we know for sure is that the Captain shut down an engine because it had low oil pressure and was sounding rough. The passengers and the cabin crew say that the cabin depressurised and that the oxygen masks dropped down, goodness knows why. Apparently the aircraft then went much lower for about thirty minutes or so and then climbed up again. Finally, after some time it let down trying to land at St Antony and ditched at the last moment. We don't know why the aircraft ditched, whether it was because they had run out of fuel or if there was a flying control problem."

Ronald cut in. "Peter, I thought there was a crook, a drug baron, on board with his team and something happened up front?"

"Yes, that's quite right but we have no idea if that had any relevance to the accident. Personally I think it's unlikely as they wouldn't have any weapons, assuming Gatwick security did their job."

"Were any of the gang in the survivors?"

"Good question. Not sure yet. However, let's talk about the electrics. How is it possible for the crash recorders not to work?"

Benson interjected, "But as I understand it the flight data recorder did work until shortly after they shut the engine down.

Then there was some data on the main crash recorder but nothing useful."

"Yes, that is what the AAIB data analysis people are saying."

"Well AAIB haven't sent me the exact list of the data that was recorded but it sounds as if some of the 28V DC supplies were missing."

"Is that possible?"

"I wouldn't have thought so unless there was some physical damage to the aircraft wiring."

"How about an electrical fault?"

"I would have to see the good data and look at the actual layout of the aircraft wiring. I'm surprised AAIB haven't sent it to us yet. On the face of it the whole thing is impossible. The aircraft can't fly unless the electrical system is working."

"But what about failures?"

"There are no flight failures which would account for loss of data to the flight data recorder."

"What about if the aircraft wasn't serviceable when it took off?"

"I don't understand you. If it wasn't serviceable it wouldn't have taken off."

"Shouldn't have taken off."

"Surely we must know. Anyway nothing would have prevented the data going to the recorders."

"Should have prevented."

"Peter, you didn't come all this way just to hear me say this."

"No, Jimmy, I wanted to make the point that something very unusual must have happened. Maybe something you haven't thought of." He nodded, obviously thinking hard. "Mind you, you're quite right in a way. I also came out to talk to the dispatcher of the flight in question to see if there was a problem."

"Was there one?"

"Yes, there was a problem but he wasn't party to it. There was a discussion between the captain and the duty pilot after which the aircraft left."

"So what do you want?"

"I'd like you to think if there might be any possible faults which, if not rectified, might account for lack of data."

"Well I must know what the recorder did have, so I'll know what was missing."

I looked at Ronald. "Surely it would be in order for you to ask AAIB for that information as quickly as possible?"

"Peter, yes I'll do that immediately. We've got to get to the bottom of this problem before the Company suffers any more." He suddenly smiled. "Shall I tell them it was your idea?"

I smiled back, shook my head but didn't bother to reply. The last thing I needed was Tom Falconbury thinking I was trying to do his job. We talked a lot more about the accident and the salvage operation but made no progress. We had a quick sandwich at the railway diner not far from the office building and then Ronald took me to the 'emergency design and procedures' section where they showed me movies of a model 831 ditching in a water tank. The pictures were horrifying as the model twisted and somersaulted on occasions as it hit the water.

"Surely you've got a clip of a ditching where the aircraft hit the water neatly."

"No, we tried probably fifty times varying the touch down but it always ended up completely uncontrollable."

"No wonder the book says that ditching is catastrophic. How anybody survived on Alpha Delta is a miracle. And it was at night. Incredible."

Ronald agreed. "As you can imagine, we don't normally show these clips to anyone. The pilot must have done a super job. And at night. Amazing."

I left and made my way to the airport, not a lot wiser on what had happened to Alpha Delta. There was a message on my phone to call David Winston. The flight left on time and bleary eyed I caught the connecting flight to St Antony.

DAY 18

The immigration man grinned when he saw me and gave me six weeks without my asking. I picked up a car, drove to the hotel and collected my key. I was greeted by a waft of perfume, ladies clothes in the wardrobe and a diaphanous pair of pyjamas that were definitely not part of my kit. I unpacked, showered, gingerly moving a whole heap of stuff that wasn't mine out of the way of the basin in the bathroom so I could shave and clean my teeth. I put on a shirt and shorts and then telephoned David Winston before going down to find Helen. He was in.

"Peter, I'm so glad you called. I've just remembered something about Alpha Delta's departure. It was trivial really and I forgot to mention it to you but I realise now it might be important. After Jim started up he shut the engines down and called me. Apparently he was worried about a faulty fuel gauge and got me to check in the Acceptable Deferred Defects list. I assured him it was OK if the indication was faulty as long it was correctly shown on the Flight Management System fuel quantities page. He checked and he agreed to take the flight."

"That explains things."

"What do you mean?"

"I had a word with the dispatcher and he told me there was a delay but didn't know the reason."

"How did you manage that." He sounded puzzled. "I thought Gonzales had left us."

"Yes I know. But by chance I bumped into him in San Francisco."

"How do you mean 'by chance'? Doesn't sound very likely if I may say so."

"Well I wanted to go out to ITAC to discuss the way the aircraft's flying controls are operated electrically and, knowing Gonzales was in San Francisco, I took the opportunity to find out if there had been any problems on start up. He did say that there was a delay and that's why I was about to ring you."

"Well I'm glad its all been sorted. Is there anything else I can do for you?"

"Not for the moment, David. Thanks again."

I went down the stairs and my first port of call was the swimming pool where Helen was sitting under a large umbrella at a table with two other girls. The sun was very warm and I was glad to sit next to Helen on another chair out of the sun.

"I like the bikini."

"It's me you're meant to like." She grinned. "It's really great to see you. You may kiss me."

I obliged, to the obvious amusement of the other girls who I assumed correctly to be Worldwide cabin staff

"How did you get on?"

"Not very well I'm afraid. Full of ideas. I must catch up with Tom Falconbury to see if he is making any progress. When did you get in?"

"Yesterday. I used your room."

"I had noticed." I thought for a moment. "I must try to contact Tom. Why don't we aim to meet in the bar and then we can go out for a meal to celebrate your arrival. Where would you like to go?"

"How about Moby Dick's for a change?"

I left and asked the bell captain to make the reservation. I looked around for Tom who wasn't to be seen. I checked with the desk and found he had checked out so I went up to my room and called Tom's extension at AAIB.

"Tom, it's Peter here. When did you get back?"

"Thursday night. I'm trying to take advantage of the salvage delay to tidy things up this end. You're lucky to find me here on a Saturday. Where have you been? I couldn't find you to tell you I was going back."

"Have you made any progress? How is the salvage going?"

"The ship is in position next to the aircraft but we don't want it to start until the building is complete. Going to be another week. I plan to be back before they start. Where have you been?"

"I went out to the West Coast to talk to Worldwide and also ITAC."

"Alright Peter, that explains something. Bob Furness told me you never sit still. I've had a message from Ronald Raycroft asking for some details on the data that was on the recorder. Where were you yesterday?"

I was glad Tom couldn't see me. "That's a coincidence, I was with Ronald yesterday."

"Don't give me that. What were you doing if I may ask?"

"I was with an electrical expert. I was trying to understand how the 831 electrics work."

"Did you glean anything?"

"'Fraid not. It should all have worked. The guy did say that he was awaiting more information from you. Maybe they got impatient!"

"Yes. To be honest we should have given them more details earlier. Anyway they've got what they need right now. What's your next move? Now I've met you I'm always wondering what you're scheming."

"Well, rather like you, I was thinking of going home, but Helen Partridge has come out to visit me."

"You mean that fantastic girl who rescued all those people."

"The same."

"Why on earth has she come back? I'd have thought she would have had enough of St Antony."

"I told you. To see me. We get on rather well."

"Peter, you really are amazing. I wasn't even aware you two had met. A man of many parts."

"I'm not sure you expressed that very well. She is a lovely girl but, understandably, the aftermath of the accident is proving a trial for her. And the airline is not helping by trying to publicise her efforts to show how good their training is. I keep telling her she's not ready for the media yet. Not altogether surprisingly, she's liable to break down as she remembers what actually happened. I know you interviewed her but you did say that you wanted to talk to her again. There's a lot of horrifying stuff I don't think you've heard yet."

"Well she's got a good man to advise her."

"Thank you for that. I'd better go and try and find her. Keep in touch if you find anything you can tell me."

In fact I didn't have to find Helen as she appeared smelling of sun tan cream.

"What time did you book?"

"Seven o'clock."

"Good. Then we can take our time getting ready. I'm really glad to see you." She definitely embraced me.

"I didn't think I wanted you to come out but actually I'm delighted. As it happens there isn't a problem. You've chosen a good moment since the salvage hasn't started."

"Listen Peter. Whenever I come to see you it's always going to be a good moment."

I decided not to argue, grinned and found the sun tan oil wasn't as bad as I feared though I was looking forward to it being replaced by perfume.

We left in plenty of time and managed to find Moby Dick's again. There was a parking slot not too far away and we strolled back to the restaurant. Nothing seemed to have changed but this time Helen decided to sit so that I couldn't see all the diners arriving.

"Did you say oysters, Peter?"

"No, my dear, I didn't. I'm having jumbo shrimp and filet steak."

"Well I'm having the scallops and the steak."

Just then two diners arrived and I heard Helen gasp. She stiffened up and went very pale. She was looking at the guests as they came in and sat down. They got up a few moments later, presumably having changed their minds, and left. I glimpsed a head of hair which almost certainly belonged to Philip Smithson and the back of the other guy definitely reminded me of Jacko.

"I'm sure that was one of the survivors in my boat. He saw me looking at him as he came in and then he dug the other guy in the ribs who looked at us both. The guy with the blonde hair dragged him out. It was as if they didn't want to be recognised." Helen looked at me. "Perhaps it was just as well they left. I remember now if I'm right that he was one of the absolute bastards fighting to get out of the aircraft and pushing other people out of the way. If he's the one I think he is, he got knocked out hitting his head on the door sill. I was forced to help the man who knocked him down getting his unconscious body into the slideraft and clear the way for passengers to escape. What's the matter, my love? You look as if you've seen a ghost."

"I've been rather stupid. Actually it is you who've seen a ghost and we may be in trouble. In fact I'm wondering whether you shouldn't go straight back to England to-morrow."

Helen stared at me in misbelief. "Tell me what's the matter."

"The guy you recognised, the survivor, is a very famous crook and thought no-one would know him. He is ruthless and is trying to change his name and remain incognito. He is relying on everyone thinking he is dead and has taken on a new identity."

"But I don't know him except as one of the survivors. Who is he?" She looked at me and gripped my hand tightly. "What haven't you told me?"

"Don't you read the newspapers? The guy the police believe is a big drug runner in England, Jackson Turner, was on your flight in business class and he had some associates in steerage."

"Of course I read that, but he was killed in the crash." A look of concern came across Helen's face. "Wasn't he?"

I shook my head. "I think he survived but the problem is that he doesn't want anyone to know. One guy has already been killed, almost certainly to prevent people finding out that he has a new identity. Now you tell me that he was fighting trying to get out of the aircraft, he will guess correctly that you will remember that. Your life may be in danger."

"Wouldn't it have been better if you hadn't told me?"

"No, now you've seen him and he's recognised you, you had to know. Problem is we don't know what Mr Smith alias Turner will do. His rapid exit from here was because obviously he didn't want you talking to him and perhaps asking him his name. However, because you recognised him as a passenger he will be worried that you will talk to Worldwide and he won't want you to do that. You know the safest thing would be for you to go home to-morrow."

"Are you serious, Peter?"

"Yes, my love. I am. Believe me I'd like you to stay but I'm afraid he may try and find you."

"How will he do that?"

"He clearly remembers that you were at the aircraft escape door monitoring the escape. So he knows you were cabin staff and will easily be able to find your name from someone in Worldwide at the airport. Anyway your name was all over the local papers so he probably knows it already. The cabin staff stay in the *New Anchorage* so he will guess where you are likely to be."

"But I'm not checked in."

"Yes. That is good and he daren't go over there himself and look for you. However, someone may talk about us. The situation is complicated I think because you said the blonde guy looked at me as well, while I was looking at the menu."

"Why does that matter?"

"Well we met briefly at *Dark Blue Diving* and he probably thinks I'm a policeman or a Secret Service officer."

Our meal arrived but understandably Helen had lost her appetite. I tried to cheer her up but not with a lot of success. When it was time to leave I decided that we had better not take any chances in case Jacko or Smithson had organised someone to follow us and find out who we were. So, to the surprise of the head waiter, I asked that we might leave through the kitchen and, not surprisingly, the kitchen staff looked bemused as we threaded our way to the service door at the back.

Outside I checked that we were not being watched and then we made our way down the street to a bar. I ordered some drinks and later I called a cab. Back in our room we were rather subdued and I held Helen close until she eventually went to sleep.

DAY 19

In the morning we got up slowly and I suggested to Helen that she had a word with Becky since she had come out sub load as a Worldwide employee.

"Peter, I want to stay here and have a holiday. I don't want to go home. I need a rest."

I had an idea. "Alright, I'll tell you what we'll do. Why don't we go to Barbados and get away from here?"

"That would be wonderful," she thought for a moment "but can you spare the time?"

"I'll be alright until they start bringing the aircraft up."

On the internet I made a reservation at the Colony Club for seven nights and booked a 1400 flight with Caribbean Airlines.

"You're a star. The best thing that has happened to me. You work at my speed," a pause, "or the speed I used to move at until Alpha Delta ditched."

"Let's go and have breakfast and work out a programme. I'd better collect the car from Moby Dick's on the way to the airport."

"Is that wise? They may be watching it."

"Well it wasn't parked outside the place and a lot of the parked cars stay there all night. They won't know which was my car."

"I suppose not. Shouldn't you tell the police?"

"Probably, but let's have breakfast first."

We went outside and sat a long way from the next couple.

"You know, the only person who knows about Jacko besides us is Ben Masters, the chief of police here. He has got to decide what to do. If and when Jacko's existence become general knowledge then we can relax but at the moment Jacko thinks he has got away with it and he'll want to keep it that way."

"Peter, I'm so glad you are coming with me to Barbados. The way I feel at the moment I couldn't stand being by myself even for a second. I'd be worried stiff."

I called Ben when we got back upstairs and explained what had happened.

"You're probably right to leave straightaway."

"When are you going to tell Cindy about Jacko?"

"I'm not sure I like the implication in that remark, Peter. For the moment I think we need to keep Jacko's survival under wraps until we can nail him or Smithson for something."

"Have you told anyone in the UK yet?"

"Not yet. If I do the news will get out. Once more than one person knows, it's no longer a secret and the UK police these days seem to leak everything to show how good they are."

I broke the news to the front desk that we were checking out and then we started packing. Helen looked excited about going to Barbados.

"I'm looking forward to a lovely recuperation, just the two of us."

"So am I. It will be a relief to get away for a bit. I've discovered that accidents are never simple and straightforward."

"Is that what Mandy used to say?"

"Please, Helen, leave her out of it. The fact is aircraft accidents are terrible, not only for the passengers and their relatives, but also for the airlines and the aircraft and engine manufacturers. Millions, if not billions, of pounds are at stake and all sorts of organisations and firms get involved. And the problem is that all the big battalions are only looking after their own particular interests. And if that isn't enough, in this case there are drugs and crooks involved. The only people who gain are the lawyers."

Helen carried on packing. "Peter, are you keeping this room?"

"You have to be joking. I shall be broke after the Colony Club without keeping on an empty room. As they say in the auction room, everything must go."

My financial comment seemed to cheer her up. "It will be worth every penny. It sounds great and I like the idea of a suite. Ideal place for a honeymoon. Hope they've got a big bed. How are we getting to the airport?"

"I thought we might go by taxi with the bags, you drop me off in Cape Harbour to pick up the car and I'll meet you near check-in after I've got rid of it."

We checked out and the bell captain called a cab. From force of habit operating outside the UK, I noted the driver's name and licence number as he loaded our bags into the back of the cab and then the driver dropped me off at my car near Moby Dick's. I walked round it and checked, it seemed OK. I looked underneath the car as best I could and then opened the boot. All seemed normal so I got in and drove to the airport. It only took a moment to check in and I walked over to the Caribbean check-in. There was no sign of Helen.

I went to the first class check-in where there was no line and asked if Helen had checked in but she hadn't. Suddenly I began to get worried and I rang Ben. For a moment I thought Jearl wasn't going to put me through but she could tell from my voice it was important.

"Ben, Helen is missing, disappeared."

"What do you mean, Peter? Where are you?"

"She went by cab after she left me to go to the airport and to Caribbean check-in while I checked in my car with Hertz. We were supposed to meet at check-in but there's no sign of her."

"Stay there. Rick Welcome is with me. I'll send him straight round."

I felt cold fear descending and I wondered if I would ever see Helen alive again.

* * *

Rick Welcome arrived incredibly quickly and he listened intently as I told him our movements exactly.

"There's been no report of a taxi being held up. Did you check that the cab was a real one?'

"It looked like a regular St Antony taxi, Rick. I've got all the details here."

I took out my note book and copied the driver's details plus the car's plate number on to a blank sheet which I tore out and gave to Rick. He phoned the information through to the police station and held the phone listening, presumably while the person at the other end was checking. As the information came through Rick looked concerned.

"You're sure. How long ago." A pause. "Two weeks. OK, Thanks. Try and find the car as soon as you can." He put the phone back in his office and looked at me. "The driver details were from a man who died of natural causes two weeks ago."

"Where will they take her, Rick? Did Ben explain the problem?"

168

Rick nodded. "I've no idea. To be frank, and forgive me for saying this Peter, if they've got any sense they ought to get rid of her straight away. Mind you that driver will be in trouble. They probably didn't anticipate that you would be travelling with her and he wouldn't have known what to do." He smiled. "We have one advantage, however. They wouldn't have expected the driver's number and the number plate to be taken."

"Rick, I think the problem is that Jacko fought to get out of the aircraft and the last person he would have wanted to see is the girl who saw him pushing everyone else out of the way and who was supervising and helping people to get out. As you know he got concussion or something like it when he left the aircraft. He must have been convinced that Helen would report the encounter in Moby Dick's to Worldwide and he didn't want people to start talking to him. I don't think he thought it through. Just because Helen recognised him as a survivor didn't mean that she would know who he was. If he kills Helen it will make the police look for an explanation. Jacko's best bet would have been just to ignore Helen."

"You may be right but whatever we think isn't going to help. We've got to find where Helen is as quickly as possible," and then he added grimly, "while it is still light."

"How about going to Smithson's house? Or to *Dark Blue Diving*?"

"Without a search warrant? We'd never get one. There isn't enough evidence and Philip Smithson seems to know the heavy breathers."

"This is ridiculous. You can't just sit idly by."

" I'll talk to Ben."

He got straight through but I couldn't hear all the conversation with the airport noise. It seem to take a long time before they finished.

"Peter, Ben already had people watching Smithson's house and he has just put men to watching *Dark Blue Diving.* He's also issued a warning to his people to look out for the cab. There's not much more he can do."

I nodded but felt wretched and frustrated, feeling I should do something. Rick interrupted my thoughts.

"Peter, the best thing you can do is to go back to the hotel, rent a room and wait. I'll take you there."

Luckily the hotel was not full and I went up to my new room. All I had was my laptop with my emergency travelling kit and I felt desperate. I cancelled the reservation at the Colony Club, then called Hertz and booked a car. I told Jearl that Ben could contact me on my mobile and then went by cab to collect the car.

I drove to Paradise Harbour and went into the café. It was very busy but I found a table where I could look across at *Dark Blue Diving* and ordered a coffee. There were some divers returning from one of the boats and I thought I could see Alvin Goddard with the group. A police car was in the parking lot with a driver inside who clearly also had a good view of *Dark Blue Diving*. My concern was that the driver could have taken Helen there before Ben had got his people into position.

A green Ford Fiesta arrived and parked well away from the police car and quite close to the café. To my surprise Jacko got out and sat down at the only free table, which was next to mine. Surreptitiously he kept on looking in my direction but I ignored him.

My phone rang and I walked to the quay as I answered the call. It was Ben. "We've found the car. It was in a parking lot in the middle of Cape Harbour. No sign of the driver or of Helen Partridge. We're having the car checked for finger prints, not that we expect to find any."

"What are you going to do?"

"I'm about to send Rick and Malcolm Strang over to *Dark Blue Diving* to ask if they can help and look round the facility. I don't expect them to agree but it will be interesting to gauge their reaction. Where are you?"

"I'm in the café at Paradise Harbour and would you believe Thomas Smith is at the next table having a sandwich."

"Peter, be careful."

I decided not to mention that Jacko had been looking at me in case Ben reckoned I'd be safer in the UK. "Will be. Presumably I'll see Rick arrive in a moment."

Back at the table I ordered a sandwich. Jacko got up, walked back to his car and drove out of the harbour. Shortly afterwards Rick arrived in his plain blue Toyota Corolla and parked next to the police car. The police driver, who I assumed to be Malcolm Strang, got out of his car and they both walked over to *Dark Blue Diving*. They seemed to be there for about three quarters of an hour before they finally emerged. Then they drove off in their cars. There was nothing more I could do and I went back to the hotel, feeling very distraught.

About an hour later Ben called. "Would you believe they were allowed to look in the whole building? They didn't find anything of course."

"Then Helen must be in Smithson's house."

"No, Peter. She could be at several other location but not at *Leewards* or *Dark Blue*. As you know we've been watching Smithson for some time since we believe he is involved with drugs and we are pretty sure he wouldn't have her anywhere near his house. The last thing we want to do is to alert him to our suspicions by searching his house, not that we could get a search warrant. We want to catch him red handed one day but we're not ready yet."

I went down to the bar and had a drink. As it got dark I drove over to Paradise Harbour and parked the car in the reserved slot next to the *Discover St Antony* hut so I could watch *Dark Blue Diving*. A man arrived after about forty minutes and went into the building. I crouched down hoping that the car would appear to be empty with the poor illumination from just two lights close by the *St Antony Fish Sales* kiosk. There was no moon. After some time a door opened in the building and some light shone through. A man came out and stood absolutely still, apparently checking that there was no-one about. He saw my car, came over and stood very close to the car. Realising he was about to discover me, I decided to make the first move and suddenly pushed the door open, hitting the man as he was fumbling with his torch. I could see him reaching for what I guessed correctly to be a gun but I had already leapt out of the car and hit him as hard as I could on the face followed by kicking him in the stomach. He screamed with pain and dropped motionless to the ground, whimpering in agony. I picked up his gun and then shone his torch in his face. It was Alvin Goddard. He started to move and against all my fair play instincts I kicked him again in the stomach. He moaned and didn't move.

I called Ben's number and after a bit the duty officer answered. He wouldn't put me through to Ben but agreed to give him a message after I threatened the guy with losing his job. Ben came back on my phone almost immediately. I explained the situation.

"Peter, why can't you leave things like this to us? I told you the place was empty."

"Well the place clearly is not empty. Do you want me to go inside? I've got a gun now."

"Alright, I'll be along as quickly as I can with Rick. Will you be able to look after the guy you hit?"

"Ben, I think he may need an ambulance. I had to hit him very hard as I didn't want to be shot. You'd better get one."

All went quiet apart from Alvin moaning. Then the door in the building opened again and another man came out and shut the door behind him. I hid behind the car and the man heard Alvin groaning. He also had a torch and cautiously made his way towards Alvin, holding a gun in his other hand and looking towards the car. As he bent over to look at Alvin I shone my torch at him.

"Turn towards the building and drop your gun and your torch."

He hesitated and I fired in the air. I think he must have heard the bullet. I heard both the gun and the torch drop.

"Now walk towards the door."

The man slowly obeyed until he reached the door.

"Now drop your phone."

He reached inside his trouser pocket and dropped his phone. We could both hear the sound of an ambulance which rapidly came to *Dark Blue Diving.* Two paramedics appeared and stood back nervously. I told them to go to Alvin lying by my car but get some handcuffs first.

A moment later we could hear and I could see the lights of cars approaching. They parked by the ambulance and Ben and Rick appeared. Rick took a gun out of his holster and waved me away. He spoke to the man I had been covering.

"Lower your hands behind your back."

Rick produced some handcuffs. He placed them expertly on the man's wrist. He picked up the man's gun.

"OK. Now get in the back of that car."

The guy turned round looking very scared and got in to Rick's car.

I handed Ben Alvin's gun and he looked at me.

"OK. You did a good job, Peter. Now, just for once keep out of this. We'll deal with it. I'll get more of my people out."

"Please get a move on Ben. We still haven't found Helen."

"How do you know she's there?"

"I don't, but I think the two of them were about to dump her in the sea."

Ben started phoning, presumably for reinforcements. After what seemed like forever three more policeman appeared and covered the back and front of the building. Rick hammered on the side door and went inside holding a gun. Ben followed with one of his men. Then Ben came out and called me in.

"She's alright. Rick's just cutting her free."

I went in and saw Helen getting up from a stool holding what looked like a gag of some type. Rick had clearly just finished untying some ropes which presumably had been tying her down. She looked very shaken and her face looked a mess where the gag had been. I helped her over to sit on a chair. She was obviously relieved but very nervous and I did my best to reassure her. She didn't say anything but grabbed my hand. I suddenly realised my hand was hurting where I had hit Alvin as hard as I could and my ankle felt bruised where I had kicked him.

Looking around the room we were in I could see how Rick and Malcolm had missed Helen in their search. There was a dummy corridor about thirty inches wide along the whole length of the building with what was virtually an invisible door on the wall of a toilet situated near the back door of the building. I saw Ben looking inside the corridor. It was almost full of a whole load of brown boxes and I noticed with some relief, our two suitcases and Helen's handbag. The stool near the entrance to the corridor had clearly been inside with Helen on it.

At this moment Philip Smithson suddenly appeared. He went up to Ben who he obviously knew.

"Thank you for calling me over, Masters. What on earth has been going on?"

"That's what we want to know, Sir. Would you please explain what these boxes are in this hidden corridor?"

"What hidden corridor? What boxes? What on earth are you talking about?"

Ben showed the corridor to Smithson who looked very surprised.

"I've never seen this corridor before in my life."

"We believe the boxes contain drugs. I must warn you this is extremely serious Sir."

"Masters, be very careful. Are you accusing me of having drugs? I've just told you I've never seen this corridor before in my life. Clearly, some of my staff having been trading in drugs, if these are drugs. Don't let's assume things without checking."

"Mr Smithson, I am accusing you of trading in prohibited drugs and warn you that anything you say now may be used in evidence against you."

"This is quite ridiculous. I shall get my solicitor over here right now and talk to the Minister of Home Affairs in the morning."

I guessed the Minister of Home Affairs was Ben's boss. I had to admire Smithson. I almost believed he was telling the truth. Ben however was not to be put off.

"Mr Smithson, would you please go down to the Central Police Station with Sergeant Welcome. We shall be asking you to make a statement."

Smithson looked speechless with rage but went out with Rick. Ben looked at me. "Can you look after Miss Partridge, Peter? We shall need a statement but I guess it can wait until the morning."

I looked at Helen. "I'm not sure. I think she should go to the hospital for a check-up." Helen shook her head but I ignored her. "Could you ring the hospital and warn them? Oh, can Helen have her handbag and may we collect our suitcases in the morning?"

Ben said we could have all our cases straightaway and one of his men carried them for us.

Helen stood up gingerly and leaned on me as we went slowly over to the car.

"Peter, I'll be alright. I don't need to go to the hospital."

"Helen, whether you are well or not is irrelevant. The police will want to know how you are after what you have been through."

Reluctantly Helen stopped arguing and we went to the hospital and to the out patients. To my surprise the doctor who appeared was Rupert Stanton who I knew from my previous visit. He looked at me, knew we had met, but couldn't remember where or when. He looked at Helen and then took her away.

It seemed ages before they reappeared. She was clutching a bag which I guessed contained medicine and she looked a bit happier.

"I told you I was alright."

"You will be when you have some sedation, I guess, and a very good rest."

Rupert Stanton nodded. "Yes. There's some nasty bruising but nothing's broken. I think she may have some bruising of the jaw where a gag has been tied very tightly." He looked at me. "Bring Miss Partridge back if you are not happy. And I do remember you. There was a car accident. Driven off the road or something like that."

I nodded, thanked him and I took Helen back to the hotel. She was very quiet and held my arm very closely as we went up to my room. She lay on the bed staring at the ceiling and I went down to collect the bags. She hadn't moved and I took the bag from her with the medicines. There were three different types and the only one I recognised was ibuprofen. I looked again at Helen and saw she had bruising on both her arms. I opened the packs and offered the pills to her with a glass of water. She turned, looked at me and smiled.

"I'm sorry."

"Don't apologise. I'm the one who should be apologising for asking you to go in the taxi alone. Here, take these pills and then you'd better get some sleep."

She nodded. It took several attempts before they disappeared and then she went into the bathroom to sort herself out, returning wearing the flimsy pyjamas. I could see the bruising more clearly on her face and more marks on her side and legs. She held me for a moment and then collapsed on the bed. I sorted the bed clothes out and turned out most of the lights. I took my clothes off and as I got into the other bed I could hear that Helen was already asleep.

DAY 20

I picked up the *Announcer*. Cindy had excelled herself at the bottom of the front page. 'Crash hostess rescued from kidnappers.' The article went on to describe how she had been found by the police. However there was very little detail, not surprisingly since only Helen knew what had happened. She hadn't told anyone and, I guessed watching her breathing deeply with eye shades on, wasn't likely to for some time.

Ben came on the phone. "You've seen the *Announcer*?" I murmured agreement. "I'm sorry. But we got him this time."

"Who Ben?"

"The guy who has been leaking everything that happens in my office to Cindy. I've charged him and fired him."

"Ben, you know what I find curious about the article?"

"Yes, there's no mention of Smithson."

"Right."

"The Editor is scared of him. I told you. Smithson knows too many movers and shakers."

"What did you do to him last night?"

"I had to let him go on bail."

"And Alvin?"

"He's tucked away in prison but we need a statement from your Miss Partridge if we are going to keep him there."

"Ben, she's sedated. Fast sleep. I don't think you are going to get a statement to-day. But somehow you've got to keep Alvin in prison. Has he made a statement?"

"No, he hasn't said a thing We keep asking him who was telling him what to do but he won't talk. I think he's afraid of Smithson too."

"Ben, have you got *Dark Blue Diving* guarded?"

"Yes, but not for much longer. Smithson is asking for his place back and swearing all this is a complete surprise to him. We've taken all the bags away and if it is cocaine then it's worth millions of dollars. Why do you ask?"

"I think there may be something there from the crashed aircraft."

"Peter, I have to admire you. You get involved in things that don't concern you and all of a sudden you come up with a winner.

And I haven't forgotten it was you who found Miss Partridge and incidentally the store room with all the bags."

"Hey, Ben, you can take all the credit. I'm not looking for rewards. I just want to know why the aircraft crashed and how we're going to keep Helen Partridge safe."

"There's not likely to be another go, Peter."

"Why do you say that, Ben? Jacko will do anything to prevent people knowing he's alive. It was only by chance that I found out what had happened. Can't you confront him with the situation?"

"I could but I'm trying to crack this drug cartel and he's obviously in the thick of it."

"But you've got the drugs now."

"Peter, you may be a good insurance investigator but you don't know anything about drugs. That lot we found in that hidden corridor is only a fraction of the traffic through St Antony."

"Well you've stopped that link in the supply chain."

"But I don't know yet if it was coming in or going out. If I can watch Jacko I may learn something."

"But I thought Smithson was the key here."

"Possibly, but even if he is the key man here, he is only a link in the whole chain and there will be the small fry. I'm afraid I can't pull Jacko in just yet."

"But he'll know from Cindy's article that Helen is alive."

"I know. She'll have to disappear somewhere for a bit until we've sorted out Jacko. Why don't you two go to Barbados as you planned after she has made a written statement?"

"Only after I've looked round *Dark Blue Diving*. And I can't leave here until you put a guard on my room."

"Be at *Dark Blue Diving* at 1100 and I'll send Rick round there. I'll have a girl round to watch Miss Partridge at 1030."

My hand and ankle felt very sore and I had to get showered and dressed very gingerly. Helen opened her eyes, looked at me and then shut them again. I went over and kissed her and she smiled.

"I'm going to order breakfast. Do you want anything."

She nodded and whispered. "I didn't have anything after I left you. They were going to drown me."

"I know, my darling. I'll order something and you can graze."

Room service duly arrived with two full English breakfasts with one tea, one coffee, one orange juice and one apple juice. The waiter laid it all out on the table and left but not before I got him to leave a tray behind.

Helen opened her eyes. "Smells great. I thought I was never going to be able to eat again I felt so sick. Maybe the pills did work." She sat up and looked at the table. "You can bring me apple juice and scrambled egg to start with but my jaw is very sore. Can you cut it all up into very small mouthfuls?"

I obliged and was glad to see her eat. I had a little toast but didn't feel too hungry. The coffee tasted good but I didn't get much as Helen took it over so I settled for the tea. I produced the pills and Helen dutifully swallowed them. I removed the tray and sat next to her.

"If you stay there I shall get better quickly. Have you got a book to read?"

"I've got to leave in a bit." Helen started to look unsure of things. "But there's a police lady who is going to sit with you. Then I thought we might go to Barbados."

"When?"

"When you feel fit to travel." She started to get up but it obviously felt uncomfortable. "Don't be silly. Maybe to-morrow if you're good."

She smiled. "If I'm feeling better I may not want to be good."

"Well, we'll just have to see."

I felt a sense of relief. Clearly Helen was not feeling desperate but I didn't want to rush her and I couldn't let her out of my sight until we were well away from St Antony.

There was a knock on the door and a police woman came into the room. She was quite young which was a plus as far as I was concerned and looked extremely capable. Her name was Alice Sanchez and I was slightly surprised to see she was carrying a gun. After looking carefully round and inspecting the outside of the window for possible access, she sat down in the easy chair and I left for *Dark Blue Diving* feeling reassured that Helen would be safe.

Rick met me outside the building.

"We've having to let Smithson have his place back by 5pm to-day. The bags do contain cocaine. It's high quality stuff probably destined to be shipped to Europe."

"Why did it have to be landed here first?"

"We think that large amounts are regularly landed here and then it is parcelled up for different 'sellers' in different countries. The lot we found was destined for France as far as we can see from the markings."

"I can't believe you weren't able to 'hold' the building for longer."

"Well we searched everywhere but we couldn't find anything else and Smithson's lawyer convinced the judge that there was no reason why we should still be in the place."

"What about all his paperwork? His computer? His CD's?"

"We were allowed to take his computer but only for forty eight hours. There were a few CDs in his office which we also took. The firm's paperwork was in the general office and it looked completely genuine."

"Will forty eight hours be enough to sort things out?"

"Hope so. We've got our local expert working on it now and we've already made copies of all the CDs and a mirror image of his hard drive. We're going to run a computer which will be exactly like Smithson's. Strangely he didn't seem worried about our taking the machine."

"He must be using the internet for storage."

I needed to get on. "May I look around?"

"Yes, but please be careful."

The brown bags in the corridor had disappeared and it was completely empty.

"May I look everywhere."

"Go ahead."

I went in to Smithson's room and looked in every nook and cranny but there was nothing unusual. From there I looked in all the other rooms but found nothing. There were all sorts of pieces of diving equipment which I had to move to make certain I hadn't missed anything.

"Is there a store anywhere?"

"Outside abutting onto the building and hiding the corridor."

I went outside and the store was incredibly full but well organised. Rick appeared obviously getting impatient, but finally I spotted what I had been looking for, a bright orange crash recorder tucked away right at the back of the store covered by bright yellow life jackets. I didn't take it out as it might have fingerprints and

179

anyway AAIB needed to see where it was and get the data analysed straightaway.

I turned to Rick. "Surely this gives you a reason for holding on to the building? That orange device is almost certainly the missing recorder from Alpha Delta and it needs checking before it is moved. The big question is how did it get there? I'm sure Smithson will seem as surprised as anyone."

Rick got his phone out and called Ben who wanted to talk to me.

"Are you sure that piece of equipment is from the aircraft that ditched? How can I convince the judge so that we can get an extension of occupying *Dark Blue Diving*?"

"Do you want me to come and give evidence? I could explain how it got there."

"Why not tell me?"

"I could but wouldn't the explanation be more credible coming from me? Anyway it would be a lot quicker."

"I won't argue. You'll need to come straight over to Cape Harbour to the Courtroom. It is in Independence Way. Do you think you will be able to find it?"

I left Rick and drove straight to the Courtroom with the aid of my satellite navigator. I went to the enquiries desk and the man behind the counter signalled to a very smart looking lady talking to some men in the large reception area.

"You must be Peter Talbert. I'm Lindsay Joseph, a solicitor in the police department. Ben Masters has asked me to apply for an extension of the occupation of *Dark Blue Diving* but I'm not sure we've got a case. I gather you found part of the crashed aircraft in the store and that it is necessary to examine it carefully before moving it and also to make sure there is nothing else hidden there."

"Right. Do you really need me to say that?"

"Yes we do, as Smithson's solicitor will contest our application."

We had to wait for about an hour before we were called in to a small room. There was a man already there, clearly of white Caucasian descent, dressed in a dark blue suit which, in my judgement, must have cost a lot of money. I took him, correctly as it turned out, to be Smithson's solicitor and he was assisted by a junior man who I assumed to be locally trained. To my horror I saw

Cindy Smart in the public spectator area and she waved to me, much to the surprise of Lindsay Joseph. There was a further delay until the judge, clearly a local man, appeared in conventional European clothing and with a lady assistant.

The formal proceedings were started and Joseph made the application for a three day extension so that the AAIB could be present. Smithson's man pointed out that the crash recorder from the aircraft had already been found and the piece of equipment in the shed had nothing to do with the crashed aircraft. Joseph then requested that I be called as an expert witness.

I explained my background, experience and who I was representing. The judge seemed satisfied but Smithson's lawyer said that I was biased, not an expert and that only someone from the aircraft manufacturer or the airline could testify on the matter.

I got the impression that the judge wasn't too keen on high powered New York style lawyers and invited me to speak.

"Mr Talbert, explain to me about the part you found and why it is so important."

"Well your Honour, the ditching of this aircraft has enormous financial implications for the passengers, their dependants, the airlines and the aircraft manufacturers. It is true that I am here because I am looking after Hull Claims interests, but in these matters my main desire is always to find the truth and to help, if I can, the UK Air Accidents Investigation Branch to find the reason for the ditching. The AAIB are primarily interested in finding why the aircraft crashed and what happened afterwards. They do not consider insurance implications and that is why Hull Claims needs to be represented, since if the airline has not complied with the correct operating and maintenance conditions then Hull Claims may not be completely liable.

"On the Thursday morning, following the accident on the Tuesday night, the AAIB inspector heard the transmissions from the wreckage of two crash recorders but on the Saturday morning only one transmission could be heard. When divers went down to recover both recorders, only one recorder could be found. There can be very little doubt that the crash recorder I found in the *Dark Blue Diving* store was the one installed in the crashed aircraft."

"Are you suggesting, Mr Talbert, that the recorder was removed from the aircraft when it was underwater?"

"Yes, your Honour. I believe that the recorder was removed illegally. I understand from the St Antony police that lights were seen in the water round the aircraft structure the second night after the ditching, that is the Thursday night and it is logical to assume that some one from *Dark Blue Diving* removed the recorder from the aircraft. It is imperative that the UK AAIB see this recorder where it is at present, check that it did come from the crashed aircraft, check for fingerprints and then send it back to England to look at the data. Furthermore, the AAIB inspector will want to check the whole store to make sure there is nothing else from the aircraft."

The judge interrupted me and looked at Joseph. "Is it right about the lights in the water on the Thursday night?"

"Yes your Honour, we can bring witnesses to confirm Mr Talbert's statement."

The judge looked at Smithson's solicitor. "I think we have heard enough to make it clear that more investigation is required at *Dark Blue Diving*. The police can occupy the facility until the UK Air Accidents Investigation Branch inspector has examined the recorder and declared himself satisfied. Meantime, I suggest that every effort must be made to find out how the recorder got into the store."

Smithson's solicitor was not to be put off. "The UK AAIB are only investigating the circumstances of the ditching at the request of the St Antony Government. We wish to appeal your decision, your Honour."

"By all means appeal but in the meantime my order stands. You should be aware that whoever investigates this accident, it is vital to find out if the recorder came from the crashed aircraft, why the accident occurred and, of course, whether *Dark Blue Diving* was involved."

The judge left the courtroom and then we all filed out led by Smithson's solicitor. Cindy I noticed had gone. Joseph thanked me and then got on the phone to Ben. I indicated that I would like to have a word when she had finished.

"Ben, what is really concerning me is keeping Alvin Goddard safe. If anything happens to him you would have very little hope of indicting Smithson."

"Peter, you are trying to teach your grandmother to suck eggs. We're doing all we know to get Goddard to tell us the whole story but he refuses to say anything."

"Does he have a solicitor?"

"Yes, but I don't think Goddard trusts him. The solicitor is asking for bail and I don't think Alvin wants bail. I think he is hoping we are going to charge Smithson, while keeping him inside until after Smithson is in gaol."

"That's very understandable. Is the lawyer very smartly dressed and does he look as if he comes from New York?"

"Yes. Was he at your hearing?"

"Yes he was. Ben, I'm sorry if I was a bit naive but Alvin is probably in great danger. Judging by what happened to the crook who knew Jacko was alive, I think Alvin's life expectancy outside prison while Smithson is free must be very short."

"No worries my friend. I'm very concerned as well. Alvin is clearly very scared."

I gave Joseph her phone back and returned to the hotel. I went up to my room and found Alice Sanchez sitting in the corridor.

"Miss Partridge is asleep. I thought it would be safer if I guarded the room from the outside since it is impossible to get in through the window."

I made to open the door with my digital key.

"Mr Talbert, I got the hotel to change the settings so that no-one, not even a staff member can get in. This is the only key."

She produced the key from her pocket and we went inside. Helen was half awake and smiled.

"You were very quick."

"Hardly. It's 5pm. You've been asleep for several hours and you look so much better."

I turned to Alice. "Thanks so much for looking after Miss Partridge. Hopefully we won't need you again."

She gave me the key and left. I sat on the bed. Helen looked at me. "Do you think it's going to work?"

"What do you mean?"

"I mean us. You and me. I feel I may go the same way as Mandy. Tragedy and accidents seem to be your way of life and now I'm in the middle of it."

I looked at Helen and then held her close. "I'm sorry all this is happening. But nothing like it has ever happened before. If you are up to it let's go to Barbados to-morrow."

Helen nodded and held on tight. Then she slowly relaxed and smiled. "Alright you're on. I think I'm ready to eat something and then we'd better think about packing."

"Are you taking your pills?"

She nodded, got up, dealt with the pills and then went to have a shower. I took the opportunity to call Tom Falconbury at AAIB. He had left but I got him at home.

"I've got a surprise for you. I've almost certainly found the voice data recorder."

"Peter, that's wonderful. Where was it?"

"In a diving school's store."

Tom was speechless for a moment. "Peter, you obviously know something that I don't. It so happens I'm coming out to-morrow so you can expound your theory."

"Excellent. I got the judge to agree that nobody goes near the recorder until you've seen it. The situation is a bit difficult to explain."

"I saw something in the Mail about a kidnapping. Who was it?"

"It was Helen Partridge. You know the hostess who saved all those people. I told you she came back to see me." I hesitated. "Look, I can't sort it out with you over the phone. Unfortunately we will have left by the time you arrive. We're going to Barbados for a few days. Helen has had a very difficult time here and needs to recuperate."

"I don't follow you. What do you mean?"

"Tom, it's all tied up with the lost recorder and Jacko." I thought for a moment. "I've an idea. How are you travelling to-morrow? Direct or via Barbados?"

"Via Barbados. Why?"

"Why don't you night stop in Barbados so we can have a chat and you can travel on in the morning?"

"OK. Where shall we meet?"

"If you stay at the airport I'll pick you up from the hotel and we can eat somewhere."

"Done. I'll email you my hotel and my flight details. Let's aim for 6pm from the hotel unless I say different."

Helen was clearly listening to the conversation as she put on a top and rather short skirt which didn't do her figure any harm. I didn't wait for her to ask but kissed her appreciatively. "Wow, I'm not sure I feel like going down straight away."

Helen grinned and held the door open for me. We went in to the hotel's à la carte restaurant and Helen managed quite a good meal.

"You were brilliant arranging to see the AAIB man at Barbados."

"Yes, it was lucky he was coming out that way. Hope you don't mind that we will be talking shop over dinner."

"I'm not sure I think of it as shop since I'm so involved. Unfortunately I think I'm a piece of the action."

"Yes, I'm afraid you're right in a way. Anyway I'll try and keep the discussion as short as possible."

Back in the room Helen started preliminary packing for both of us and to my amusement it was clear that we were definitely sharing our bags and that, in this matter, I was surplus to requirements. However once she had things under control to her satisfaction she didn't mind letting me help her undress, though I couldn't help noticing she didn't pack those clothes until the morning.

DAY 21

For once the day went almost as planned. We got up, had breakfast, checked out, went to the police station where Helen made a statement, drove to the rental return at the airport and then wheeled our bags to Caribbean check-in. As we were waiting for the flight we both wandered over to the news stand to get something to read.

"Peter, isn't that you on the front page of the *Announcer*?"

I tried to look the other way, hoping no-one else had heard Helen's clearly enunciated question which was rather too loud as far as I was concerned. I picked the paper up and sure enough Cindy had got hold of some rather youthful library picture of me under a headline *'Accident investigator close to solving crash mystery.'* I scanned the article which was a factual report of the courtroom hearing the day before. At the end Cindy had attributed me with superhuman powers of detection; I hoped Tom Falconbury wouldn't read the article.

"Are you?"

"Am I what?"

"Close to solving the crash mystery?"

"No I'm not. I've got a few ideas but that's not the same as having a watertight case."

"I thought it was AAIB's job to decide what was the cause of the accident."

"Bingo. Yes it is. And that's why we're talking to Tom this evening."

"You're talking, I'm listening."

The flight was called and I hurriedly folded the paper up so that no-one would see the front page. However I wasn't exactly over the moon as the cabin staff went down the cabin before flight offering newspapers including the *Announcer* to all the passengers, with my face staring out of it.

In Barbados we collected our bags and a car and drove to the Colony Club. At check-in we got one of the honeymoon chalets.

Helen whispered to me. "Great. It won't matter if we make a noise."

I looked at her and decided that she was making a very rapid and full recovery. She grinned and didn't look at all abashed. I avoided looking at the girl who had checked us in though I'm sure she had heard it all before.

We unpacked, went for a swim and arrived at the Novotel where Tom was staying in plenty of time. We had a drink and Tom duly appeared looking very wide awake in a blue shirt, blazer and fawn trousers.

"Why don't we eat here, Peter? They don't seem very busy and I won't be able to keep awake for too long." I nodded and he added "I'll have a beer." to my unspoken question.

We went straight to a table.

"Now then, Peter. What have you been up to? What have you discovered?"

"Tom, I've felt for some time that there was something puzzling about the missing cockpit voice recorder which you couldn't find. Another thing that puzzled me was the underwater lights that were seen round the aircraft wreckage. I wondered if the recorder had been removed."

"But that's impossible. Why?"

"I'm not sure but probably to prevent anyone hearing the conversation on the flight deck."

"If you're right we are going to know what really happened when the data is played back."

"Don't be too sure about the data. The same fault that affected the first recorder you have, may also have prevented data being recorded on the CVR. You clearly need to get it back to UK as quickly as possible and see what's on it."

"I should be able to send it back to-morrow night."

"Let's hope so. There will be formalities with the police before you can examine it and I know the police want to check the box for fingerprints."

"But who took the recorder out of the aircraft?"

"That's easy. The recorder was in *Dark Blue Diving's* store. Smithson must have organised it and I believe that his man, Alvin Goddard, must have done the actual diving. He's in custody at the moment over drug issues and won't admit anything."

"Peter, your theory about who did the removal is obviously right but we've got to find out why. However, first of all we must examine the recorder you found. There's nothing I can do now. If you'll excuse me I'll go to bed."

"Wait a moment. What's happening to the salvage?"

"We're starting that on Thursday. That's why I've come back."
He paused. "But unless something significant is on the tape we are
no further forward in finding out why the aircraft ditched."

Tom left looking tired and a bit disconsolate. In the car Helen,
who had clearly been thinking about the conversation, questioned
me. "Peter, you gave him a lot to think about. Did Smithson really
take the cockpit voice recorder. Why would he want to do that?"

"Come on let's get back to the hotel and go to bed."

"Why won't you tell me?"

"Because I'm not sure exactly. Let's go."

"Wait a moment." She gave me a very provocative kiss.
"We're in the honeymoon suite. You must be romantic. Let's go for
a swim under the stars first."

"You are meant to be recovering from an incredibly nasty
experience. I'm not sure you ought to be exerting yourself."

"Come on. Don't shoot yourself in the foot. A swim first will
do you good."

"But we haven't got our bathing costumes."

"Well that's it, then!"

DAY 22

We had a quiet day. I took Helen shopping in Barbados and I bought her some incredibly expensive tiny tubes of make up which apparently would make her look even lovelier.

"I shall have to ring up my stockbroker and get some shares in Dior."

"Don't be a cheapskate. How else do you think I'm going to be able to hide all the bruises. Keep the receipt. I'm sure John Southern would allow it."

"Keeping madam happy, $400."

"Keeping mistress beautiful, $100 would be more accurate."

I gave up the discussion I wished I had never started.

Tom called while we were having dinner. "I managed to get the recorder away. There were no fingerprints on the box according to your friend Rick Welcome. I told your theory to Bob and he agrees that Smithson must have removed the recorder but we can't think why he should have done it. He had nothing to gain. Bob asked me to discuss the problem with Masters."

"Let's hope the recorder worked. Salvage still on for to-morrow?"

"Yes. The temporary hangar looks good and the air conditioning is fine. We've got a mortuary in the hangar and the specialist doctor is joining us from the Cape Harbour mortuary."

"Sorry I can't be with you."

Helen had been listening to our conversation.

"I've come to a decision. I'm really enjoying this holiday but it's time I pulled myself together and started work again. I shall go home at the end of the week you've booked here."

I thought about what she'd said and felt relieved on two counts. Firstly, having her around in St Antony was going to be difficult for me and possible dangerous for her. Secondly, it was good news that she was feeling better. The ditching followed by the kidnapping, near murder, had put a horrendous strain on her and it was great news that she was able to recover.

"Peter, you haven't said anything."

"I know. I've been thinking. Obviously we're having a great time here but if you're sure you feel strong enough then I can only applaud your decision." I squeezed her hand. "I shall miss you."

"I know you will but only for a moment and then you'll be right in the middle of it again interfering, suggesting, looking and probably doing rather well. I shall be looking forward to your return."

I didn't argue as she was almost certainly right.

We went into the news stand on the way to breakfast. The *Barbados Times* was there and I spotted a small news item on the front page *'Key accident witness commits suicide in custody'*. My heart sank as I knew what I was going to read. Alvin Goddard was dead. I showed Helen.

"That's the guy that was going to drown me?" I nodded. "Do you believe it was suicide or do you think he was murdered?"

"My dear. That is a very good question. I hope Ben knows."

Right on cue Ben phoned. "Peter, have you seen the papers?"

"I've just read it. Was it suicide?"

"For the moment it looks like it, though our doctor is checking more carefully. He apparently took a drug overdose. How he got it I don't know. All I do know is that it leaves Smithson still untouchable."

"By the way Helen is going home from here which should make your life easier."

"Yes, it will take one problem away though I'm sure Smithson wouldn't agree to let Jacko have another go. What about yourself? Are you coming back?"

"At the moment I'm planning to be in St Antony next Tuesday unless AAIB have solved the reason for ditching. Hopefully the aircraft should have been salvaged by then."

"See you then."

As I rang off I looked at Helen. "Hope you didn't mind that bit about you not going back."

"Not a bit. That's why I suggested it. What happens next?"

"I thought we might try and have breakfast before someone else calls."

My phone rang and I nodded to Helen to find a table. It was Tom on the phone.

"You were right. There was no data in the memory."

"How about the timing?"

"There was no timing that made sense."

"Was it the correct recorder. Do the serial numbers match?"

"Yes, it was the correct recorder."

"What about the memory module? Was that the correct one?"

"Peter, you ask the most searching questions. I don't know yet. But I'm having it checked. The problem is that the memory modules don't have the same serial numbers as the recorders. We're trying to find out if the airline records the numbers of the memory modules. Bob said you always make things difficult."

"Not at all. I just don't trust anyone and there is a lot of money and reputations at stake." I paused. "What are you going to do now that there's nothing on the module?"

"Peter, nothing I can do. We'll have to wait until the wreckage is in the hangar."

I found Helen sitting at a table outside the restaurant but in the shade.

"I haven't ordered. What do you fancy." I looked at her in very short shorts and a bra top. Only a very keen observer would have noticed the bruises. She must have done a wonderful job with the Dior long wearing concealer we had bought the other day. She smiled, "Sorry, Peter, it's got to come from this menu."

"You don't look very sorry."

"What did Tom have to say?"

"Would you believe that there was nothing on the memory?"

"Then you're no further forward?"

"Not sure about that. I've got an idea or two ..."

"...but you're still not going to tell me."

"How did you know?"

"We may not be married but I think I've got you weighed up. I don't mind you keeping that sort of thing from me but don't imagine you can get away with anything else. Mandy may have put up with your shenanigans but not this one."

"I'm not sure you understand what happened."

"I don't want to, thank you. As long as you're absolutely perfect we'll get on fine."

I picked up the menu in self-defence, grinned and read it carefully.

"How about melon, scrambled egg, dry white toast and coffee."

"That's fine. What are you having?"

The waiter came over and I ordered the same for both of us.

"Peter, had the box been opened?"

There was no doubt about it, Helen knew the right questions. She could see I looked appreciative.

"Don't know. Definitely a very good question. AAIB are trying to find out. The memory could have been changed. In fact the more I think about it, I'm not sure getting the memory out would be at all difficult. For a start the manufacturer gives a full description on the internet."

"Why would the manufacturer want to do that?"

"To display how well made the box is compared with the competition. I told you, the AAIB like crash recorders where the memory is easily removable so that they can analyse the data in an identical box."

"If you say so, but surely the manufacturers won't want to give their design secrets away. They have to careful not to lose their competitive edge."

I looked at her. "You know you still haven't told me where you got your degree and what your speciality was."

"Alright I'll tell you. It was at Trinity College, Cambridge and I read Natural Sciences specialising in Chemistry."

"You're joking. Why on earth are you an airline stewardess instead of using your degree?"

"I couldn't get a job I really fancied and so I decided to do some travelling at someone else's expense first. Mind you, like most jobs it's very hard work, particularly with the time changes."

"It seems such a waste. Anyway why did you tell me you read English?"

"That was when you were trying out long words on me and I didn't know you."

"Now I don't know what to believe except that you seem to know everything and are lovely to boot."

"Let's keep it that way. That way you can't relax. But you haven't told me who you suspect of taking the memory out."

"Well it could be the Worldwide electronic specialist who is still out here as far as I know."

"But why?"

"Maybe Worldwide didn't want AAIB to find out something which might affect the insurance claim."

"That's a dangerous game. But why would someone get Smithson to do it?"

"That's a very fair question. I'm working on it."

"How did you get on with their chief of maintenance?"

"He was helpful up to point." I looked at her. "I'm not sure I'm going to let you go back home. You've just reminded me of something. Stan was going to let me speak to the crew chief who dispatched the aircraft."

"Why do you want to talk to him?"

"Well I'm still not convinced the aircraft was fully serviceable when it left. Winston says it was the fuel gauging. There was obviously something not quite right. The dispatcher didn't or couldn't help. I wondered if Jim Scott had told the crew chief why he shut down the engines."

"But Winston says it was fuel gauging."

"I know but perhaps the crew said more to the crew chief."

Our breakfast had arrived so I decided to wait before calling Stan Bellow. When it was over we went back to our room and I called him.

"Sorry, Peter, I'm afraid I never got round to finding the crew chief who dispatched the Alpha Delta. I'll try again to-morrow."

Helen shrugged her shoulders. "He wasn't much use."

"Tell me about it."

"Peter, the situation as I see it is that, for some reason we don't really know, the aircraft ditched. You tell me that it might have been a technical problem, insufficient fuel or something to do with Jacko and his people being on the aircraft. We know there was a delay on departure, apparently due to a fuel gauging problem. We know the Captain shut down the engine in flight because the airline had a recording. We know the aircraft had a pressurisation problem and let down. What we don't know is why it ditched. The whole thing is confused with Jacko, his survival and the fact that he thinks I recognised him as Jackson and not just as a fellow survivor. But we still don't why Smithson removed the cockpit voice recorder."

"Very good summary. Time we swam or something."

Stan Bellow rang the following day.

"Peter, I've got the crew chief who despatched the flight here, Henry Thompson. I'll put him on the phone now."

I wasn't sure that I wanted to talk to Thompson with Stan Bellow listening but there was no alternative.

"Henry, I gather there was a problem when Alpha Delta started up to go to Barbados?"

"Yes, that's right Mr Talbert. When both engines were running there was a pause of a few minutes and then Captain Scott told me there was a problem and shut the engines down."

"Didn't he tell you what the problem was?"

"No. He said he was going to talk to Ops. After about fifteen minutes he said that he was going to take the aircraft and then a few minutes later we went through the start up procedures again after he had got clearance from air traffic."

I went round the start up sequence again with Thompson but made no progress at all. I asked him to put me back to Stan Bellow.

"Could you transfer me to Sandy Thomas, Stan?"

Slightly to my surprise Thomas answered straightaway.

"Sandy, Peter Talbert. I don't think we've met. I'm phoning in connection with the accident to Alpha Delta."

He said "Go ahead." But it might have been 'drop dead'. I definitely got the feeling he didn't want to discuss the matter.

"The dispatcher, Ricardo Gonzalez."

"He left for San Francisco. By chance, just after Alpha Delta had left, David Winston asked me to send out someone immediately to sort out a problem in San Francisco."

The answer seemed very pat and I hadn't even asked the question. However there was nothing more I could do and I rang off feeling very frustrated.

"No luck, my love?"

"Not really. Jim Scott didn't tell the crew chief the problem."

"But you know it was a fuel gauging problem, don't you?"

"I wanted to double check if I could."

"You do like to be certain, don't you."

"You bet. In an accident when the crew are killed it is particularly necessary to make sure the cause of the accident is definite and not a surmise. It is so easy to blame the pilot and then design faults may possibly go unnoticed and unchanged."

"Why did you ask to speak to the other guy?"

"I'm still intrigued at the speed the dispatcher was sent to San Francisco."

I decided to ring Michael Longshaw who had done such a wonderful job helping Linda in the life raft. He was in which surprised me.

"Michael, Peter Talbert here. I'm ringing about the ditching."

He didn't sound too pleased. "Go ahead."

"Helen Partridge who was the cabin attendant on the other life raft is going to be interviewed on the TV and she is thinking of mentioning the splendid job you did."

"Peter, I'm damn sure you know perfectly well I wouldn't like that. I've been looking you up. You didn't tell me you are well known in the aviation world as a very smart insurance investigator."

"Helen Partridge does not want the interview to sound as if she was exceptional. She wants to give you credit as well."

"That's as maybe. If I know TV interviewers they will want to concentrate on Helen Partridge and not dilute the interview. Come on, Peter, why did you really phone me?"

"I am advising Ms Partridge a little on the interview because as you know interviewers can be very awkward with their questions."

"Like asking Ms Partridge if you and she are just good friends?"

I ignored the remark and carried on. "You clearly are newsworthy. In fact, unlike you, I haven't been doing any research but I did wonder what you do for a living and following on from that I wondered if you could tell me a bit more about the flight?"

"You're not threatening me are you?"

"I don't understand."

"Don't believe you. You've worked out that I was working on the flight, haven't you? And you are pressurising me to tell you more about it."

"Well I wouldn't put things quite as crudely as that but I was alerted when you decided to call me back after I first called you and I was intrigued when you weren't prepared to tell me your job in the Government. I came to the conclusion that you were probably on the flight as a marshal or to observe Jacko and his henchmen or both."

"So what if I was?"

"Well AAIB have been told that there was a lot of activity in the business section of the aircraft and they are wondering if it has anything to do with the ditching. You clearly had some form of weapon on you, a knife or more likely some form of stun gun, and if there was a fracas in the business section you would know all about it."

"So what are you looking for from me? You know very well that you won't get a written statement."

"No, all I want is for you to tell me if there was something unusual happening in the business section. I've got some ideas of the real cause of the ditching and I don't want AAIB chasing red herrings."

"Surely AAIB has to investigate what really happened, not you?"

"Absolutely, but I'm acting for an insurance company and the reasons for an accident and the way it is reported are very important for them. It's just possible they may not be completely liable for the cost of the Hull and the passenger claims."

"Alright, I trust you not to shoot your mouth off. I was on the flight to watch Jacko, Geoffrey Hudson and Thomas Smith."

"What about Toby Makepeace?"

"Absolutely no comment. Not relevant."

His reply seemed rather terse and rapid. "If you say so, Michael. Anyway what happened up front?"

"As you know I was travelling economy, in the front of the rear section, and there was a lot of activity in the business section. But it was nothing to do with Jacko's mob. They were in the back with me and they stayed there."

"When did the activity start in the business section?"

"I've been thinking about that quite a bit. I reckon it was after we had depressurised and let down to some low altitude."

"Thanks a lot for that. I wanted to be certain that the activity could not have caused the problem."

"Hold on, Peter. How can you be certain? I know it did not cause the engine failure but what was happening up front might have made matters worse. Maybe AAIB are on to something."

"Michael, a very interesting observation. Thanks for all that. I'll try and persuade Helen not to mention you."

"Helen? You mean Ms Partridge don't you?"

I had the definite feeling he was giving as good he got. "Michael, touché. Thanks so much for your help."

The next few days seem to pass very quickly and Helen made a very good recovery from her bruising and also, I judged, from the mental strains of her kidnapping as well as the ditching. On the Sunday night I took her to the airport to catch the Worldwide flight to Gatwick so she could start work.

"Where are you going to stay for your course?"

"I'll commute from Portsmouth. Why?"

"I just wondered if this would help?"

She looked down, thought for a moment, kissed me and took the spare key of the house I always carried. "It's rather like an engagement ring. You're lovely."

The flight left almost on time and I idled Monday away.

In the morning I flew back to St Antony and to the New Anchorage. I checked in but there was no sign of Tom so I called his mobile.

"I'm in the new hangar they've just built. Come on over and have a look. Go past the West Atlantic Airways hangar and you'll come to a barrier. We've got some guards there and I'll tell them to let you in if you've got your passport with you."

"Have you got it all up?"

"Come and see."

I drove over and the guard at the barrier, after a very careful check let me through. I couldn't believe my eyes. There was a brand new hangar, just large enough for medium sized airliner, standing on what was obviously freshly laid concrete. The hangar was obviously temporary in that the sides were uniform, built in identical sections, without any bells and whistles. There were doors at each end but, presumably to keep things simple, they appeared to be straightforward double doors, opening outward. There were builders still working, erecting what seemed to be an eight foot fence around the whole complex.

The hangar doors were shut and I made my way to a single entrance door let into the side of the hangar. There were two very noisy air conditioning engines each of which had a huge flexible pipe let into the walls of the hangar. I opened the door and met a blast of cold air as I entered so that I rapidly shut the door. There was another guard waiting inside and again there was a very rigorous check.

In front of me was a pile of wreckage which in spite of the air conditioning was giving off a smell reminiscent of bad seaweed. I noticed that there seemed to be one or two security men wandering around the hangar. The guards must have told Tom I was coming as he appeared and led me to an office with about four desks, computers, filing cabinets and the rest of the clobber which makes up a nest of offices. He sat at what must have been his desk and pulled a chair over for me.

"This is amazing, Tom. I can't believe it could be done in the time."

Tom looked pleased. "Yes, I'm a bit amazed myself. We hired quite a lot of local labour initially to help put the wreckage in approximately the right position but now we've cut right down; I've got quite a large AAIB team inspecting the wreckage."

"What about the bodies?"

"We've got a temporary mortuary at the other end of the hangar and we've got one of our doctors plus some specialist UK undertakers identifying the bodies as best we can. We're now independent of the Cape Harbour mortuary but of course we have to keep the St Antony coroner informed. He had the original list from Worldwide and he is keeping it up to date. In fact, the doctors are doing a first class job and they are hoping that they will be able to account for all the bodies, but obviously some of the identification is proving a bit difficult. A lot of dental records and the like are being requested from the next of kin where we can find them and of course it will all take time."

"Have you found anything interesting in the wreckage?"

"To be honest, I don't think we have."

"Did you manage to get all the wreckage?"

"I think we've got most of it. There will be bits and pieces of course and I've asked the divers to continue to search and pick up all the bits they can see from the bottom. Luckily it is just within their diving range. We've put the bits they've picked up in a pile over there and then we try to identify the correct location for the pieces. Why don't I take you on a conducted tour?"

Tom gave me an identification badge and then he led me out into the hanger. At first sight the wreckage looked completely haphazard but in fact the pieces had been placed correctly longitudinally but some pieces, which should have been on top, had to be placed alongside the lower pieces. Luckily the pieces of the aircraft which had been salvaged were quite large, though extremely twisted and deformed.

"How difficult was it to salvage the pieces without damaging them, Tom? Did the cranes cause any problems lifting?"

"You've raised a good point. The nose section had broken completely from the rest of the aircraft and that probably explains why the fuselage filled so quickly with water from the front. Consequently, the front was lifted very easily and in some ways has not been damaged as much as the rest of the aircraft. The main fuselage was still connected along its whole length and it was quite impossible to lift it in one piece. We had to make a decision and cut the fuselage very carefully into three sections in order to get it up out of the water; we were then able to move each section along the road on transporters to the hanger."

"How did you actually get the bits into the hanger?"

"Oh, that was relatively easy. We had some long low trolleys and we used them to slide the sections into position and then we used a crane to lift the bits off the trolley, slide the trolleys away and then lower the pieces into position." He paused. "Of course the whole thing had to be done with special care because some of the bodies were still strapped to the seats, some of which were no longer attached to the fuselage and a lot of bodies at the rear were loose. All very difficult. We have not informed the next of kin yet until we are a bit better organised."

"I think you have done and are doing a wonderful job but how are you coping with the locals and the media?"

"Well we briefed them before we started and we are about to brief them again. There are quite a few local next-of-kin and very understandably they are very keen to have the bodies of their families handed over to them. However, we have to be absolutely certain of the correct identity before we release a body and, to be fair, the next-of-kin are very understanding. We don't want any mistakes."

"You seem to have quite a few guards."

Tom's face clouded. "Yes, we have had a problem. It took us several days to lift all the wreckage and we started getting break-ins at night. I couldn't believe it was happening at first. There seemed to be no rhyme or reason for it until I spoke to Ben Masters who told me that there was at least one item of extremely valuable jewellery aboard. He gave me the name of a reliable firm which now provides 24 hour watch on the hangar. And you probably noticed we're having to go to the expense of erecting high fences round the whole place. Such a waste of money, but with all the bodies being examined and identified we can't allow anything to go wrong."

"Was there any damage done with the break-ins?"

"I'm not sure. Unfortunately at first we didn't take pictures each night before we finished. We were wondering if some of the stuff that came from the overhead compartments had been looked at. As you can see some of the lockers are still shut even though the structure has moved. Others are wide open. We now take pictures every evening before we leave to make sure if there are any more break-ins we can see if anything has been tampered with."

"May I look round?"

"Help yourself but please don't touch anything without consulting Gordon Wessex over there, he's in charge of the wreckage analysis."

Tom went back to his office and, starting at the back of the aircraft, I had a careful look at the wreckage. I found it very difficult to learn anything and I suspected it was necessary to be trained in accident inspection to be able to draw any conclusions from inspecting the wreckage. Along the main fuselage there were broken wires everywhere all mixed with pipes, seats, straps and oxygen masks. I found it very difficult to believe that anything useful could be learnt from it. As Tom had said, a few of the doors of the overhead stowage compartments had not come undone so presumably some of the passengers belongings would still be in place. I wondered if this would help the AAIB in any way. Sometime I supposed, when AAIB had finished, these belongings would have to be handed back to the owners, if that were possible.

Tom looked at me as I re-entered the offices. "Did you learn anything?"

"Only that if you can learn anything from the wreckage you are a better man than I am."

"Actually, it's amazing what can be gleaned from it. I'm not very good at it but our experts are out there in the hangar."

"Well let's hope they can sort something out."

I left Tom and went back to the hotel and called Ben. Jearl said he was busy and would call me back. I tried calling Helen at home but there was no reply. My next call was to Charles Hendrick at Gatwick. Mary Turner answered the phone and put me through.

"Charles, I'm back in St Antony and I've just been looking at the wreckage in the new hangar that AAIB have built."

"Have they learnt anything?"

"I think you'd better ask them that question but I don't think so."

"Peter, how can I help you?"

"Do you happen to know if Worldwide keep a record of the allocated seating position of the passengers with the passenger list?"

"I don't know. Why do you ask?"

"You know Jackson Turner was on the aircraft. I would love to know where he was seated."

"He's dead isn't he. Does it matter."

I didn't feel it was the right time to share what knowledge we had of Jacko with Charles. "If you could find out where he was sitting it might be very helpful."

"I'll see what I can do Peter. Where are you? Still in the same hotel?"

"Yes. No change and my mobile and my email will always find me."

"OK."

We rang off and shortly afterwards Ben came on the line.

"Welcome back. What do you think, Peter?"

"About what? Alvin Goddard?"

"That's a real pain. The doctor thinks it was suicide. It was an overdose of cocaine. I don't think we'll ever find out where he got it from. I told the supervisor to watch him like a hawk. A fat lot of good that did. I've had to give up charging Smithson and he's got *Dark Blue Diving* back. Apart from making life a bit harder for him we've achieved nothing. And he's bad mouthing me behind my back to the heavy breathers in the Government. What do you think about the new hangar?"

"It's a brilliant construction job but I'm not sure what to think about the break-ins. I can't think that Jacko is organising a search for his diamond in the hangar."

"I think you're absolutely right about that as he has disappeared."

"Disappeared? When? Where did he go?"

"We think he left two days ago because we've been watching the house as best we can without being noticed and he hasn't been seen since then."

"Do you think he's left the island?"

"Don't know."

"Wouldn't there have been a problem leaving since he obviously didn't get the passport stamped on entry?"

"Don't know, Peter. Depends what arrangements have been made with the High Commission."

I rang off and out of curiosity I spoke to Dorothy Henshaw in the High Commission.

"No, Mr Talbert, we made no special arrangements with St Antony immigration. We assumed that common sense would prevail. They have a copy of the passenger list."

For some reason I decided to have a go at trying to see if I could find out if Jacko, alias Thomas Smith, had left the country. I rang Dick Bartholomew, head of immigration who I had met sorting out the disappearance of the WAA aircraft.

I managed to find him and asked what happened when a survivor left St Antony without an inbound stamp in their passport.

"Good question, Mr Talbert. I've been telling my guys to check with the passenger list and there should be a copy there for them to check. They should mark the list as a survivor leaves. Why do you ask?"

"I'm trying to check what happened to a survivor I happened to know, Thomas Smith."

"It will take me some time to check because of course there are all sorts of ways people can leave the island, legally and illegally. Your Mr Smith could have got on a small boat to Antigua and we would never know. Why do you ask? Is it in connection with the aircraft that crashed in the sea? I assume you are here investigating it."

"Yes, it is in connection with the ditching. Mr Smith is no longer staying where he was when he came out of hospital and apparently he left without telling the airline where he was going, as all the survivors were asked to do."

"Alright Mr Talbert, I'll see what I can do."

I tried Helen again and this time she was at home.

"Hello, Gorgeous, what are you up to."

"Peter, what are you up to. When you call me terms of endearment from afar I get suspicious."

"So far I've only been consorting with Tom and talking to the head of immigration ---"

"---as one does! Are you being deported?"

"I'm looking for a missing survivor whose name you can probably guess."

"Good Lord. Has he gone walkabout?"

"Yes and Ben doesn't know where."

"Couldn't he still be on the island?"

"You bet, but I thought it was worth a check in case he's decided to go to Florida or somewhere. Where have you been?"

"Shopping. I'm off to do my ground test as a first class purser later on to-day."

"But you've only been home two minutes."

"I know but they reckon I can pass the ground test."

"Do you have to write exams?"

"Yes, I most certainly do."

"When you're a first class hostess, will you still be slumming in the New Anchorage here or do you go to an even more expensive hotel, if that were possible here?"

"No, I'll still be in the New Anchorage and I expect I'll have to share."

"Any preferences?"

"I'm trying to decide."

"I'll keep my spare bed free just in case."

"And the other side of the one you're in, if you don't mind. Must fly."

The phone went dead and I decided to ring Bob Furness.

"Tom and his team have done a marvellous job on the temporary hangar, Bob."

"So I understand. He's sent me some pictures. Looks very good. Mind you it wasn't cheap. How are things with you, Peter?"

"So so. Waiting on Tom to sort the whole thing out."

"I'm not sure I completely believe that. After all it was you who found the recorder, thank you very much. I'm sure you know you may have to wait for Tom's final report for some time at the present rate of progress. As usual we are going to have to issue an interim report and we'll have to concentrate on the ditching behaviour and the survival procedures, which were brilliant by all accounts. It does show that emergency crew training is worth doing. The survivors have those two cabin attendants and their training to thank for their lives."

"You're right there. I've got to know one of them quite well and met the other in hospital. I suppose I rang you just to check that nothing had changed with the recorders and their memories."

"We've made no progress with the recorders or the QAR. In fact the QAR manufacturer has told us that they can't get anything from the recorder which is a great shame and they've sent it back to us. Anyway Peter, please drop in next time you are in the UK."

There was nothing more I could do so I went down for a swim and a very late lunch. When I got back the message light was on. Bartholomew had called.

"Mr Talbert, we cannot find any trace of Thomas Smith. Of course it doesn't mean he hasn't left the island. It is just that we haven't a record of his going."

"Mr Bartholomew, thanks very much for trying and getting all your people to look."

I rang off and decided to call Michael Longshaw.

"Sorry to worry you again but I've got a problem or perhaps we've got a problem."

"Go on. I'm listening."

"The guy you were watching on the flight out actually survived."

"How do you know? Are you certain?"

"Yes, Michael. I am certain. I wish we could meet up. I don't like talking over a phone like this."

"I agree. If you go to the High Commission and ask for the duty security officer, I will arrange for you to have access to a secure phone. How long will it take you to get to the High Commission?"

"About twenty minutes."

"Make it forty and it should work out OK."

I took my time driving to the High Commission. Anne was at the desk but before I could sign in and ask for the duty security officer a lady wearing a smart pink suit and white blouse got up from a chair in the waiting area. She had a badge on a loop round her neck with her photo and I could read her name 'Frances Jones'.

"Mr Peter Talbert?" I nodded. "Please come this way."

She led me to the elevator where we went down one floor and then along a passage and through an unmarked door. There was another door inside a small room which was protected by a security sensor. However, first the lady introduced herself and asked to see my passport which she examined carefully and then smiled.

"Mr Talbert, I gather you want to talk to the UK, a Mr Longshaw." I agreed. "He should be ringing here in a few minutes. Let me show you how to operate the phone."

Ms Jones swiped the security sensor and opened the door. The inside room had no windows but was obviously air conditioned and had a table and two chairs. The table was well equipped with paper, trays and pens and a special telephone with some unmarked switches on the front.

"You start the conversation normally and then when you are told you select this switch up. When this light goes from red to green you are in business. I will wait in the outer office until you've finished. Are you likely to be long?"

"I shouldn't think so. I'm just passing over some information." I smiled. "A paper rather than a book should be perfect."

Ms Jones allowed a returning smile and indicated that we should sit down and wait. Unlike most people in this situation she made no attempt to chat. Luckily we did not have long to wait as the phone rang. She checked that Michael Longshaw was at the other end with some security interchange and then handed the phone over to me.

"Peter, if you can hear me OK select the secure switch." I did as instructed and sure enough the light went from red to green. "can you hear me OK still?"

"Fine, Michael. Wait a moment please."

But Frances had already left and closed the door.

"Michael, Jackson Turner survived as it turned out. He fought his way out of the aircraft but he was concussed and had to go into hospital for a few days. He wasn't able to give his name initially and he was visited by Geoffrey Hudson who must have told him that Thomas Smith was dead. Jacko knew that Smith was a loner with no next of kin and saw his opportunity to change his name. He got Hudson to tell the hospital that his name was Smith and then he got the consular lady to give him a passport."

"How on earth do you know all this? Did the local police tell you?"

"Not exactly. You remember Helen Partridge, the cabin attendant?"

"The one you're advising on her TV appearance? Oh, yes."

"We were having dinner together when she recognised Jacko straightaway in a restaurant as the passenger who fought his way out in a terrible way and he apparently recognised her. It's a long story but I had got some pictures of Jacko and the consulate gave me a picture of Thomas Smith."

"You did well, Peter. I'm surprised the consulate didn't check digitally with the Passport Office that Jacko really was Thomas Smith."

"You must know better than I do, Michael, but surely it depends on when Smith's passport was issued and whether all his details were recorded digitally. Weren't the Government hoping that the passport office could be the initial developers of the national identity card? My understanding is that the computer system is barely up to speed and politically the whole concept is in the balance."

"You're right. Anyway it is all irrelevant at the moment. Jacko became Thomas Smith. Then what?"

"He went to stay with a local villain called Smithson, Hudson got murdered and Helen was grabbed and nearly got drowned, presumably because Jacko didn't want anybody to know he was alive. To cut a long story short I'm ringing you because he seems to have disappeared. I've been in touch with immigration here to see if there is any trace of his leaving St Antony but they can't find anything. I'm particularly worried in case he is in England and tries to find Helen who is staying in my house. You see he doesn't know that his trick has been discovered. Ben Masters, the chief of police here, is keeping Jacko's survival under wraps because he thinks it will help him in catching Smithson who is big in drugs."

"Peter, thanks for all that and I will pass all the information on. You say Masters has not told the UK about Jacko being alive?"

"Yes, that's right. I wanted to make sure you knew the situation so that you could explain it carefully to the people at your end."

"That's great Peter, but if you take my advice you had better tell Masters straightaway about our chat or you'll be in trouble."

"Yes, I shall. However I'm worried about Helen. Do you think a good way for your people to find Jacko is to watch my house?"

"Possibly, but as I understand it Jacko is not wanted for a crime. However it might be sensible for your Ms Partridge to find somewhere to live for the moment which is not on record. To be frank, there is absolutely no evidence that Jacko has come to UK to have another go at your Helen. More likely if he is in UK it will be because he has some unfinished business. Perhaps he needs to transfer funds from one place to another. Let's face it, he could be anywhere in the world."

"Alright. I'll think about it. That's about all I have for you. If I have any other ideas I'll call you."

"Peter, you should be a detective."

"That's what Ben Masters says and I keep having to remind him that as an aviation insurance investigator I am a detective. I don't think he's convinced."

"You'd better rush off and tell Ben about our conversation or he won't let you be a detective. Thanks again."

I rang off and opened the door. Frances led me back to the lobby where I thanked her and left. On impulse I drove round to the police headquarters and asked for Ben. He wasn't there but Rick was. I explained about Bartholomew not being able to find Jacko leaving and about my conversation with Longshaw.

Back in the hotel I reckoned that Helen would have finished her exam and I called her mobile. She answered straightaway.

"Did you pass?"

"Absolutely. I'm having a training flight to-morrow would you believe on the flight to St Antony. So stand by your bed for a full inspection."

I decided there was no point in bringing her up to date with Jacko's movements since she was about to start travelling and I could discuss it all with her the next day.

Down in the bar I found Tom and we had a drink. There were no developments and I went to bed.

DAY 29

Ben called me after breakfast and asked me to come down.

"I need someone to talk to and I know I can trust you. Smithson is getting at the Minister of Transport and I'm getting worried about my job."

"Ben, that's crazy. You're doing superbly."

"That's as maybe but Smithson has got the ear of these people."

"You need to catch him red handed."

"Right. I suppose that's why I called you. You always have such way out ideas that seem to bear fruit."

"Ben, if Smithson is still trafficking drugs, where will he be keeping them? Surely not in *Dark Blue Diving*?"

"No. He wouldn't risk that."

"Do you think he is still in the business."

"Yes I do. We are monitoring his phones including his internet traffic. We can't read the messages because they're all scrambled but every few days the traffic increases to a peak and then dies away."

"Have you given the scrambled traffic to anybody."

"You bet. We've given samples to the CIA and your secret service, so far without success."

"In fact the traffic is building up again. We don't know how the stuff is coming in or how it is going out. However, it may be that he is using private aircraft. We have alerted air traffic to watch for unidentified planes, the coastguard and also the customs but so far we've drawn a blank."

"What about boats, Ben? Surely that is the most likely? Are you watching all the time?"

"Well we check all the boats we know about including the visiting cruise ships but it's so difficult to check all the smaller boats. There are so many islands close by and a local fishing boat or yacht can easily drop into Antigua, for example, and come back here and we would be none the wiser. We've asked the harbour authorities at Cape Harbour and Paradise Harbour to alert us if they see anything suspicious but so far we've drawn a blank."

"Surely if you suspect Smithson, the most likely place for the stuff to be dropped off and dispatched from is his place by water."

"We think that and we've tried watching but we don't have the funds for a 24/7 monitoring operation. Furthermore, I've got a feeling that somehow Smithson knows when we have search boats out. Someone is leaking the information."

"Where do your boats come from?"

"Cape Harbour."

"That's not really ideal, is it?"

"Perhaps not, but that's the way it is."

"Do you always use the same people?"

"Yes we do. Customs have a boat and we alert them as necessary. We've got a boat out to-night."

"It may not be at night. Have you ever stopped a boat going to Smithson's jetty?"

"Yes we did once. We didn't find anything and all hell was let loose. The head of customs and I got a ticking off for even suspecting such a stalwart supporter of the local community. Believe me, Smithson is a very clever operator."

"Pity I can't be on your boat to-night, not that it's anything to do with me. I would have liked to have gone along just to watch but Helen comes in to-night."

"Miss Partridge?"

"Yes Ben, Miss Partridge. She is training to be a first class purser with Worldwide."

Ben made no comment. We went round and round the problem but made no progress. I left and went for a swim.

Helen arrived on time, very full of herself. The flight had gone well and, fortuitously, the Prime Minister of St Antony had been in the first class cabin with the First Secretary. He had been well briefed by Worldwide and so he congratulated her on the rescue work she did with Alpha Delta. He had pressed her to come and see him in his Office and the First Secretary had given her the contact details to make certain it would happen. She was telling me all about it in the bar with the girl who had been training her, Sandra James.

"Sandra, how did she do?"

"She was super. She handled the PM beautifully. He was almost purring."

"I didn't know she could do that."

Helen grinned. "Only with nice, polite men who aren't rude."

I looked at them both. "Did he make any other references to the ditching?"

"Yes he did, my dear." Helen took over the conversation. "He said how worried he was that the cause of the accident had not been discovered yet. He knew the wreckage had been put in a special newly constructed building and he was planning to visit it in the next day or so when he could fit it in."

"Sounds great. Tom will like that. Let's hope he has some good news for the PM."

"Are you going to be there?"

"Of course not. It's nothing to do with me."

"Well you found the recorder."

"Didn't do much good, did it?"

"Well, I'll take you along to meet the PM."

"You'll do no such thing. You will go there wearing your most snazzy suit and smile as you are having your picture taken with the boss. And the good news is that Cindy can write it all up and remind everybody what a good job you did." Helen didn't look convinced. "When are you thinking of contacting him? If it were done when 'tis done, then 'twere well it were done quickly."

"Give over. I'm not going to kill him. And, would you believe, I'm not going back until Sunday."

"Good Lord, it's alright for some. Seriously, memories are short and Worldwide, like the PM, would love the publicity." A thought struck me. "Sandra, when are you going back?"

"Same flight as Helen. I'll be supervising her."

"So if Helen was delayed to meet the PM you could do her stint?"

Helen butted in. "Peter, don't be so horrible and stop trying to be a Worldwide scheduler. I am going back Sunday, come hell or high water." She turned to Sandra. "I'm sorry. Do you see what I have to put up with."

"It's not a problem. Actually I think Peter's right and you should try and arrange a meeting and see what happens."

Tom came in to the bar and saw us. He knew Helen of course from his first interview and Helen introduced him to Sandra.

He pulled a chair over and turned to me. "Ben tells me that there were some lights on where the aircraft was last night."

"How very strange. Presumably somebody is looking for something. Very odd since you may well have whatever has been lost in the hangar. If it is a piece of jewellery the chances of finding it at the bottom of the sea must be nil."

"Perhaps there is something else that we haven't found."

"How would they know?"

"By the way Peter, the local Prime Minister's office was on the phone to-day. The PM wants to visit the hangar."

"So I understand."

"How did you know?"

"Helen here told me."

Tom looked puzzled and we explained the situation.

"Peter, are you going to be there?"

"Thanks for asking, but it is your party."

"Well come along anyway and I'll introduce you after I've done my people. After all, you did find the missing recorder."

"That's exactly what Helen said but it didn't do much good, did it? Anyway thank you again for asking. If the visit happens and I'm around then, yes, I'd love to be there."

I could see Helen was almost out on her feet and she excused herself, rapidly followed by Sandra. I followed a little later but by the time I went into the room Helen was sound asleep with the desk light thoughtfully left on.

DAY 30

"Why don't we go sailing to day?"

Helen was sitting, fully dressed, on my side of the bed with a cup of coffee.

"Is that mine?"

"Certainly not. You'll have to get up to get yours." She pointed to a steaming cup by the telephone. "And then you can find a boat at the same time."

"But it's only seven o'clock."

"Wrong it's eight o'clock and time you got up."

I levered myself up, thought for a moment, found my phone and rang *Discover St Antony*. "Beverley, do you rent yachts? Peter Talbert here."

"We most certainly do. They are not ours but we rent them on behalf of the owners. What do you need?"

"How about a 36 to 40 ft ketch with in-mast reefing?"

"Can you manage that by yourself?"

"It's not for me. It's for my partner."

There was a pause. "You're just going along for the ride?"

"There's no answer to that, Beverley."

"When do you need one?"

"How about 10.30 to-day, for three nights, back on Sunday?"

"That's what I like about you. You always give me plenty of notice."

"We'll come to the office."

"No, don't do that. I'll meet you in the restaurant with the necessary paperwork. There's not much wind. Make sure you've got plenty of SPF, sun hats etc. What are you going to do about food?"

"I don't know. Any suggestions?"

"Tell you what. I'll get the restaurant here to do you a package. We often do that. Do you want anything to drink besides water?"

"Some wine and perhaps a few bottles of beer. I take it there is a fridge on board?"

"And a small freezer but you have to run the engine frequently to charge the batteries. Mind you the batteries seem huge for the size of boat."

"See you at 10.30."

I rang off and Helen nodded approvingly. "You're definitely not going along just for the ride. My crew has to work. Get a move on. I'm starving and need breakfast."

We sat outside as usual, in the shade but getting the morning breeze.

"Why did you ask for three nights? I only suggested a day sail. You do realise that if the PM wants to meet me to-morrow you've blown it?"

"Not at all. We'll just come back and then continue sailing. It's nice to have the option. It's such a wonderful opportunity."

"Who's Beverley Peter? You sounded as if you knew her."

"She's a lovely tall blond 92, 55, 87."

"Inches I trust?"

"Absolutely, darling. Actually I rented a RIB from her a couple of times when I looked at Smithson's house and the wreck. By the way, have you got the PM's number with you?"

"Of course not. Anyway it's too early to phone. Officials don't start until 9am. You seem very keen for me to see him?"

"Well, I think you deserve more recognition and he will be very keen to do it. Standing next to a glamorous female is always good for a political career."

Helen looked at me thoughtfully. "And you might want his help in other matters?"

"You never know. Time spent in socialisation is seldom wasted."

"I thought that was reconnaissance. Anyway, if I do go I plan to take a taxi."

"I'm not letting you ride in a taxi by yourself ever again. You'll have to let me take you. Why don't we go up now, you phone the PM's office and then get ready to leave."

Up in our room she dialled the number and in what seemed a very short time a rather worried Helen agreed to an appointment, not for the next day, but for the following Monday, at 11am, at the PM's office, entrance at Government House. The secretary must have been very well briefed.

"Should I have done that? I feel awful having to ask Sandra to stand in for me."

"Give her a ring."

Helen called her and explained the situation and Sandra agreed immediately. She also, very sensibly, said she would inform publicity as well as scheduling. She reminded Helen to explain the situation to Becky Samuels.

"Well that's fixed. Well done, darling. You'd better ring Becky before you forget. I've got the number here."

"You seem to have the number of all your female contacts immediately to hand."

"You could say that." I handed her my phone with the number showing and she called Becky and explained about the re-scheduling and the reason.

"All done. Let's go."

We packed a small bag, went to Paradise Harbour and ordered a drink. Beverley appeared and joined us. "Hope this boat will be OK. It has slab reefing, not in-mast." I nodded agreement. "As I said you're probably going to need the iron topsail if you want to get anywhere to-day, there's not a lot of wind. The boat has an electric mooring winch but it only works when the engine is running. You could make Antigua before it gets dark --- by the way we want you back here safely berthed by Sunday night as the owner needs the boat for a long trip starting the following afternoon. The restaurant will have the food and drink I ordered for you ready by 11.30 or soon after."

"Has the boat got radar?"

"Yes, of course. What do you want that for?"

"It's safer if we are not in harbour by dusk. Boats these days tow enormous barges miles behind them and it frightens me."

"You have to be anchored by dusk unless we give you special permission so that won't be a problem. One other thing, we do our schedules at 1600 and 0800 each day and you must check in with us by radio or telephone so we know where you are and can tell you about the weather and what we want you to do."

"Beverley, that's absolutely fine. Can we go to the boat?"

I checked what wine and beer the restaurant was supplying and then we followed Beverley to the marina and out on one of the fingers to *Northern Cross,* a very modern wide beamed ketch.

"By the way, the security code to get to the boat is 3754. Better note it down. Here are the keys for the boat. There are some trolleys by the marina office for bringing out your bags and food"

"She looks great, Beverley. How old is she?"

"This is her second season but she's barely been used. The navigation equipment is bang up to date."

We went on board and Beverley showed us all the gear. She checked us out on the electrics, the fridge, the freezer, the electronic chart, the radar, the engine, the winch and the sails.

"There is a furling jib as you can see. In fact there is a spinnaker and another jib which you can set inside the big jib if you are really keen, but we will charge you for any damage if you use those sails. Anything else you need to know? Anyway, you can always call me if you think of something."

"What about charts, GPS, navigation tools?"

"In the table here there are charts and somewhere there should be a ruler with a protractor, but you won't need anything like that. It's all done for you on the electronic chart; there's a large repeater of the one in front of the helmsman on the nav table here. The GPS outputs on to the chart. You can display the radar on the chart as well."

"But I need dividers to measure distances and a parallel ruler or protractor for headings. What happens if it all goes wrong?"

Beverley looked at me. "Not many people these days are like you. They believe in the infallibility of digital technology."

She started searching though all the papers and finally produced a pair of dividers and a protractor.

"OK, we'll take the boat then."

We went back to the shore, picked up our food and drink from the restaurant, which was in large polystyrene containers, put them on a trolley and said au revoir to Beverley.

"Will you be able to get out without hitting anything?"

Helen reassured her that she would be able to manage. "I might need help if it's windy when we come back. I'm not sure about my crew. He's so argumentative."

Back on the boat we stowed everything and started the engine. I cast off the ropes and Helen slowly eased the boat out of the finger, past an old gaff rigged boat alongside on the next finger and we emerged into the relatively open waters of the harbour. As we went past the breakwater we could see Beverley on the other side watching and waving.

"Get those sails up, Peter."

"There's no wind, Captain."

"Yes there is, to starboard. I assume we're going past the spot where the aircraft ditched. The sea breeze is freshening all the time. And pass me the chart for a moment --- don't worry I won't let it go."

"It's on the display. You don't need the chart."

"You know the displays are never bright enough when the sun falls on them. I'll have the chart, please. And what heading shall I steer?"

We decided on our initial track and Helen brought the boat into wind. I went to the mast and wound up the mainsail fully and adjusted its setting while Helen trimmed it for a narrow reach. Once done I went aft and unfurled the jib. The boat heeled gently over in the light breeze and we were on our way. I managed to hoist the mizzen with its sheet fully out without having to go into wind and then we could feel the boat accelerate as I pulled the sheet in. Helen reached forward, pulled the slow running cut-out and switched off the engine. The silence was wonderful and she sat down, steering the boat from the rim of the wheel. I sat next to her and we both revelled in the experience. I put my arm round her but not for long.

"We're here to sail remember. The wind's veering and getting stronger. You need to slacken off the jib and you can't do that sitting here holding me."

In fact Helen had to stand up behind the wheel to sail the boat properly and for the next hour or so we sailed, first past the wreck marker buoys for the aircraft and then along the shore. We could see the coastguard boat cruising round the buoys and we kept well clear.

I pointed out the end of the runway to Helen and, as we went by, I showed her *Leewards*. As we cleared Cape Fearless, I got the chart out and worked out a course for Antigua. Despite Beverley's foreboding the wind was 15 knots, now conveniently on the beam, and we creamed along at about 9 knots with the boat lifting slightly out of the water.

"Peter, this absolutely great. Only a few cumulus and the visibility unlimited."

"You're terrific. Where did you learn to sail like that?"

"I told you, Peter. Portsmouth and then at Cambridge. Mind you this is the biggest boat I've sailed, though it sails almost like a dinghy. Pass me the sun blocker and I'll put the autopilot in."

She took her shirt off displaying a very chic and very small black bikini.

"Did they charge you for that? There's barely anything there."

"Are you complaining? Anyway it doesn't work like that, the price varies inversely with the area of the bikini. Come on. You had better rub my back with this sun screen oil. My back I said, no side trips or you'll spoil my bikini. I could take it off but I'd burn horribly. I'm well able to do the rest, thank you. And I'd better do yours as well. Not that we're going to sunbathe deliberately."

The wind started to drop and I re-trimmed the sails. We could make out Antigua low on the horizon. I took over from Helen, who went down to produce some lunch, and I put the auto-pilot in again.

"Peter, you've been watching that motor yacht or boat on the port side like a hawk, the one we've been overtaking."

"It looks familiar but I can't place it. Don't know where it's going and it doesn't seem to be in a hurry. It looks as if it is aiming, not at the harbour, but towards Rendezvous Bay."

"Why should we care? I sometimes think you get paranoid about things."

"Sorry. I just had a feeling."

"Well keep your feelings for me."

Helen took over the helm.

"Where are we going, Peter?"

"Antigua."

"Don't be stupid. Which marina?"

"I thought we'd go to Catamaran Marina in Falmouth Harbour. The other marina there and English Harbour are too developed for us. Have you been to any of the marinas there?"

"No. Worldwide doesn't fly to Antigua for some reason."

"I think for a yacht of our size we'd do better in Catamaran. I suspect their charges may be less as well. We can go to Nelson's Dockyard from the marina if we want to."

"What's our ETA?"

"1700 if the wind doesn't drop any more. I'd better call them to make sure they've got a berth."

I tuned the RT transceiver to Channel 68.

"Catamaran Marina, Catamaran Marina, Catamaran Marina this is Northern Cross, Northern Cross, Northern Cross."

"Go ahead Northern Cross, this is Catamaran Marina."

"We are from Paradise Harbour, St Antony. We are a 38ft ketch. Have you a berth for to-night?"

"Northern Cross. Can't manage to-night. OK for to-morrow. You can anchor off Pigeon Beach to-night, clear of the buoyed channel. You are welcome to come ashore with your dinghy and use our facilities. Drop in to the office."

I put the microphone back in its holder.

"Darling, that sounded really friendly. Actually in some ways I'd prefer to anchor if we are not too far from the marina and the fleshpots. Marinas can be very noisy."

"Great. That's what we'll do. Hope Beverley won't mind. Better check."

I called Beverley using my telephone since we were out of RT range with Paradise Harbour but in the telephone cell phone range of Antigua. She agreed that where we were going to anchor was fine.

Antigua got steadily closer and we could see Shirley Heights behind English Harbour.

As we came under the lee of English point Helen brought the boat in to the North East wind and I dropped all the sails. I got her to give Bishop Shoal a wide berth to starboard and then very cautiously, with our eyes riveted to the echo sounder, we dropped our anchor as close as we dared to Pigeon Beach. The anchorage was very well protected and there was only one other boat nearby. In fact it was a good way away so there wasn't going to be problem if we started swinging on our mooring.

"That was a really great sail and I've got a super crew at last."

"No, I've got a super crew, Peter."

"Well who gets the drinks, the skipper or the crew?"

"You do."

After a quick drink and shower, we lowered the dinghy from its stowage on the rear stanchions and, as advised by Beverley, we locked the boat. The outboard started first time and we went over to the marina. It was quite small, unlike the other marina in the harbour which was clearly filled with enormous yachts. After checking in at the office we had a drink at the café by the marina entrance. However, we decided we might as well eat on board since we had plenty of food and didn't feel like weaving our way, full of good spirits, back to the boat in the dark.

After we had eaten I looked out; there was no wind and everything was flat calm. We decided to take the dinghy outside the harbour before going to bed. The sea was like a mirror and incredibly we could see the stars and constellations clearly reflected in the water. It was fantastic. And then I realised there was a boat without lights just off Rendezvous Bay and I could hear a dinghy somewhere by the shore.

"Peter, let's go back. It's great out here but I'm ready for bed."

"Can you see that boat over there without lights?"

"Not really. Why?"

"I think it's the Smithson's boat. You know, the boat we overtook this afternoon."

"No, Peter. I don't know. What makes you so sure it's his?"

"I looked at it the other day when I was fishing. I didn't remember until just now that it was Smithson's."

"What's it doing?"

"I don't know but I happen to know that parts of the beach at Rendezvous Bay are very awkward to get at."

"You think its something to do with drugs, don't you? Are you going to tell Ben?"

"When we get back."

We motored back to *Northern Cross* and went to bed.

DAY 31

In the morning we had a leisurely breakfast and then decided to go for a sail before we took a berth in the marina. Helen had a go at the electric winch and after weighing anchor we motored slowly out of the harbour.

"That winch is fantastic. I've never used one before."

"Beverley said we must charge the batteries after using it."

"If you paid as much attention to me as you do to Beverley we'd have a great time." But she made it clear she didn't really mind. "Will Beverley mind if we tow the dinghy and not hoist it back on its stanchions?"

I ignored her and got Helen to unfurl the genoa so that we drifted slowly past Rendezvous Bay with the light north easterly wind behind us.

"My love, you won't see anything now from out here, even if there is anything to see. Anyway the boat's gone."

"I know. Why don't we rent a car and have a look?"

"Because, Peter, can't you get it into your lovely head that you are not a policeman. If you must do anything then call Ben now." I nodded. "OK, I'll get the sails up. Come on, get into wind."

We tacked back and had a quick look in to Half Moon Bay, with its great beach and over developed hotels, before running back to Falmouth Harbour. I called the marina on the RT to get our berth but they were full of apologies and explained that the boat they expected to go didn't leave so they couldn't accommodate us. Actually I think we were both glad to anchor back where we had been before.

Helen went straight down to our bunk after we had eaten but I couldn't resist getting the dinghy out and going outside the harbour. The stars still shone down, undiluted from the lights of earth. I stopped the outboard engine and there was complete silence. The warm breeze was almost still and though I strained my eyes I could not detect any boats waiting off the shores of Rendezvous Bay. Reluctantly I restarted the engine and slowly motored back to the boat, realising how fortunate I was in so many ways. Helen didn't stir as I joined her down below.

DAY 32

In the morning we made our way slowly back to St Antony. The wind started to veer and we had to pinch to windward to clear the Cape. As we cleared the headland we were able to bear away and we sailed past *Leewards* towards the harbour. My phone rang.

"Peter, what are you up to?"

"Ben, I'm having a few days holiday and currently going back to the marina."

"Well I don't want you hanging about Paradise harbour to-night."

"I don't understand. Why on earth not?"

"Let's just say you tend to interfere in things that don't concern you. I can't stop you going in but I should warn you that if you leave your yacht then my people may want to interrogate you in Cape Harbour."

"OK Ben, I get the message. Have a good evening."

Helen had been listening to my end of the conversation.

"What on earth was all that about? What did he want you not to do?"

"Stay in harbour to-night."

"That's ridiculous. Why on earth not."

"I think he must have got wind of a drug run to-night and he's got a lot of his people in the harbour."

"But it wouldn't be *Dark Blue Diving* surely? Not after what has happened."

"No, but maybe there is a boat involved. I don't know but we'd better do as we're told. In fact it so happens that I was looking at a spot that might just do."

Helen looked at me suspiciously. We went back again past *Leewards* and could see the same boat that had gone to Rendezvous Bay on our way to Antigua moored to the pier.

"Alright, I agree. It's the same boat. Why haven't you rung Ben?"

"Because I think he must be on to something and probably knows all about the boat."

I showed Helen the spot I had in mind, about three miles past *Leewards* in a deep water pool very close to the beach with no houses near on the shore.

"Why do you want to watch here? You're mad."

Helen came in to wind, I furled the jib, dropped the mizzen and then went up to the main mast and dropped the mainsail. She started the engine and we came in, close to the land so that we were completely hidden from *Leewards*. As she gave a touch of the astern gear and the boat stopped going forward, I dropped the anchor using the winch. I secured the chain on the windlass and went aft. Perfect peace.

"Come on now, Peter, out with it. Did Ben tell you what he was going to do? When I suggested sailing you didn't argue but agreed straight away and you embellished the whole idea by extending the rental to three nights. You must have had an agenda which you haven't mentioned yet."

"Not really. I just liked the idea of sailing and three days seemed better than one. Obviously Ben suspects that on occasions Smithson is using his jetty and his boats but so far he hasn't been able to catch him at it. Presumably to-night he's got some information and is active in Paradise Harbour. Since Ben won't let us in, I think it's reasonable to watch. I never thought we would have the opportunity."

"Peter, we shouldn't be doing this. It's crazy. Drug runners are armed to the teeth and will stop at nothing. They would have killed me given half a chance. This drug business is absolutely nothing to do with you."

"It might be in a way if Smithson is involved."

"I have to tell you I'm not convinced." She stopped for a moment and looked at me. "I suppose in some ways we're very alike. You never give up. Surely this boat can't do what you want?"

"Yes it can. That's why I checked the boat had radar and chose this spot for anchoring to see if it was suitable. It's nice and close to the shore so we won't be spotted by any passing boat but we can watch the world go by."

"Are you sure? Isn't it a bit close to *Leewards*? That electric winch is great but it makes a hell of a noise. They may have already seen or heard us. If anyone from the boat we saw in Antigua spots us we'll be in trouble. Just as well I don't have to sleep to-night to get ready for a return trip to-morrow. However, I do feel tired. If you want to stay awake all night instead of cuddling me, that's up to you."

The radio buzzed. I looked at my watch --- it was 1615. Beverley came on the radio.

"*Northern Cross, Northern Cross* this is *Discover St Antony*."

"Go ahead, *Discover St Antony*"

"Where are you, Peter?"

"We're anchored close to the shore a few miles North of the end of the runway. Do you want Lat/Long?"

"No, just checking. Did wonder where you would go. Luckily for you what little wind there is will drop to-night as it gets dark or I might have made you go round to Cape Harbour. See you to-morrow."

I turned off the radio and switched on my mobile phone to check there was a good signal. Helen had been listening to the exchange. "Well she obviously knows that something odd is going on."

"I think Ben must have warned her as well."

I got out the bottle of Jacob's Creek fizzy wine which I'd ordered and put it in the fridge. We drank it as the sun set and then I produced some Trinidadian chicken pelau which I'd heated in the microwave.

"This is great. No more cooking for me."

"Don't bet on it, my love."

It got dark very quickly and I could see Helen was tired after helming the boat most of the way across from Antigua. She got into one of the double berths in the rear of the boat and went to bed. I turned out all the lights and went on deck to watch. Like the previous night there was no light pollution, the sky was clear, there was no moon and millions of stars shone down. I could barely make out Orion's Belt with all the stars shining through.

DAY 33

About midnight I thought I heard the dull sound of engines coming from over the water and switched on the radar which woke Helen up. She came up next to me to look at the screen.

"What's been going on?"

"Nothing at all, looking at you."

"Stop complaining. What's happening?"

"Helen, put some clothes on for goodness sake. I'm trying to concentrate."

She came back with a pullover on.

"Look, dear. There's a small echo coming out of Paradise Harbour."

She went on deck and came back. "I think I can make out the lights of the boat where the echo is."

"There's another faint radar echo just beyond the harbour close to Lightning Head almost on the land. I wonder if that's something to do with Ben?"

"Surely they would be more careful. If we can see the echo then so can all the boats."

"Not sure about that. We are close in to the shore and are able see Lightning Head beyond the harbour. The radar on any boat out to sea might not be able to see that echo because the reflection from the Head would swamp it."

"But the boat coming out of Paradise Harbour would see it."

"Only if the boat has working radar. And even then they wouldn't know anything about the boat. After all it is just a guess on my part."

We watched the boat coming out of the harbour. It headed straight for Cape Fearless and disappeared. Nothing else seemed to be happening.

"Tell you what, my love. I'll do an hour while you have a rest. Set your phone so you don't oversleep."

"That seems a bit unfair, Helen. Why should you support my wild goose chase?"

"Because I'm lovely and it's a beautiful night. Off you go."

I never made my hour as forty minutes later Helen woke me.

"A big echo has appeared from the South East and is heading our way."

We looked and the echo stopped about eight miles offshore. Then as we watched an echo reappeared round Cape Fearless and headed for the new echo. It must have gone alongside and then about thirty minutes later it started heading towards Paradise Harbour. Helen looked for its lights but she couldn't see any. The faint echo we had been watching near the shore started to move towards the echo going into the harbour and then the echoes coalesced and disappeared.

Helen pointed excitedly. "Look, there's a very faint echo coming out of *Leewards* very quickly and going to the big echo."

We could hear the engine noise very clearly.

"It must be going very quickly. It's got to be a RIB."

It was only at the big echo for about ten minutes and then it started towards Cape Fearless. Almost simultaneously the big echo started to move away quite quickly in the direction from which it had come. I wondered what was going to happen next when suddenly a searchlight shone on us. Incredibly the big boat which we had seen on the *Leewards* jetty must have crept along the coast so we did not see its echo. It was very close indeed and the searchlight swept backwards and forwards along the boat. Then the light went out and the boat crept further along the coast to Cape Fearless. The captain must have known the coast like the back of his hand.

"What are we going to do now, Peter."

"I'm damned if I know."

"Why has the RIB gone towards Cape Fearless?"

"All I can think of is that it has taken a load of drugs on board and is going to give it to that boat that just went by us. Presumably Smithson doesn't want any drugs in his place and he can't use *Dark Blue Diving* any more."

"In that case hadn't we better weigh anchor in case the RIB comes after us on the way back to *Leewards*?"

"You're absolutely right." I thought for a moment about what might happen. "You know, if that happens we'll have to go to the jetty at *Leewards.* If we stay at sea they could sink the boat and us in one fell swoop. Call up Ben as quick as you can and tell him what is happening. With any luck Ben will have some people watching the house. Take my phone, its got his number, and give me yours."

Helen got through and I could hear her struggling with the duty officer, yelling it was an emergency, trying to explain what we were doing and asking for Ben. Suddenly I heard the faint roar of an engine. I rushed forward and winched the anchor up. As I returned, as quickly as I could to the wheel, I could see white foam, even in the darkness and the engine noise was getting very loud. I opened the throttle fully and started snaking towards *Leewards* and the jetty. The RIB soon caught us up and we heard what we assumed to be shots. It tried to come alongside but it couldn't make it as I was steering so erratically.

It seemed to take forever for the jetty to appear. I tried to bring the boat alongside in the dark but there was a sickening crunch and the boat came to an abrupt stop. I throttled back as a local man I hadn't seen before appeared on the deck from the RIB holding a gun. He clearly didn't know what to do. Helen meanwhile had tied a rope from the stern to the jetty. The bow had made its own arrangement and seemed tangled with some stanchions on the jetty.

A cultured voice with a very clear English accent announced. "Come onto the jetty with your arms in the air."

It didn't take a lot of imagination to realise it must have been Smithson and as we climbed from the boat I could see his blonde hair, even in the dark. He shone his torch in our faces, first at Helen and then at me.

"You had better come inside with me." He turned to the gun man. "Cover them very carefully, Jacob. They're a very tricky pair."

We followed him down the jetty to the shore and then climbed up into the house. He took us into a small room, turned the light on and looked at us.

"I've seen you two before. This time you've interfered once too often. Give me your phones."

I handed over Helen's phone.

"I left mine on the boat on the table. Do you want it?"

She made to move but Smithson indicated she was to stay where she was. It looked as if he was about to issue some instruction to Jacob so it seemed important to give him a situation report.

"Mr Smithson, if you take my advice you won't get Jacob here to kill us and have two more murders on your hands. Your house is surrounded and the police know about the new delivery of drugs which your RIB put on your big boat. I've just spoken to them and they will be here with a search warrant in just a few minutes, despite all your efforts and your heavy breathing friends in Cape Harbour. I think the penalty for murder is even greater than for trafficking in drugs." I added to emphasise his predicament. "The police are also meeting the trawler that pretended to bring the drugs in. I'm sure some of the crew will spill the beans."

Smithson looked at us and was clearly undecided. Jacob didn't look too happy but, in my judgement, would probably shoot us if he was ordered to. Luckily he sensed there was a problem. I looked at him as I spoke.

"And by the way, Masters is wondering what you have done with Jacko? Did Jacob here kill him for you? Have you got rid of the body yet? Did you weigh him down and get this guy here to dump him in the sea or have you still got the body somewhere?"

Smithson stared at us, trying to decide what to do. He turned to Jacob who was looking decidedly uncomfortable after my last remark. "Keep these guys in this room. You can close the door, shoot them if they try to get out. I'll be back in a minute to deal with them."

Smithson turned round and disappeared down a corridor, taking a phone out of his pocket at the same time.

I turned to Jacob. "You won't see him again. Your best bet is to give yourself up. Smithson is going to run. He won't get away and you might get your sentence reduced."

"Shut up." Jacob clearly didn't want to think things through. He went out of the room, keeping us covered, and locked the door. There was no furniture in the room and we had to sit on the hard cement floor. There was a long wait.

"Do you think it's safe yet for me to produce your phone?"

I looked at Helen in amazement.

"You said you left it in the boat."

"Well he was a Brit. I reckoned he wasn't about to do a strip search."

"That was incredibly risky, darling, but well done. Where is it?"

"Never you mind. I'm not letting you look for it. Do you think Jacob is going to come back?"

"Not sure. Probably not. Why don't we take a risk and try and get Ben and then hide it again? Of course it may not work in this room without any windows. Let's listen."

We could hear nothing and Helen reached down in her clothes and produced my phone. The signal was weak but usable. I rang Ben's number but there was no reply. I sent him a text message 'At Leewards, the sooner the better.'

"You'd better put it away again."

She smiled. "You can if you like."

I looked at her and raised my eyebrows. "You're impossible. I hope somebody's going to rescue us."

She took the phone and hid it again.

"What was all that about the drugs going to Antigua? And Jacko being killed? You made it all up."

"Nonsense, just reasonable hypotheses."

"You must be in a dream world." I was pleased to hear that there was doubt in her voice

"Well as I see things, somebody must have known that Ben's lot were going to be on the prowl last night. The shipment must have been very large and very important. It was probably too late to delay the boat so they decided to use another boat as a decoy. Probably a fishing boat they had used before. I expect a lot of money changed hands. Then, while the boat was being inspected in Paradise Harbour, the RIB rushed out and collected the drugs for onwards transfer to the large boat at the jetty, the one we had seen before at Rendezvous Bay and the one that shone the searchlight on us. It was just bad luck for them that we were watching."

"Bad luck for us you mean, Peter. What on earth is going to happen next? That Jacob guy doesn't look as if bumping off a couple more people would worry him."

"Not sure I agree completely. I thought he looked concerned."

"Hope you're right. But you inferred they had killed Jacko?"

"I'm sure they bumped him off and I think I know why. Smithson wanted to get hold of the diamond. It must be worth a fortune."

"You're making it up." She looked pensive. "Ben doesn't know yet about the boat that went round Cape Fearless to Antigua, if it is Antigua."

"I'm not sure where it is going. Possibly Guadeloupe. I don't believe the boat will get very far. I'll tell Ben when he appears."

"If we're not dead first. That duty officer did not fill me with confidence. He didn't seem to know who Ben was." A pause. "Well perhaps I exaggerate a little."

We waited for what seemed like ages but in reality was probably only about an hour. Then to our surprise we heard the roar of an engine.

Helen produced the phone and I called air traffic. The duty controller answered.

"Peter Talbert here. There's a helicopter taking off from the shore just north of the eastern end of your runway. Can you track it until it disappears? The police will want to know where it was heading."

A surprised controller acknowledged my call.

"Jacob isn't going to come back now. If he's still here he'll know Smithson has scarpered. We must talk to someone."

I tried Ben again but it was already 8am and Jearl answered. I asked her to put me through to Ben but he was not there. She said she would get him to call me. All was quiet and Helen looked at me.

"What's happening?"

"I suppose Ben's getting a search warrant because he doesn't want to put a foot wrong where Smithson is concerned."

"Well what about some concern for us?"

"I'm getting a bit fed up with all this excitement."

My phone rang.

"Where are you Ben? We're locked in a room in *Leewards* with a hit man called Jacob waiting to get rid of us and Smithson's left the island in a helicopter."

"I've just heard about the helicopter. Don't know where it's going."

"I've asked the tower to track it. Hope you don't mind."

Ben sounded as if he was choking.

"We'll be with you shortly. It's taking time to get a judge out of bed to get a search warrant. The bad news is that there were no drugs on the trawler, *Swinging Low*."

"I know. They pulled a trick on your people. While they were searching the trawler Smithson's RIB went to the boat and then put

231

the drugs on Smithson's 40ft boat that was managing to keep hidden going very close to the shore and Cape Fearless."

"Well we must get the boat with the drugs on if we're going to convict Smithson. You seem to know everything as usual, Peter. Where is it going."

"Well get us out of here and I'll tell you my idea."

After what seemed an age we could hear sirens getting louder and then stopping, apparently outside. There was a hammering on the door, a splintering noise and then voices. We yelled and the door was unlocked. Rick appeared with a smile all over his face.

"Thank God you're both alright."

"Did you get Jacob?"

"As far as we know there's no one else in the house."

"He must have decided to run before he was caught. Pity about Smithson getting away."

"Not sure. At least he can't try and influence the politicians if he's not here. May be a blessing in disguise. We can charge him in his absence so he'll never dare to return."

"But don't you need to find some drugs?"

"Yes, we do. But you told Ben they were on Smithson's boat, wherever that is. Not much chance of finding it, though we have alerted Antigua and Guadeloupe."

"Nonsense. Take me to the airport and the Coastguard. If they've got a plane we can search for the boat. It can't have got that far. It's a heavy old displacement boat, only good for 10 knots at the very most, probably 9. I'll be able to recognise it."

Rick called the Coastguard in Cape Harbour and asked them to authorise a search plane to try to find the boat.

"What about the yacht, Peter? Beverley will kill us when she sees it. Goodness knows what damage we've done. How are we going to get it back."

I looked at Helen. "We'd better have a quick look to see if it can be moved."

We went with Rick down to the jetty and looked at *Northern Cross.* The yacht looked a mess. It had been very badly damaged in the bow. There were two holes right through the hull above the waterline, one on each side, and the genoa had been cut very badly by the jetty railing so that the forestay didn't look too happy.

I looked at Helen. "Well you can't sail it back by yourself. Why don't you get Beverley to come over, look at it and then she can decide what to do."

"How can I? I don't have a phone and you are about to leave me here."

"Alright, I'll phone her now before we leave."

Beverley agreed to come over and we left Helen with one of Rick's men in the house while we went to the airport. The Coastguard plane, a twin engined Beechcraft, was ready and Tony Wilson, the Coastguard's senior pilot, took me out to the plane.

"Where are we going, Peter?"

"We need to start searching from Cape Fearless towards Guadeloupe and Antigua."

We took off and climbed to 5,000 ft. The visibility was superb and we could see for miles. Instinctively I favoured going towards Guadeloupe because the boat had been to Antigua two nights previously. I got Tony to fly on a line parallel to the coast and we gradually left Cape Fearless behind and towards the French island. Thinking about what was happening, the boat we were looking for would not want to approach Guadeloupe closely during the day. It probably would be going quite slowly, maybe only 5 knots. Presumably there was a spot, like Rendezvous Bay in Antigua, where the drugs could be landed at night.

We could see quite a few motor boats and I got Tony to drop down two or three times to check on certain boats that looked possible. Finally I spotted the boat we were looking for, heading for the north eastern shore of the island, probably only about half way across. I was so confident that it was the right boat I decided not to ask Tony to go low over it and possibly alert it but merely to note its current GPS position and heading. I asked him to get their operations to phone Ben so that we could talk, with the help of the coastguard operator.

"Ben, you'll never catch him from St Antony, how about alerting the island?"

"Not much else we can do. Do we know the name of the boat?"

"I don't. Isn't there anyone you can ask? Won't the boat be registered in your marine department under Smithson's name or *Dark Blue Diving?* Ben, to be on the safe side why don't you get the coastguard aircraft to watch the boat until the French

Coastguard have intercepted it. He won't have to remain airborne all the time as the boat can only move very slowly."

We flew back, the aircraft refuelled and Tony went back to shadow the boat. I called Helen and then realised I was wasting my time since she had lost her phone but before I could cancel the call Helen answered.

"You've got your phone back. Where was it?"

"On Smithson's desk. He must have dumped it there before he escaped. I'm with Beverley at *Discover St Antony*. Your car's OK. Are you coming over?"

"Where's *Northern Cross*? What did Beverley say?"

"Why don't you shut up for a change and come and collect me? If you come straightaway we'll be in the restaurant."

I said my farewells and caught a cab from the airport to Paradise Harbour. I saw Beverley and Helen looking very relaxed with long drinks in front of them.

"What on earth have you got there?" The girl serving the drinks came over.

"I'll have whatever she's having."

They grinned. "Not sure that's possible. It's a rum punch."

"*Northern Cross*? How bad is it? Where is it?"

"Your concern is to be applauded. We motored it back very carefully and it's in its berth."

"But what about the damage, the insurance?" I looked at them both and they were smiling. "There's something you haven't told me. What does the owner say?"

Helen looked at Beverley. "Shall we tell him?" She nodded. "You'll never believe this. The owner's gone away. The boat belongs to Smithson. And it's insured anyway."

"You're joking? Alright you're not. Amazing."

"What did Ben say?"

I saw Beverley looking at the car park. "You can ask him, he's just coming over."

"Peter, how many times have I told you not to interfere. Thank God you did. Let me buy you a drink."

"Two drinks. I couldn't have done it without Helen, here. But later or we'll get smashed and I'm driving."

"Seriously, Peter. Thank you so much. Apart from anything else you've probably saved my job. I think there was a serious bit of financial persuasion taking place to get rid of me. Anyway we can talk about it all later." He turned to Beverley. "You didn't hear any of that but we'll be responsible for any damage to the boat."

We all smiled and Ben looked puzzled until we broke the news to him. He looked as misbelieving as I did.

"Are you sure?"

Beverley nodded.

"I'll have a coffee. You people seem to pushing the boat out. Actually I'll have a sandwich as well. I've been up all night."

"Ben, so have we, come to think of it. I'll have a sandwich as well. Helen looks as if she's eaten." She nodded.

"Have they caught the boat yet?"

"It's going to take a few hours. They've got a large RIB going out from Point à Pitre. They've also got a customs plane about to take over the tracking of the boat. The French police have been after the drug dealers on the island for ages and they are hoping they can get the crew of the boat to talk."

"Knowing the way the French do things I wouldn't like to be the crew if they don't talk. By the way, what have you done with the crew of *Swinging Low?*"

"We charged them with abetting drug running, which really scared them, and then we released them on bail. They admitted receiving $500 Caribbean dollars each but they swore they didn't know anything about anything. They just stopped by the drug boat for about thirty minutes, the time that was specified by the person who paid them. They didn't see anyone."

"Ben, were they paid in full?"

"No, they've only got half and would you believe, they're not expecting any more."

"Where did Smithson go?"

"Don't know for sure but air traffic said the helicopter was heading for Antigua. I've told their chief of police that there is a warrant for his arrest but I'm not holding my breath. The helicopter could have landed at so many different places."

"I think Antigua is very likely, Ben, not that I know what I'm talking about. Anyway you're bound to find out where he went."

"Why?"

"Because presumably he was flying the helicopter himself. He must have left it somewhere."

"He may not have been flying it. We don't know everybody who lived and stayed in *Leewards*."

"Well at least you can check whether he has a valid licence with the SRG in Gatwick and The Ministry of Transport here should know about the helicopter, who owns it and the registration. I favour the helicopter going to Antigua because there's a very good service to the States and Europe and he's probably got a Swiss bank account and a false passport."

"You're probably right. I'll make sure Antigua has his photograph and all his details. Mind you, I'm not sure I want him back."

"That's what Rick said. But he needs putting away or he'll start again somewhere else. But I'm pretty sure it won't be with Jacko."

"How do you know?"

"I've got an idea he had Jacko killed."

"Here we go again. How can you possibly know that?"

"Well I've been thinking. I had thought that Hudson was killed to prevent anybody knowing that Jacko was still alive. But I'm thinking now that what might have happened was that when Hudson found Jacko in the hospital, remember he was unconscious, he found the diamond. I've always felt that the diamond was so valuable that Jacko would never let it out of his sight and my bet is it was strapped to his body."

"But he wouldn't be allowed to leave the UK with it like that. He would have been caught by the scanner"

"Possibly, but all that would have happened if he was searched was that they would have found the stone and there is no crime in having a diamond. More likely he would have been wearing it and then once on the aircraft he would have strapped it on. Anyway, Hudson probably saw the stone while Jacko was unconscious and took it."

"But Jacko would have been desperate when he came to."

"Well there was nothing he could do. He would think that the stone and its strap obviously got disconnected during the ditching. Or he might have suspected the hospital staff. You need to get someone to ask them if he had something strapped to him when he was admitted."

"But that's no reason for Smithson to get rid of Jacko."

236

"Maybe Jacko told Smithson that he'd lost the diamond during the ditching. How about if Smithson realised that Hudson had the diamond? You told me Hudson's clothes had been undone even though he was shot."

"Yes, that's right. But you're guessing."

"Yes I am. But it would explain Hudson's death."

"But not Jacko's, assuming he is dead."

"I wonder. I think Jacko then began to suspect Smithson of taking the diamond and maybe he was unwise enough to accuse Smithson. Perhaps Smithson decided Jacko had to go and judging by the look on Jacob's face when I asked if the body had been weighted and thrown overboard or was in the house somewhere, I must have been pretty near the truth. Jacko was probably proving an embarrassment. We're never going to know."

Ben nodded. "You could be right. Anyway I'd better go and get on with some work instead of chatting to you two, dreaming up fantasies. We've got to find Jacob to tie Smithson in with the drug running. And the Guadeloupe police have got to find the boat and the drugs." He looked at both of us. "Anyway thanks so much for everything. Hope you find out soon why the aircraft ditched."

Helen smiled. "He's a nice man. Wish all policemen were like him. And I bet he wishes that he had lots of helpers like you."

"Peter," Beverley looked at me, "why is it whenever I rent you a boat you always do something you shouldn't?" She grinned at Helen. "I thought he just wanted the boat to take advantage of you."

"Wish."

"I should have known better though. Peter, why you should decide to help Ben I can't imagine."

"Well he wouldn't let me come in to the harbour last night so I had no alternative."

"There's always an alternative --- like minding your own business. Anyway, remember Peter you're on my proscribed list from now on. You can take me out to lunch but not to sea."

We went back to the hotel and lay by the pool dozing in the shade. Sandra came by and said hello and good-bye in a loud voice. "Good luck to-morrow with the PM."

Helen squirmed slightly "Speak up, they missed that in the far corner of the pool."

Sandra departed and we went back to the room for a bit before we had a drink in the bar and a sandwich.

"Here's to us."

Tom appeared. "What are you two celebrating?"

"Being alive."

Tom looked puzzled but we didn't enlighten him.

DAY 34

We got up slowly and went down to breakfast. To our surprise the *Announcer* was full of the capture of the drugs approaching Guadeloupe. Cindy was having a field day. Ben had obviously decided not to involve us and very sensibly took all the credit for finding the drugs. He made sure that Smithson was mentioned as often as possible. *Leewards* was Smithson's house and Smithson had left the island by helicopter and a warrant had been issued for Smithson's arrest. Interpol had been informed.

My phone rang and I left the table to take the call.

It was Ben. "Hope you don't mind not being in the paper and my getting all the credit?"

"Not at all. You needed to sort the politicians out and, more important, your own job. Well done. Did you find Jacob?"

"Yes, we guessed he would try to hide with Goddard's family and we found him in a cellar. By the way, you weren't wrong about Jacko. We found his body in *Leewards* cellar next door to the room your were in. He'd been dead for a couple of days."

"I almost feel sorry for him."

"And we also found Tom Smith's passport amongst some of Smithson's papers."

"That's great."

"The grapevine is telling me that Miss Partridge is seeing the PM this morning?"

"Trust you to find out. Surely you aren't going to be there?"

"No, but I'm going a little bit earlier to be thanked."

"That's really great, Ben. We're so pleased, Miss Partridge and I."

"I think you're pulling my leg. Alright then, Helen."

"May see you there. I'm escorting Helen in the taxi; I'm not letting her go alone even if Smithson has gone."

I started back to the table and the phone rang again. It was Cindy. "I'm having breakfast. Call you later. Don't mean to be rude."

I told Helen about Ben.

"What was the second call? You soon shut him up."

"Her up. It was Cindy and I said we'd talk later."

We went back upstairs and Helen put her war paint on and her best suit with a fairly short skirt.

"You look terrific."

"Well you don't. Go and smarten yourself, even if you are only the consort."

I obliged with a lightweight suit and I managed to find my one and only tie. We went downstairs and took a cab to Government House. We were ushered into a waiting room and then we were both invited in. I tried to explain I was only the escort but apparently I was expected as well.

We were introduced, Helen as the cabin attendant who saved all the lives during the ditching and myself, much to my surprise, as the person who helped catch the drug dealers. The PM concentrated on Helen and allowed photographers in to record the meeting. Then he turned to me.

"I gather we owe you a double round of thanks, Mr Talbert. You rescued West Atlantic Airways when one of their aircraft disappeared some years ago and the night before last you were able to tell Ben Masters about the drug smuggling, at some risk to yourself."

"I was delighted to be able to help, Sir. You have a wonderful island here and long may it stay the same."

"Mr Talbert, you know as well as I do that nothing ever stays the same. There will always be change; all we can do is to strive to keep this island as a wonderful home for those who live here and a magnet for tourists to enjoy our good luck."

We chatted for a bit and did the photograph routine, with and without Helen. The whole thing didn't take long and we went outside to be greeted by Cindy.

"The photos were great. Can we have a story?"

"Have you got a car here?"

"Of course."

"OK. Then you can take us back to the hotel and we'll buy you lunch."

Helen looked at me and didn't say a word. She thought it was chutzpah but I thought it was a fair trade.

We chatted over lunch while Cindy had her pencil and pad going like a lunatic.

"What's this story about a boat you rented and the drug runners?"

"You must ask Ben. It's his story."

"Have you sorted out why the aircraft ditched?"

"It's not my job Cindy. That's for AAIB but I've got some ideas. I'll have to go back to the UK though to check things out." I saw Helen raising her eyebrows. "I'll try to give you some early info if it works out. Some leads anyway, which you can chase up with AAIB."

"Can I say that you two met as a result of the accident?"

I looked at Helen. "I don't see why not. We are now good friends, just."

Helen kicked me under the table and looked at Cindy. "He's impossible but I'm putting up with him for the moment."

Cindy beamed. "What a wonderful quote. Thanks so much."

We waved her goodbye. "She's a super reporter and I like to help when I can."

"I agree. What happens next, wonder boy?"

"You're going to find out when you're scheduled for going back and I'll go back on the same flight. Then you can organise an upgrade for me."

I think Helen had forgotten for a moment that she was on call. She pulled her phone out, texted scheduling and then we went up to get changed for a swim but we didn't make it. I heard the attention noise from her phone.

"To-morrow night from here. Let me call Becky to see how full the flight is."

She went into the bathroom so I couldn't hear the conversation.

"If you book business class she'll fix the upgrade."

I duly went to my computer and made the reservation. There was a message from Ben waiting when we got back asking if we would like to go to *The Royal Restaurant* in Cape Harbour that night at 7pm. I had always wanted to have a meal there but I knew it was ridiculously expensive. I rang him straight back and said we would be delighted. I wanted to make sure he wasn't paying but it would have been terribly rude to mention it. Anyway, on reflection Ben probably was paying and it was a splendid way of saying thank you.

Tom came on the line. "The PM is coming down this afternoon at 1530. Are you free? It would be very nice if you were there."

I looked at my watch and reckoned it would be OK.

"Off you go Peter. I'll have to swim without you."

I didn't have to change as I was still wearing my PM suit from the morning. I managed to get there just in time and Tom showed the Prime Minister round the airframe and the mortuary. I could see he was very impressed. Then Tom introduced him to his staff and then to me.

"We met this morning, Mr Talbert. What have you been doing down here?"

Tom interrupted before I could get a word in.

"Mr Talbert found the missing crash recorder. Thanks to him we now have a chance to discover what really happened to the aircraft."

"Well Mr Talbert, you seem to have done a lot of very good work."

"Thank you, Sir. I've been very lucky."

"No, Mr Talbert, more than that. Some luck perhaps but I suspect hard work played a very large part. Thank you once again and please make sure my office knows how to contact you."

The Prime Minister had a final chat to Tom before leaving but one of his aides came up to me to find out my contact details. The moment the Prime Minister left I drove back to the *New Anchorage* where Helen was already worrying about what I was going to wear that evening. We finally agreed a shirt, trousers and the tie.

"And you'd better take a jacket as well. You know how cold these places are."

I didn't have to worry about her. She always looked great, not that I was biased. We caught a cab downtown and were ushered into the dining room overlooking the harbour. The restaurant was built on quite high ground so the view was dramatic. There was a cruise boat in the harbour, its lights gleaming everywhere. Our table was by the window and Ben's wife Diana was there to meet us. We had a superb evening, but as I left I definitely had a feeling that St Antony was already beginning to slip away from my immediate sphere of contacts.

The phone rang at 7am. It was Ben.

"Peter, Smithson's been found in Antigua."

"How?"

"Their police spotted a helicopter registration V9-SMI in a field near All Saints. It was being towed in to a barn. They recognised the St Antony registration and phoned last night while we were having dinner."

"Why didn't they call you?"

"They did try but I had decided to turn my phone off for once. When I woke up this morning I saw the missing calls."

"What happened?"

"They surrounded the property, it was a farm apparently and then went in without a search warrant based on spotting the plane. Smithson was there and guess what?"

"They found more drugs."

"How did you know?"

"Ben, I told you Smithson's boat had been at Rendezvous Bay with a dinghy going ashore. Presumably their police got the person or people at the farm?"

"Absolutely. And we've applied to have Smithson extradited."

"Extradited? That's ridiculous. Can't they put him in a boat or plane and bring him straight back?"

"You would think so but Smithson has demanded to have a lawyer and it's getting very difficult, apparently." I could hear a phone ringing wherever Ben was. "Wait a moment Peter, I'll call you back."

Helen was awake by now and had been listening to the last part of our conversation.

"That's great, my darling. You never believed they'd catch him."

"He's not here yet. He's slippery as an eel. The fat lady still hasn't sung."

The phone rang again. It was Ben again. "He's here. In our police station in Cape Harbour, clamouring for a solicitor and yelling foul. Tom Somers, my opposite number in Antigua, told his men to fly him over here and damn the lawyers. I think he wanted to get rid of Smithson and reckoned that he wouldn't be able to do anything once he was here."

"Good for him. So presumably all Smithson can do is to apply for bail."

"Yes, but I don't think he is going to get anywhere. All his heavy breathing friends seem to have deserted him."

"Ben?"

Ben stopped me.

"Peter, I recognise that note. What wild scheme have you got now?'

"If you could find Jacko's diamond who would it belong to?"

"You really ask the most amazing questions. I don't know. How about his next-of-kin?"

"But Thomas Smith doesn't have any next-of-kin. We know that already. If he was intestate wouldn't the Government get it?"

"Which Government? UK or St Antony?"

"Ben?"

"Here we go again, I know that tone."

"Ben, you said you found a body at *Leewards*. What have you told the coroner?"

"Haven't got round to that. I've got to write a report. What are you getting at?"

"Well you've got some decisions to make. Was it Jacko or Tom Smith that died?"

"We know it was Jacko?"

"Do you? Have you checked the fingerprints?"

"Peter, you were the one that put us on to Jacko surviving. You were the one who said he was Tom Smith."

"But you haven't checked. Does it matter either way? The UK police won't care though if the body is Tom Smith. You'll just have to ring them up and blame me for making a mistake."

There was a long pause.

"Ben are you still there."

"I've been thinking. You're quite right, Peter. The body is Tom Smith's. I've got his passport. I'll advertise here and in UK to make sure there are no next-of-kin. By the way, do you have any ideas about Smithson? You mentioned to me he might have Tom Smith's diamond."

Helen poked me and grinned. She could obviously hear both ends of the conversation.

"Well it might be interesting to ask your guys at the police station where his effects are."

"It's funny you should say that. Apparently Smithson was most reluctant for my guys to search him and he made them list everything."

"Would you like me to come to the station? It won't be a problem."

"I thought you were leaving to-day."

"We are but not until this evening. I'm on my way."

Helen grabbed me. "I haven't had breakfast yet."

"But we had a big meal last night."

"That was last night. And I'm working to-night, not sleeping, being waited on foot and mouth."

"Don't you mean hand and foot?"

"I know what I mean. " She relented. "Don't be long and there might be time for a French breakfast."

I threw some clothes on and went to Ben's office.

"Have you found it yet?"

"No we've looked through all his effects. By the way he's not looking at all well."

"Have you got the doctors to X-ray him to find out what's the matter?"

"Peter, surely you don't think he swallowed it?" I nodded. "It might kill him. It's meant to be huge. At least 3.5cm in diameter."

"Well clearly he hopes he might get away with it. You'd better take him to the hospital and see if he needs to be cut open."

"But his lawyer will object."

"He certainly will if Smithson dies. He'll be losing his meal ticket. Go for it."

Ben shrugged his shoulders in despair as I left him and drove back to the hotel.

"You were quick. You must be hungry."

"Only for a petit dejeuner."

"Well that's bad luck for you. I've changed my mind and fancy the full monty."

"So do I."

"Let me rephrase that. Turn round, open the door and lead the way downstairs."

We sat outside as usual but for the last time. Helen looked around.

"It sad really. In spite of everything, my love, I like it here."

"We'll come back for our honeymoon."

"Peter Talbert, I think you have forgotten something."

"Alright then on holiday."

"You've blown it." But she allowed me to kiss her.

We packed and went down for a swim. I met Janet Underdown who was going to be supervising Helen on the way back. Then Ben phoned again.

"The doctor's have advised an immediate operation. There is a very nasty stone of some type in his stomach and the doctor thinks he might die. The stone might cause an obstruction."

"What does his lawyer say?"

"Nothing."

"When is he going in to the theatre?"

"Right now."

"Call me back when its all over."

"You bet."

But Ben didn't call until we were at the airport. Helen was goodness knows where, preparing for the flight and I was in the first class lounge.

"Its huge. It might well have killed him. How he swallowed it we'll never know."

"How many carats?"

"Well over a hundred apparently. We haven't had it valued yet. It must be worth much more than a normal diamond as its green."

"Where is it now?"

"In my safe and it's going to stay there until we sort out Tom Smith's will."

The flight was called and Helen welcomed me on board as if she'd never seen me before. She showed me to my seat, took my jacket and offered me a glass of champagne.

"No thank you my dear, I've got nothing to celebrate. And I'm not keen on drinking when I'm flying."

"But didn't they find the diamond, Sir?"

"Sorry, I forgot. Yes, they did. Ben called me to let me know."

"Then I suggest Sir that you drink up and shut up."

I saw Janet Underdown watching with amusement.

"You'll fail your supervision if you talk to your passengers like that."

"And you won't be getting any meal service if you don't behave yourself. Sir!"

DAY 36

Helen saw me off the aircraft in her most professional manner.

"Goodbye, Sir. Hope you enjoyed the flight." However she spoilt it by saying "I'll pick you up in front of arrivals. My car is in the Worldwide employees park. I'll phone you as I approach the terminal."

It all worked like clockwork. Because she was crew she cleared immigration and customs more quickly than I did even though I was in the premium fast line for admittance and I was a UK citizen. Conveniently, as I got my bag from the carousel my phone rang. I just made it as she pulled up and we drove back to Kingston. However, when I opened the front door and went inside I stopped. Looking around I realised that Helen had indeed been staying in the house. Everywhere I looked I could see changes that clearly she had made.

"You're doing a great job, my love. It's beginning to feel like home already."

"Peter, it's only temporary. I think we should move to something larger. We're both working, you're doing rather well and I feel Mandy is watching us here."

"I'm too tired to think about that now. You must be exhausted and I didn't get too much sleep. Let's go to bed."

"But it's only 9am. I'm not that tired."

"Well you should be. Alright let's go to bed, if you feel like that."

I managed about four hours sleep but then decided I'd better do some work. Helen, in spite of her protestations was still asleep. I showered, got dressed and started work on my computer. There was a tap on my shoulder and Helen was standing there with a tea and not much else.

"That's great, but you'll freeze."

"I wanted a cup of tea before I got up. And I've just remembered there's something I haven't told you."

"Well I can't take it in when you're dressed, or should I say undressed like that. Put something on and we'll have brunch."

I waded though my emails and Helen returned looking very smart and clearly ready to go out.

"Where are you going?"

"We are going out."

"Why."

"Because we can't have breakfast here as we don't have any food in the house. You're taking me to the Cannizaro hotel in Wimbledon for lunch."

"What a great idea. I never seem to think of things like that."

"Peter, I know. It's one of your weaknesses. You're OK for dinner but no good for breakfast or lunch."

We made good time using the back roads.

"Helen, what was it you hadn't told me?"

"Let's sit down first."

Helen chose a table not in the middle of the diners, much to the disgust of the head waiter who wanted to put us with everyone else. We ordered our drinks and chose our meal from a very extensive menu.

"Worldwide want me to be interviewed live to-morrow night."

"How do you know?"

"I got a message on the plane."

"Do you feel up to it? Have they told you the questions?"

"They are going to to-morrow afternoon. I've told them that if they try any tricks I won't play ball."

"That sounds very sensible."

"Oh, by the way, I told them that you would be there."

"Wait a moment, me or your partner, unidentified?"

"I said partner, but I had to give your name and it seemed to ring a bell."

"In the circumstances that's not altogether surprising, is it? I am very happy, nay delighted, to go with you but I don't want to be part of the interview."

"Of course not but I may need advice. Thinking about what you said some time back, do you think I should try to change the way I look?"

"Why don't you wear something rather unattractive and change your hair style a bit? Don't let the make-up people smarten you up. But it's up to you, darling. If you don't mind being recognised then go for a full frontal or whatever it's called."

"Peter, you're quite impossible. I'm sure you don't mean that. Anyway I look better sideways. However, I think I'll go for your first suggestion."

After our meal we went home and I got on with my work. I realised that I had never spoken to Gatwick air traffic control and I had no contacts. Being a member of the Guild of Air Pilots and Air Navigators I decided to call the office to get help. Kristy answered the phone and I explained I needed a contact at a senior level.

"Well Howard Backhouse is a member of the Guild and I happen to know he is a senior air traffic controller at Gatwick because he organised a Guild visit recently. Why don't you call him."

She gave me his contact number at work as well as his home and mobile numbers, she clearly wanted to chat.

"Peter, are you involved with the aircraft that ditched? That was a strange accident. Do you know what went wrong?"

"Kristy, I'm retained by Hull Insurance. It's not my job to find out causes. AAIB do that. However, I don't believe that they have a watertight explanation yet."

"So you want to talk to Gatwick air traffic just for practice?"

"Kristy, you've been very helpful. Thanks a lot."

"I think you're ignoring me. All the best."

We rang off and I called Backhouse at Gatwick. My luck was in as he answered the phone. I explained that I was retained by Hull Insurance and asked if it would be possible to listen to the conversation between Alpha Delta and air traffic.

"Peter, you're very fortunate, as we've recently gone over to digital recording instead of tape so we can find recordings in a particular time frame and frequency quite quickly. Can you give me the call sign, date and rough time?"

I passed the details over. "Howard, what I would like is a print out of the conversations on the ground frequency and then on the tower frequency with times. Is that possible?"

"Why don't you come over here and then you can hear what you want and we'll give you a print out? When can you come?"

"To-morrow morning at about 10am?"

"OK. Bring your passport and accreditation and I'll collect you from air traffic reception."

DAY 37

After arriving at Gatwick, I made my way to the control tower reception and obtained a pass. Howard appeared and introduced himself. He was wearing a blue suit, looked very active and I guessed he must have been about sixty years of age. We went along a corridor into what was a small technical meeting room equipped with computers, a pair of loudspeakers and a large printer. Howard made a telephone call and a young looking thirty year old lady called Yvonne appeared, obviously very efficient. She was carrying a pad with some notes.

"I checked this morning that the recordings you want were all in order. In fact it was easy to find as we had already given the recordings to AAIB. I'll play the Clearance Delivery frequency exchanges first and then we can hear the Ground Control. Do you need the Tower frequency as well?"

"Not sure yet, Yvonne. Let's see how things go."

The recording started with one aircraft after another communicating with the air traffic controllers in a seemingly unending stream. I had to listen intently to separate 442's RT from the other aircraft.

"Gatwick Delivery. Worldwide 442, stand one eight, ITAC 831 with information Delta, QNH one zero zero nine, request start."

"Worldwide 442, Delivery, expect about a fifteen minute delay"

There was a gap of about twenty minutes then.

"Worldwide 442, Delivery, start approved. Cleared to Barbados, Seaford Four Mike Departure, squawk three four two zero."

"Cleared to Barbados, Seaford Four Mike Departure, squawk three four two zero, Worldwide 442."

"Worldwide 442, contact Gatwick Ground one two one decimal eight for push back"

Yvonne had to change to the playback of the Ground frequency and find the next exchange with 442.

"Gatwick Ground, Worldwide 442, stand one eight, request push back"

"Worldwide 442, push approved. Advise ready to taxi."

A gap of about four minutes.

"Ground, Worldwide 442, ready for taxi."

"Worldwide 442, taxi holding point Alpha One, 26Left. Follow the Virgin Boeing 747."

"Taxi holding point Alpha One, 26Left. Follow the Virgin Boeing 747, Worldwide 442."

"Worldwide 442, Ground, call Tower one two four decimal two two five."

Yvonne changed frequency again to the Tower and we listened to Alpha Delta taxiing out and taking off on the Tower frequency but there was nothing unusual that I could detect.

"Yvonne, I don't need the print out of the RT to the Tower."

She smiled. "Great, that'll save a lot of paper" and she gave me a print out of the RT. It was very lengthy because it had the communications from all the aircraft.

"How do you get the print out, Yvonne?"

"Oh, we have a piece of software which does the conversion. It's not perfect but if there is any doubt, like with a pilot with poor English, then we listen carefully and edit as required. In this case there were no problems."

I looked at the print out and though everything was perfect, there was something troubling me. I felt I had missed something. There were no timings.

"Yvonne was this the first dialogue with 442? Is it possible they called earlier? Can you give me the timings?"

She consulted her records and wrote the time of the first transmission on the print out she had given me.

"The first call from the aircraft is about thirty minutes later than I expected. Was there an earlier transmission?"

Yvonne looked surprised but didn't say anything. She went back to the computer and turned round after a few minutes.

"You're right Mr Talbert. I'm extremely sorry I missed it. I'll play it now, if I may."

I nodded.

"Gatwick Delivery. Worldwide 442, stand one eight, ITAC 831 with information Charlie, QNH one zero zero eight, request start."

"Worldwide 442, Delivery, stand by"

Almost immediately there was another call from air traffic

"Worldwide 442, Delivery, start approved. Cleared to Barbados, Seaford Four Mike Departure, squawk three four two zero."

"Cleared to Barbados, Seaford Four Mike Departure, squawk three four two zero, Worldwide 442."

"Worldwide 442, contact Gatwick Ground one two one decimal eight for push back"

"Ground, one two one decimal eight for push back, Worldwide 442"

Yvonne changed frequency again.

"Gatwick Ground, Worldwide 442, stand one eight, request push back"

"Worldwide 442, cleared to push stand one eight"

There was a pause of about three minutes.

"Gatwick Worldwide 442. There will be a delay. We are having to shut down our engines. We have an electrical problem. Will advise."

"Worldwide 442, Ground. Start and push cancelled, call Delivery when ready again"

"Yvonne, absolutely first class. You've found exactly what I wanted. Can you print out this second lot as well with the timings of each call?"

Yvonne went back to the computer and the printer burst in to life again. She gave me both the print outs, this time with the timings. She tried to apologise but I cut her short.

"Just a thought. Has anybody else heard this first playback?"

"Not as far as I know."

Howard had been watching and listening but saying nothing. As we came back into reception he looked at me.

"You reckon you've got the answer, don't you?"

"Well I've got a theory that might explain what happened."

"Are you going to try it out on AAIB?"

"I expect they've worked it out ages ago."

Howard didn't look convinced. I made my farewells and went back to the station, Victoria and my office. I called Charles Hendrick who wasn't in but I spoke to his secretary.

"Mary, I need to speak to the pilots on the last flight Alpha Delta did before it ditched. The flight was about ten days before the ditching because the aircraft was called in for maintenance.

253

Presumably Flight Operations have the records? Can you send me a text message with the pilot's number?"

Mary agreed. I looked at my watch. I only had forty five minutes to meet up with Helen at the TV studio. I got the timing just right as Helen had arrived a few minutes before me. I did a double take. Her hair was brushed right forward with her lovely long hair in plaits. She was wearing a shapeless pair of trousers with an equally shapeless top.

"You look perfect."

"Don't be rude."

"I'm not. You will do a really great job and you won't be recognised outside the studios."

Helen didn't look too sure but before we could debate her appearance the interviewer, Tracey Stapleton, came in and gave Helen a list of questions and she had a copy for me. I could see her looking at Helen and wondering what I saw in her. The questions looked straightforward but I'd seen Tracey in action. She was very attractive, very fluent and I didn't trust her.

Helen looked at me. "What do you think?"

"Providing Tracey keeps to these questions you'll be absolutely fine. Remember you did an amazing job and it's only right that people should appreciate what you did. And don't let's forget Worldwide did a good job training you."

Tracey nodded "I want to bring those points out, Helen."

I looked at her. "Tracey, a couple of things. Firstly, please don't labour the scramble to get out. It clearly was survival of the fittest which is not surprising. It was a very traumatic time for Helen here." Helen nodded. "And please no fishing trips at the end. Helen will walk out if you start asking her how she met me and that sort of stuff. I don't exist as far as this interview is concerned."

Helen looked surprised. "But Peter, you've seen the questions here."

"I know. But I've seen it all before. What happens is that the interviewee starts to relax at the end of the interview and that's when unexpected questions are asked."

Tracey had the grace to look a bit uncomfortable. "But Mr Talbert, you are newsworthy. You are a well know airplane insurance investigator. The public would like to know that you and

Helen are more than just good friends. That you met while you were investigating the ditching. It's a great story."

"Not to-day it isn't. We're serious, one word out of place and Helen will stand up and leave."

Helen agreed. Tracey looked furious and then tried a different tack.

"Can we interview you separately? Do you know why the aircraft ditched?"

I looked at her. "As a matter of interest, yes I think I do know what happened but AAIB have got to do some investigation to prove it."

Helen looked at me. "When did you find out?"

"This morning as it happens, but I haven't informed AAIB yet and there is work to be done to prove my theory."

Tracey didn't know what to do. She knew she was sitting on a great story but she also knew I was not going to co-operate if she put a foot wrong.

"Tracey, I hate TV interviews but I'll do you a deal. I'll let you interview me in a day or so when AAIB have done what is necessary, but only if you treat Helen fairly."

The bargain was struck and Helen disappeared to be made up and I went to watch the interview on a large screen. I was glad to see that the make-up people had failed to alter Helen's appearance. To be fair to Tracey she played the interview right down the middle. By the time she had finished there could be no doubt what a wonderful job Helen had done and how good her training had been.

"Helen, it's a remarkable story. I know the survivors will be immensely grateful for your courage and expertise. A wonderful example to us all."

Helen smiled and didn't look too uncomfortable and the interview finished. I went back to the waiting room and almost immediately I got a text message; Jim Scott had been the pilot of Alpha Delta's previous flight as well and the message gave me the name and telephone number of his first officer, Ken Bradley. Mary had added that Jackson Turner had been sitting in the back row of the business class section.

Helen re-appeared. She had sorted her hair out and had changed into a very smart pair of trousers and close fitting jumper. She looked fabulous.

"Was it alright?"

"It was great. Really. It was just as well you looked as you did or you would be headline news in the Sun, if not on page three."

"I'm glad to say you're biased."

"Seriously though. Tracey did a great job."

"Thank you sir, she said." I hadn't heard her come in.

"Helen was very good and it makes a great story."

"When will it be shown?"

"Not sure. Should be at 9.30 to-night but it was so good they may show clips on the news bulletins."

I could see Tracey looking at Helen and then at me. She clearly wasn't concentrating. She looked at me. "Did you put her up to looking the way she did?"

I smiled at her. "You've just heard Helen and interviewed her. She's got a mind of her own." Helen grinned. "She does what she wants. You don't seriously imagine I can change her."

"I have to tell you that I am not convinced."

"The problem you have Tracey is that most of the people you interview are either celebrities or want to be celebrities. Furthermore, you are a celebrity yourself, presumably you like it and you've got used to it."

Tracey looked at me, nodding slowly. "I hate to agree with you but you're right. It is very difficult and very expensive to get away from it all once it has started. I'm a single mother with a young daughter and I don't like being chased by the paparazzi. Probably Helen should be grateful for the way you advised her how to look. Mind you, Worldwide may not be so pleased --- they would have preferred her to look as she does now, like an up market model."

It was time for us to go but Tracey felt she had to remind me. "When can I interview you?"

"I'm not sure exactly. I've got a lot of work to do and telephoning, but don't worry, I'll keep to the deal."

We went home and I produced some smoked salmon with fresh bread and butter. Helen produced a lovely Chablis.

"We've both been shopping, Peter. But what about the accident?"

I switched the news on as we sat down, just in time to see Helen on the box. She shuddered.

"Did I really look like that?"

"You bet. Wonderful. Listen to it. You were superb."

The clip finished. "I look terrible."

I shook my head. "But you sounded really great."

Helen repeated herself. "What about the accident? What happened?"

"Hang on. Thank you for reminding me. I must make a telephone call."

I dialled the number Mary had sent me. I introduced myself and started asking questions.

"Ken, did you realise you were on the flight before Alpha Delta ditched?"

"Yes I did, Peter. To be honest I've been rather concerned. We had an electrical problem on the flight. The No 2 alternator stopped driving its 28V TRU. It didn't matter because the failure only occurred at the top of the descent. As you know there are five other 28V TRUs. Jim told me to put the snag in the defect report but I forgot. The next day I went to Australia which took ten days and as I knew the aircraft was due for maintenance I didn't bother to report it. When the accident happened I was rather worried wondering whether it was due in some way to the same electrical fault we'd had. However, I was sure the fault would have been sorted when the aircraft had its ten day maintenance."

"Have you told anyone about this? AAIB for example?"

"No, nobody. I've been too worried, to be honest."

"Don't blame yourself. Maintenance should have found and rectified the fault. But you'd better write a report because AAIB will be on to you very shortly."

I rang off.

"I only heard your side of the conversation but it sounded as if you've struck oil."

"Possibly. I'll try my theory out on you before I phone Tom." She nodded. "This morning I listened to the conversation between Alpha Delta and ground control at Gatwick. At first the girl there only gave me the second sequence of the Alpha Delta calls. I looked at the timings and realised that there must have been an earlier sequence. She went away and found it. There was a very significant transmission in the first lot, *'We have an electrical problem'.*"

"But I thought you said that there was a fuel gauging problem?"

"I didn't, David Winston did."

"Aren't there any recordings?"

"You ask super questions, my dear. No. The airline doesn't have to record its Ops frequencies and AAIB aren't worried as they reckon on hearing the conversation on the cockpit voice recorder. However, in fact Worldwide does record the Ops frequency used in flight but not the ground one."

"David Winston wasn't telling you the truth then?"

"No, I think he lied. He realised that I would eventually find out about the delay on start up. Whether he knew I had been interviewing the dispatcher in San Francisco I don't know but it seems a bit of a coincidence that he asked me to call him immediately afterwards. Anyway, when I spoke to him he started telling me about a trivial fuel gauging problem which caused the start up delay.

"What I think happened is that Jim Scott started up and had an electrical problem and he was persuaded by David Winston to break the rules and take the aircraft when the flight should have been cancelled for maintenance. You see, Jim Scott had had an electrical problem on this aircraft on the previous flight and it was almost certainly the same one. One of the alternators didn't work properly but I think in reality it was probably a more sophisticated fault than that. However, whatever the fault it must have been an intermittent one since it clearly worked during the engine runs or maintenance would have fixed it."

"Why did Winston lie?"

"Because he realised that he should never have persuaded Jim to take the aircraft. His whole career would have been ruined. He wanted to be Chief Pilot, at least."

"But the missing recorder. Did he organise that?"

"Yes, I'm sure he did. He knew it was essential that no-one could check what was actually said between the Captain, Jim Scott, and himself. He must have been desperate but he had an amazing piece of luck because he had met Smithson when he was scuba diving on holiday in St Antony."

"Peter, you're romancing. How on earth do you know that."

"I saw a picture of the house, *Leewards*, in a family snapshot in his office, though of course when I first saw it I did not realise it was *Leewards*. Winston had his scuba diving gear next to him That's when I knew I was on to something. He realised he would be in trouble if his conversation with Jim before departure became public knowledge. He rushed out to St Antony and asked Smithson to get the recorder out. He was lucky that Alvin Goddard was a brilliant diver and was able to find the recorders and get the right one out."

"But the recorder. It doesn't make sense. Did Winston change the memory module? Why did he bother if the recorder was not going to be found?"

"A very good question. Clearly they were going to put the recorder back but for some reason, like they were being watched, they didn't do it. He must have got a memory module he'd taken from another recorder --- remember he was an electronics expert. He did the swap and that was it."

"What did he do with the valid module?"

"Yes, that's the key question. If we are very lucky he may have taken it back with him to the UK, hoping to put it back in the recorder he pinched from the other module."

"But it would be written on."

"Wouldn't have mattered as the data would have been overwritten straightaway."

"Amazing. But if he has the module and it is found, then all this will be confirmed."

"Yes, it should be. If he has the memory module then that will be incriminating in itself. In addition, we should be able to hear the conversation at the start of the flight since things only went wrong after the engine was stopped and the TRUs started being switched. There will almost certainly be a lot of missing data on the cockpit voice recorder after the shut down but that won't matter."

"That's brilliant, Peter. You've found the reason for the ditching."

"No I haven't, my love, though its kind of you to say so. In fact you've again reminded me of a job I have to do. You see what I've found out is that it looks as if Winston caused the accident by making Jim take the aircraft when he shouldn't, but we still don't know what was actually wrong."

"When did you first suspect Winston?"

"I'm not sure I can answer that question but when Ben told me that Smithson owned *Leewards* I realised that Winston had been staying with him and not at the *Astoria Reef*. It had always seemed strange to me that whenever I called the hotel it took them a long time to find him."

"But Jacko was staying in the house."

"Only later when he had recovered enough to leave hospital. Winston had left several days earlier."

"Well if you're right hadn't you better tell someone? AAIB for a start and ITAC."

I looked at my watch. "You're right."

"Go ahead." Helen looked at her watch and smiled. "They will have started work."

"Thank you."

I rang Ronald Raycroft.

"I think I've found out what happened to the cockpit voice recorder. I expect AAIB have told you that it has been found with no data on the module. However that's not why I'm calling. I've just discovered that there was an electrical fault on the aircraft before it took off."

"Peter, you'd better speak with Jimmy Benson but I'll get him to record the conversation. OK?"

"Fine. I'll hold while you put me through."

There was a pause of about a minute and Jimmy came on the line.

"Peter, what news? Good to hear from you."

"Jimmy, I've listened to the pre-flight conversation to the Tower and the Captain said there was an electrical fault when he started the engines and then he shut the engines down. I think he was persuaded to take the aircraft by Flight Ops. On the previous flight when the same captain by chance actually flew the aircraft, the No. 2 alternator on the left engine suddenly stopped supplying its low voltage 28V TRU but the crew forgot to write up the fault on the snag sheet. The fault was almost certainly the same one as on the previous flight."

"But that's an acceptable allowed defect, Peter. It shouldn't matter."

"Well the aircraft was on maintenance between the two flights and apparently they didn't find the snag on engine run. Clearly it would not be an allowable snag if it was the same as the previous flight; the rules say that if there is spare TRU then it has to be fixed."

"What sort of maintenance was the aircraft having? They probably didn't need to run the engines."

"Of course! I should have thought of that. That's the answer. I was convinced they would have run the engines between the two flights." There was a pause. "Jimmy, are you still there?"

"Sorry, Peter. You've got me thinking. I'm trying to think why the alternator would come off line and stop supplying its 28V TRU."

"Surely that's because the TRU was faulty."

"Maybe. I'm not sure. There must have been a lot more wrong with the aircraft than a faulty TRU."

"Jimmy, I knew of a military aircraft once which had a mechanical manufacturing fault on a bus bar and the aircraft caught fire in the air and all the crew were killed."

"We don't have to consider that sort of fault when we design an aircraft. All sorts of things could occur if there were manufacturing faults and similar failures. The whole thing would be impossible. We have to find a reason that explains not only why the No. 2 alternator on the left engine wouldn't drive its 28V TRU but also why the crash data recorders didn't have proper data."

"And why the aircraft ditched, Jimmy, when it should have had enough fuel."

"Of course. What puzzles me is that we have protection for electrical faults on the TRUs so that if a TRU fails the bus bar is unaffected. I'll have to think this thing through. I've just had from AAIB the data that was shown on the main crash recorder and hopefully it will now all make sense. What I think is very significant is that the aircraft depressurised and lost its satellite radios for sure after the engine was shut down. That would happen if part of the 28V system lost its supplies, like the battery going flat. Do you think you could get the pilot on the previous flight to send me a detailed description of what happened?"

"No problem. He'll have to write one for AAIB and I'll get him to send you a copy. Obviously you'll get one from AAIB but it will be a lot quicker from the pilot direct." I paused. "Jimmy, and Ronald if you're listening, I haven't brought AAIB up to speed with my conversation with the pilot yet. They are not aware of the No 2 alternator TRU fault. Please don't contact them for a bit. I'm just going to ring Tom Falconbury."

"Fine. I've got quite enough work to do anyway examining the fault in detail. What made you ring the pilot of the previous flight?"

"I'm not sure. I was just lucky."

Helen dug me in the ribs and made a despairing gesture.

"Well done anyway, Peter. Keep in touch."

I put the phone down but Helen couldn't contain herself.

"You're impossible, Peter. It was good thinking to investigate the previous flight when there was nothing on the squawk sheet and the aircraft had just come out of maintenance."

"Not sure about that. It should have been routine."

"AAIB didn't do it?"

"How do you know?"

"Because the pilot you spoke to would have told you."

She had a point. I realised I had better get on to Tom Falconbury straightaway but as bad luck would have it he wasn't there. I asked him to call me back as it was very important.

Helen leant over, took the phone I'd been using and pressed the call button. Then she got up and put it next to the charger.

"Nobody will be able to call."

"Perfect. Now give me your mobile."

I reluctantly handed it over. She muted the ringing tone and put the phone in my office.

"Great. Now we can enjoy the smoked salmon and the Chablis. It's all very well bringing work home but this is ridiculous. I'll lower the lights in case you fancy anything else."

"I'll fall asleep."

"Not if I have anything to do with it."

Helen was right. We did need to relax and not get drawn remorselessly into the accident investigation.

"Do you think we ought to be living in sin? My parents are very worried about it. And about you, for that matter."

Though I was getting used to Helen I did feel a bit surprised. A moment before I was investigating a very serious ditching and now I could feel myself getting into much deeper water.

"It doesn't feel like that. It feels rather comfortable."

However, I thought about things. Diana had definitely not been a success and Mandy probably wouldn't have worked. Clearly Helen was something entirely different.

"Tell you what. Why don't we go down to Portsmouth and visit your parents as soon as there's a gap so they can see the bogey man? And we can go sailing if the weather is like St Antony."

"You can obviously see pigs flying. However, you're on for Portsmouth, except it's near Emsworth."

"I think I can hear my phone buzzing."

Helen laughed. "And I can hear Santa knocking on the door."

She got up and returned still grinning with my phone.

"John Southern phoned. Why don't you call him now and then we can carry on where we left off."

"You know something? You're impossible but we do get on very well together. Maybe I should say 'yes' to your suggestion."

"What suggestion?"

"Your last one."

DAY 38

I looked at my watch. It was only 7am, too early to call John. I crept out of bed leaving Helen sleeping and turned on my computer. There was an email from Tom Falconbury saying he had tried to phone but I was permanently engaged and there was no answer from my mobile. It was far too early to call either him or John Southern. I made a cup of coffee but it was whisked out of my hands before I could taste it.

"Thank you, my darling."

"I thought you were asleep."

"Wrong again. When are you going to ring John?"

That was the thing about Helen. She kept me guessing wondering what was coming next.

"9am prompt. Can I taste your coffee? It's exactly what I fancied."

We had an impromptu breakfast though as usual I had to turn the central heating up so Helen wouldn't freeze. At 9am prompt she disappeared upstairs and I called John.

"Thanks for returning my call, Peter. How are you getting on?"

"You may not have to pay the full amount, John."

"That's really fantastic news. One of the reasons I called you was because we have a Board meeting this morning. Tell me why we might not be fully liable."

"Well I haven't discussed it properly with AAIB yet but the Captain was persuaded to take an aircraft that wasn't properly serviceable and, furthermore, the crew didn't enter an important defect they had had from the previous flight."

"How did you find all that out?"

"With difficulty. In fact AAIB have got to get the police in and a search warrant to try to prove what I say."

"Peter, did you say that AAIB aren't aware of what you've found out?"

"Well I only found out for sure yesterday and I couldn't get hold of Tom last night. However, I've had a email from him so he knows I need to talk to him."

"I don't want to mislead my Board. How confident are you that you're right?"

"99.99%. However we may need a bit of good fortune if the primary cause of the problem won't confess."

"When will you know?"

"Depends on the speed of AAIB and, I suppose, getting a search warrant. What we don't want is what seems to be the norm recently, which is the police telling the press what they are going to do and then knocking on the suspect's door at 5am with a bunch of photographers --- disgraceful."

"Any idea of what percentage saving we may have?"

"No idea at all. Way beyond my experience. And there may be an associated design fault on the electrical system. I'm waiting to hear from the ITAC electrical engineer. Maybe ITAC are liable to some extent."

"Peter, it looks as if once again we are going to have to thank you. Let me know how you get on with AAIB."

Helen appeared, obviously ready to go out pulling a large roller bag.

"What's happening?"

"I'm off to LA, back in a couple of days."

"You didn't mention it."

"Didn't want to spoil a good evening. And Peter."

"Go on."

"Don't forget to ring AAIB! And no interview with Tracey unless I'm present. She's too hot for you to handle."

Luckily she didn't expect a response from me. I decided I could ring Tom at 12.30, 8.30 St Antony time but Tom was on the phone at 11.45.

"Where were you last night, Peter? I couldn't get through."

"Never mind we've got a good line now. Did you listen to the ground control conversation between Alpha Delta and Gatwick."

"No. I got Graham Prince to do that."

"Well I believe he only heard the second conversation between the aircraft and air traffic, the actual departure conversation. There was an earlier exchange when the aircraft shut down the first time it started up and the Captain said they had an electrical fault."

"But I thought Winston said there was a fuel gauging fault."

"That's what he told me as well. Did Graham look at the maintenance sheets for Alpha Delta?"

"Yes, of course."

"Did he talk to the crew of the previous flight?"

"I've no idea. Not sure why he would need to as the aircraft didn't have any snags and it had been on maintenance. Anyway you obviously have. Go on, tell me."

"The captain was Jim Scott, the man himself. The No 2 alternator on the left engine suddenly stopped supplying its 28V TRU at the start of the descent. The first officer was told to put the fault in the defect report but forgot to do it. He didn't bother to tell maintenance later as he knew the aircraft was on an inspection."

"What are you saying? That Jim told Winston about the electrical snag? It must have been an Acceptable Deferred Defect or he wouldn't have taken the aircraft."

"Perhaps. But since Jim Scott had had the fault on the previous flight the rules almost certainly said the fault needed rectification. My guess is that Winston persuaded Scott to take the aircraft against his better judgment and, as bad luck would have it, the fault was more serious than just a left alternator 28V TRU failure?"

"So?"

"Well, then things started to go wrong for Winston. First there was the engine shut down and then all contact was lost. Remember, Winston was an electrical engineer and he realised that he would be in serious trouble if anybody found out about his conversation with Scott before the flight. He knew he had to get hold of the cockpit voice recorder and so he decided to fly out taking a memory module with him. He had the foresight to get the dispatcher, who might know something, posted to San Francisco where there was a serious problem."

"That's all very well, Peter, but how was he going to get at the actual memory module?"

"What I discovered by chance was that Winston was a trained scuba diver and that he knew a man called Smithson who ran a St Antony diving school. Conveniently for Winston, apparently Alvin Goddard did the diving and got the recorder up. As you know, there was an unused module in the recorder we found so somewhere there must be the actual module."

"But where is it?"

"Hopefully Winston will still have the real one at home, assuming he hasn't returned it into the stores."

"This is all very well. But how are we going to get hold of it? What are we going to do about Winston?"

"I would have thought you could justify a search warrant of his house. We know he lied and somewhere there is a missing memory module. I believe he would have kept it to refit in the recorder he took it from. He may even have got the recorder he took it from at home. Of course, the search must be a complete surprise or, if the module is at his home, he will have time to get rid of it."

"Peter, I'm afraid I'm a bit speechless after all that you've told me. You've obviously done a great job. I think I'll talk to my boss, Bob Furness, to get some advice and help. If we can get the module and play it back it will be fantastic."

"But remember, that's just one aspect of the ditching. The actual fault needs to be understood so we know what caused the aircraft to ditch. Sorry, I didn't mean to try to teach you your own business."

"Peter, you're quite right. No offence taken. I've got a lot to do. We must keep in touch."

I went in to my office in Farringdon Street. I had hardly sat down when Bob Furness rang.

"Peter, I gather you've been helping again."

"Do you think you can make a case for a search warrant?"

"We think so but the problem is that Tom is in St Antony. You've got the recording of what the captain said to the Tower. You know what Winston said to you. You found the recorder. You saw the picture of Winston's family with Smithson's house in the background. You know the dates when Winston was in St Antony."

"Surely Bob by now you've got the recording of the first conversation between the aircraft and air traffic talking about an electrical fault. And George Sandford knows about the wrong memory module."

"Agreed but that won't be enough. If we are going to settle this thing quickly we'd like you to be with us when we apply for a search warrant."

"Alright Bob, but you'll have to make sure that the police don't tell the press first to show how clever they are. If Winston gets any wind of the search you'll never find the module. Let's hope the application will be in camera. What time and where?"

"To-morrow Saturday, 10am, Bow Street. Jim Sampson will be our solicitor. Not sure if it will be in camera."

***

I was at Bow Street in plenty of time. Being Saturday there was almost no-one about. George Sandford was there as well as Sampson. The police made the application and the procedure went smoothly. The judge quizzed both me and George and then signed the application. I went home and tried to put the whole thing out of my mind. I had plenty of work to do giving opinions to insurance companies. There were also some airlines I had to visit. I started making out a programme. The day passed quickly but the house felt empty without Helen.

Bob Furness called me at 8am.

"I'm afraid your forecast was wrong, Peter. We couldn't find the memory module anywhere and Winston wouldn't admit anything. He said we were mad and called his solicitor."

"What are you going to do?"

"I'm not sure. Winston said he got muddled between saying it was a fuel gauge fault and an electrical fault. You had me convinced on the reason for the accident but now I'm not so sure."

"Bob, it's not over yet. The aircraft recorder was in *Dark Blue Diving* and it didn't get there by itself. You'll have to look through all the spares at Gatwick. Winston must have returned the module to Worldwide spares."

"Peter, why would he need to do that. He could have just thrown the module into the bin."

"Maybe but then there would be a module short. He's an engineer. It would be much more elegant to return the module and then its contents would be overwritten in due course. Why don't you take a team to Gatwick and get them to check that Worldwide can account for all their recorders and memory modules."

"Alright. I still think we've missed something but we'd better give it a go. I think I'll ask Graham Prince to go down to Worldwide straightaway."

He rang off and I did odd jobs during the day wondering all the time what was happening at Gatwick. Finally Bob came on line.

"We've collected up all the spare memory modules and they're over at our lab."

"Were there any missing, Bob?"

"No, they were all present and correct."

"What about recorders?"

"Actually there was one too many but it shouldn't matter."

"Don't bet on it. How do you know there was the correct number of modules? Chances are there is one short to match the surplus recorder."

"Why on earth do you say that?"

"Because life's like that. They've got a simulator at Gatwick. My guess is that the airline undertook to provide the recorder, amongst other electronic units to keep the simulator costs down and then didn't do so. Maybe the simulator manufacturer realised that they needed a special non-flight worthy unit and module so that the airline was left with a spare recorder and memory module. Anyway when will you know if there is anything peculiar about the modules?"

"In a couple of hours we hope. It shouldn't take long. Each module just has to be plugged in and the date/time examined."

"Bob, let me know how you get on."

I decided to call Ben.

"Sorry to disturb your Sunday lunch. May I ask you a question?"

"Go on, surprise me."

"Ben, did you search Smithson's house?"

"You bet we did. We scoured the place for drugs but didn't find any. Luckily Jacob spilt the beans and we're going to be able to prosecute Smithson over the drugs we found in *Dark Blue Diving* as well as the drugs on the way to Guadeloupe. Why do you ask?"

"We've lost a memory module, the one that was in the aircraft."

"I thought you found that in the *Dark Blue Diving* store."

"No, unfortunately we didn't. We found the recorder but the module was not the correct one. I assumed Winston took it back to England but I'm wondering if he left it behind."

"Rick told me that there was a lot of stuff that looked like computer gear in one of the rooms."

"What did you do with it?"

"Because the case hasn't come to court yet everything found in the house that could be significant has been labelled and is in a special store room in the basement underneath my offices."

"Can you get Rick to go through the list with me. Perhaps he could take some pictures and then email them to me. I need a metal box 4cms square, 2cms deep with a plug having about 40 pins. There will be a model number 45TH36579-1 and a serial number something like 00004328 on the side."

"We'll do what we can, Peter."

I turned on the TV to watch the news and after about half an hour Bob phoned.

"No, luck I'm afraid. All the modules were kosher."

270

"OK. Bob, I'm having a check in St Antony just in case Winston never brought the module back for some reason."

"You're convinced Winston is the fall guy, aren't you? I have to tell you we don't think there's a module short."

I said nothing but turned the TV back on. Then I got out the Sunday Times to read which I found very depressing. At about 9pm I heard my email alarm go and I checked my mail. There was one from Rick with attachments. The message said 'Is this what you are looking for?' and when I opened the attachment there were three perfect pictures of a memory module and I could even read the serial number.

It took me microseconds to get through to St Antony police. "Rick, you're a star. Where did you find it?"

"It was neatly labelled, without a description, next to some computer cards and cables."

"Can you contact Tom Falconbury in the New Anchorage and get it on to-night's flight to UK, BA, Worldwide, Virgin, any UK carrier? Make certain you've notarised your pictures or whatever you have to do just in case the module is lost. It's very very urgent. If you can't find Tom then talk to Worldwide Becky Samuels or whoever is on duty. See if you can't give it to the Captain and I'll make sure there is someone from AAIB waiting to collect it. Email me and Bob Furness letting us know what is happening."

I phoned Bob and told him the news.

"I'll email you the pictures of the module and presumably Tom will let you know what is happening to the module reference to despatch."

Bob thanked me profusely but was rather quiet. Maybe he felt he had missed a bet.

"Peter, by the way the press have got hold of the fact that Winston's house has been searched as a result of the evidence you gave when the search warrant was being obtained."

"There's always a down side. How did it happen?"

"There's a resident free lance journalist at the law courts and he contacts the papers if he thinks there's a story. He gets paid for his troubles, of course."

"Well keep me out of it. I just represent Hull Claims."

"Yes, Peter. We want to keep you out of it. However, you found the recorder and Winston, if he did lie, actually lied to you first. He repeated it to Tom later but at the moment in this country we are relying on you. I think your friend Brian Matthews has worked that out."

"Believe me Bob. I don't want to be involved. It's your investigation, not mine."

"Peter, I know, but the fact is you got there first and it's going to be difficult for that not to get known. And Brian knows your track record. I'm afraid you may not like the *Mail* to-morrow morning.

DAY 41

I stayed up late talking to Helen who was wide awake in Los Angeles so I was half asleep when the phone rang the following morning.

"Good morning. Hope I didn't wake you up. Tracey Stapleton here."

"Tracey, can't you sleep?"

"It's 7.45. I've got to get my daughter to school. I can't be a layabout like you."

"I'm not a layabout. I was up late talking to Helen."

"How lovely. Have you read the *Mail*?"

"Don't tease me. What's Brian written."

"You're the greatest, single handedly finding out why the aircraft ditched."

"We don't know for sure why the aircraft ditched."

"But it was you who suggested that the missing memory module from the crashed aircraft was in Captain Winston's house."

"But it wasn't in Winston's house."

"But you found the recorder and showed it was a dummy one. We've got a deal, remember?"

"Are you sure you want to interview me to-day. Things are still a bit in the air."

"Yes, Peter. We would like to do it to-day."

"What time and when?"

"To-day, where we met before and 1.30pm."

"But your program isn't until 8.30pm."

"We may be able to use the clips and I've got my daughter to pick up, remember. See you."

First thing I did was to send Helen a text message romancing slightly, *'Fats in the fire. Brian Matthews in Mail. Tracey interviewing me 1330. Don't worry she has to pickup her daughter at 1530.'*

I got up quickly to get the papers but to my surprise Helen sent me a reply, *'Just read Mail on net. AAIB won't be pleased. Watch it with Tracey.'*

I walked down to the newsagent. Brian's article was on the front page. I bought the *Times* and *Telegraph* as well and strolled into Starbuck's for a coffee. The *Times* had nothing but the

Telegraph covered the search of Winston's house, made it clear that no recorder was found and that Winston was protesting his innocence. It was the *Mail* article that I didn't like. Brian had pointed out that it was I who had found out what had happened and had told AAIB to search for a missing memory module. He referred back to the crash at Heathrow when I had found out the technical reason why the aircraft crashed in fog. He made me sound like some sort of a super sleuth. To my horror he had also taken a picture while I was having breakfast at the *New Anchorage.*

My phone rang at about midday. It was Bob.

"We've had a very quick look. It's the right one. The data is not much good but the voice channel on the flight deck is fine, thank goodness. I don't know what to say Peter except thank you."

"No worries. What are you going to do about Winston?"

"Well we need to listen more carefully to the play back but I expect he'll be charged later on to-day. The police have told him that the module has been found."

"Bob, I've got a problem. Tracey Stapleton is interviewing me very shortly. What can I say?"

"Whatever you think is appropriate. Good luck with her, you'll need it."

With my head whirling slightly and with some foreboding I went to meet Tracey. She met me in the lobby and I saw that Helen was right. She looked great and was being very friendly. She had a jacket over a rather skimpy plunging blouse. I couldn't believe she was going to interview me with that outfit on. The only consoling thought was that the viewers would be watching her cleavage rather than listening to me. However, I had no intention of trusting her, her reputation was too well known.

We went into the same room as last time when Helen was there and again she gave me a list of questions.

"Tracey, you look great. But if you so much as mention Helen I shall get up and walk out."

"Alright, don't be so touchy. It's a great story, you and Helen. Brian hasn't got hold of it yet."

"Are you threatening me? I'll walk out now. Be very careful asking me questions that we haven't discussed. I have a very short fuse"

"So I'm beginning to realise. I thought you were a nice man."

"I am to people who are nice to me. Come on. Let's get on with it."

I went into the make-up room but barely let the girl do anything. It just didn't matter if my stubble showed. Finally I sat down in the interview chair, Tracey appeared with her jacket not hiding her blouse and off we went. We discussed my discovery of the missing recorder and the fact that the memory module was not the one that was in the aircraft. She went on to talk about the search warrant and David Winston.

"Mr Talbert, are you saying that there is a missing memory module somewhere? Why did AAIB search the Worldwide Deputy Chief Pilot's house for it?"

"Tracey, yes I am saying there was a missing memory module."

She was on to me like a hawk and interrupted. "You said was."

"Yes I did because the module has been found in St Antony and is currently being decoded by AAIB in Aldershot. I understand that they have already established that it is the one that was in the aircraft."

Tracey was smart, no wonder she was paid a fortune. "How was it found? Did you find it?"

"It was found by the St Antony police."

"But you told them where to look?"

"Yes, I did suggest where it might be found. It wasn't very difficult."

"I'm not sure everyone will believe that. Do we know how it got there?"

"Tracey, this is now a police matter and there is nothing more I can say."

"But this means we now know why the aircraft had to ditch?"

"Not yet. We have some ideas which AAIB will be able to follow up now the memory module has been found with all the cockpit conversations." I decided to spoil Tracey. "Basically, we now know that apparently the aircraft took off with a serious electrical defect that had not been rectified, but we don't understand exactly the sequence of events that made the aircraft ditch. AAIB and ITAC, the airplane's designers, are now examining the data in the memory module of the cockpit voice recorder and, hopefully, they will be able to explain the accident. That is their job. I'm just an insurance assessor and advisor."

Tracey was a professional and wasn't about to be deflected.

"But if it wasn't for you the recorder would not have been discovered."

"I'm sure it would have been. I just happened to be lucky. I don't think we should be discussing this matter while it is sub judice."

The interview rapidly came to a close but Tracey was clearly over the moon. She knew she had a scoop with the fact that the module had only just been found. We met briefly after it was all over. She hadn't put her jacket on and her breasts were thrust forward. I remembered Helen's admonition and broke away as quickly as I could as she gave me a thank you kiss. On the way home I bought the *Evening Standard*. The headline was damning 'Pilot arrested for stealing crash recorder'.

There was a message from Bob Furness asking me to be at AAIB at 6pm that evening, but only to reply if I couldn't manage it. I left in the car at 4pm because I knew it would be rush hour time and stopped at the service area. All went well and I arrived at AAIB just before six, wondering why on earth I was there. Judging by the car park, everybody seemed to have left apart from Bob who appeared to let me in.

"What's going on, Bob? Are we having a private drinks party?"

"Possibly, but not straight away."

He didn't elaborate but led me up the stairs to what looked like a very secure area. He sat me down with a note book.

"This button starts and restarts the recording when it stops, this button stops it, this one is effectively the rewind and this button fast forwards until the next noise. It has a level selector but I've set it to normal conversation." He stopped. "One more thing. You were never here, or I'd lose my job! When you've finished, my office is up the corridor at the end."

He disappeared. I got a pen out and pressed the start button.

"Gatwick Delivery. Worldwide 442, stand one eight, ITAC 831 with information Charlie, QNH one zero zero eight, request start."

I felt the hair on the back of my neck tingling as I realised I was about to hear everything that had taken place on the flight deck of Alpha Delta. I felt as if I was eavesdropping into another world. The RT I had heard before, when Yvonne played it all in Gatwick Air Traffic, but this time I would be able to hear the crew's conversation.

"Worldwide 442, Delivery, stand by"

I knew the RT conversation I was going to hear but I held my breath waiting for the interjections from the crew.

"Worldwide 442, Delivery, start approved. Cleared to Barbados, Seaford Four Mike Departure, squawk three four two zero."

"Cleared to Barbados, Seaford Four Mike Departure, squawk three four two zero, Worldwide 442."

"Worldwide 442, contact Gatwick Ground one two one decimal eight for push back"

"Ground, one two one decimal eight for push back, Worldwide 442"

"Gatwick Ground, Worldwide 442, stand one eight, request push back"

"Worldwide 442, cleared to push stand one eight"

Listening on the recorder, the words were the same as I had heard at Gatwick but there was the background noise of the flight deck. I could just hear the engines being started though it was difficult with all the other aircraft calling Gatwick. Then I heard Jim Scott talking to his first officer Jane Brown.

"Jane, I can't get the No 2 alternator on the left engine to drive its 28V TRU. Shut the engines down please." [5]

I could hear the engines winding down.

"Gatwick Worldwide 442. There will be a delay. We are having to shut down our engines. We have an electrical problem. Will advise."

"Worldwide 442, Ground. Start and push cancelled, call Delivery when ready again"

The reply was clearly audible but there was a minute echo. The crew clearly had the speakers switched on and I was hearing the headphones and the recorder's cockpit microphone.

"Worldwide Ops this is 442. There's a problem on the aircraft. I'm shutting down. Get me the duty pilot."

---

[5] **Bold type represents crew conversation**

"Ops to 442, Roger"

There was background noise then,

"Jane, this is the same fault I had the last time I flew this aircraft. The No 2 alternator on the left engine stopped driving its 28V TRU at the top of the descent. I told Ken Bradley to put the defect on the squawk sheet but I noticed on the defect report that he never did. However the fault should have been found on maintenance but it's still there."

"Jim, I thought it was on the ADDs list."

"You're right but it should have been fixed. Anyway I think the rules say that if they've got a replacement TRU they have to change it."

Jim told the ground crew that there would be a delay and after a brief pause Worldwide Operations spoke to the aircraft.

"442 this is Ops. What's the problem?"

The voice was very clearly David Winston and I knew that at last I was going to hear what really happened.

"Ops from 442. I'm not happy about taking the aircraft, David. One of the alternators on the left engine won't come on line and drive its low voltage 28V TRU."

"442 from Ops. But it is on the ADDs list. You know that, Jim"

"Ops from 442. I know but, by chance, I was the last person to fly the aircraft and we had the same snag then. The aircraft has just come off maintenance and it should have come out clear of all defects. Presumably they ran the engines?"

"442 from Ops. Did you put a defect report in?"

"Ops from 442. I told Ken Bradley, my first officer, to write it up but it looks as if he didn't do it. But that shouldn't have mattered. Maintenance should have found the fault on engine run and rectified it."

"442 from Ops. Well they clearly didn't and as the fault is permitted you've got to go."

"Ops from 442. It's only permitted for one flight if there is no spare TRU. I would like you to check, David, please."

There was a long pause before Winston replied.

"442 from Ops. Alright, wait a moment."

There was another pause, then a buzzing sound, like the crew door warning.

"Charlotte, we've got a mechanical. I've shut the engines down and we don't know yet if we can go. Would you warn the passengers we definitely don't know and apologise for the delay."

"Yes, Captain."

There was a pause and I pressed the fast forward button. In fact I had to keep paging forward with the switch because of all the transmissions from other aircraft.

"442 from Ops. Jim, there is a spare 28V TRU for the No. 2 left alternator but it will take eight hours to change including the engine running and we don't have a spare aircraft. Alpha Juliet is on maintenance and won't be available until to-morrow. In the circumstance therefore you'll have to take the plane."

Another long pause.

"442 from Ops, are you reading me."

"Ops from 442. Yes, David. I don't have to go since there is a spare. Stand by."

"What do you think, Jane. I'm not happy about this but it will clearly cause a big delay if we don't go. We've got two spare alternators, one on each APU so it shouldn't matter."

"Your decision, Jim, but it seems reasonable to go."

"I agree but David puts my back up. OK let's do it. Get start up clearance will you when I've told David."

'Ops this is 442. We are starting engines. Out'

I heard Jane calling air traffic.

"Gatwick Delivery. Worldwide 442, stand one eight, ITAC 831 with information Delta, QNH one zero zero nine, request start."

"Worldwide 442, Delivery, expect about a fifteen minute delay"

There was a gap of about twenty minutes and there was very little conversation between Jim and Jane. Perhaps they were both a bit worried about what they were doing. Finally their clearance came through. It was the same as they had been given when they had started up previously.

"Worldwide 442, Delivery, start approved. Cleared to Barbados, Seaford Four Mike Departure, squawk three four two zero."

"Cleared to Barbados, Seaford Four Mike Departure, squawk three four two zero, Worldwide 442."

"Worldwide 442, contact Gatwick Ground one two one decimal eight for push back"

"Gatwick Ground, Worldwide 442, stand one eight, request push back"

"Worldwide 442, push approved. Advise ready to taxi."

A gap of about two minutes and there was the noise of the engines starting.

"Jane, Still no good. Can't get the TRU to go on line. Let's finish the checks and then tell Gatwick we're pushing back"

Jane called out the checks and then contacted air traffic.

A further gap of about four minutes.

"Ground, Worldwide 442, ready for taxi."

"Worldwide 442, taxi holding point Alpha One, 26Left. Follow the Virgin Boeing 747."

"Taxi holding point Alpha One, 26Left. Follow the Virgin Boeing 747, Worldwide 442."

"Worldwide 442, Ground, call Tower one two four decimal two two five."

Everything seemed routine after that and, conscious of Bob waiting in his office, I decided to page forward in bursts of about twenty minutes. Everything seemed normal until the engine problem occurred.

***

Jane was talking to Jim.

"Captain, the oil warning light is on for the right engine."

"Do you think it's a real failure, Jane?"

"Well the oil pressure gauge is very low but then it would be if the light was on"

There was a pause and then Jane carried on.

"Is it my imagination or does there seem to be a rumble. The vibration gauge seems slightly above normal."

"I agree. We will have to shut the engine down and tell Miami Center. We need to get on the ground as soon as possible but we're past Bermuda as an alternate so we can't go there. We'll have to carry on to Barbados as planned so it is now our alternate as well as our destination. Obviously we're going to have to clear the airway before we go down to avoid other

aircraft since we haven't got time to wait for clearance from Miami. I'll turn right now 45°. While we're leaving the airway I'll just inform Ops."

'Worldwide Ops. This is 442. We have a problem with No. 2 engine and we're going to have to shut it down. We're past Bermuda as a diversion so we're carrying on to Barbados. Awaiting revised clearance from Miami.'

'Worldwide Ops to 442. Copied your engine shut down message. Stand by for duty operations officer.'

There was a pause. **"Jane, I hope it's not still David. He always make me bridle. Too ambitious by half and too clever for his own good."**

"Captain, you wouldn't possibly expect me to comment."

I could hear the derision in her voice.

'Worldwide 442 from Operations. Jim, this is David Winston here. What's the problem?'

'Worldwide Ops from 442. David, we have a low oil pressure warning light on No. 2 engine and the oil gauge reading is pretty well out of sight. Also the engine sounds rough. We are going to have to close it down. Unfortunately we're having to head off 45° to the right to clear traffic on the direct route since we haven't got a clearance yet from Miami. Hopefully they are going to clear us direct shortly as there are some thunderstorms forecast to our right.'

'Worldwide 442 from Ops. Jim, we've never had an engine problem before. I suppose it is a genuine failure?'

'Worldwide Ops from 442. David. I'm Captain of this aircraft and responsible for the safety of the passengers.'

'Worldwide 442 from Ops. Jim, I wasn't questioning what you did. Call me when you've heard from Miami.'

Jim apparently did not reply but spoke to Jane.

"Give Miami a call, Jane, as soon as you can to let them know what we are doing. I'll keep an eye on the TCAS for other aircraft. There's no other aircraft showing at the moment. Oh, I'd better warn the passengers."

A pause, presumably while Jim selected the PA system.

"This is Captain Scott speaking. There is an indicated fault on the right hand engine and so, as a precaution, we shall be shutting the engine down. The aircraft will descend to about

20,000 ft and we will continue to cruise at that height. The aircraft will be flying more slowly on one engine and we anticipate landing at Barbados about fifty minutes later than scheduled."

Another pause.

"I'll start the right APU now, Jane, to make sure that we don't lose any flying controls when we shut the engine down."

I could hear a faint whine, presumably the APU starting up. "The No. 2 APU alternator hasn't come on line to drive its low voltage TRU to support the right 28V system."

"Jim, won't that mean when we shut the right engine down we are going to lose half our low voltage services?"

"I hope not. We've still got the left engine running. With any luck the APU alternator will come on line and drive its 28V TRU when both the No. 2 engine alternators lose their power as the engine shuts down."

A pause.

"The problem is that the No. 2 alternator on No. 1 engine isn't driving its low voltage 28V TRU. It's my fault for letting David Winston talk me into taking the aircraft. I'd better start the other APU to be on the safe side."

I could hear a faint whine as the No 1 APU was started.

"The APU alternator seems OK but I'm going to keep this alternator in reserve, Jane, and not connect it to either of its TRUs. Shut the right engine down now and let's see what happens. I don't like the rumbling sound from the engine; I'm sure its getting worse."

There was a distinct sound of the engine spooling down. Then a loud warning horn which I guessed was the autopilot disconnecting.

"The No. 2 APU alternator came off line. We've only got half the flying controls working. I'm having to fly the aircraft and it feels heavy and not very responsive."

'Miami Center. This is Worldwide 442.' Jane clearly hadn't wasted any time letting the air traffic system know their predicament. 'We've had to shut down the right engine. We've cleared airway to the right and are now descending. Anticipate being able to cruise at Flight Level 210. We've fuel for the planned

*destination Barbados. Please advise as soon as possible when we
can turn back direct to Barbados.'*

*'Worldwide 442 this is Miami. Select ADS C to max rate.
Descend Flight Level 210 and maintain heading.'*

"Jane, you monitor Miami. I'll talk to Ops in a moment.
But first I think we'd better try to get the controls all working
again."

There was a short pause.

"Thank goodness, Jane, I've reselected the No. 1 APU
alternator and I've got all the flying controls back. However,
I've just noticed a message on the system screen. It says we're
only charging half the batteries. I'll switch on the No. 1 APU
28V TRU."

"Jim." Jane's voice sounded very worried. "What did you
just do? The 28 volt DC load shedding light has come on and
we've lost a lot of our supplies. And it looks as if there is still no
feed at all to half the batteries."

"Jane, I tried to use the No. 1 APU alternator to drive its
low voltage TRU. The indication looked good. I've switched it
off now. Is that any better"

"I'm afraid not."

"You're right, the display is saying 'No charging supply to
the right batteries. Connect an alternator to a 28V TRU.' I'd
better try feeding the TRU from the alternator on the other
APU."

"But Jim that might make matters worse."

"It should be alright. Let's try."

"You were right Jim. I think we did get some supplies back
but we're still without our satellite radios."

"Miami Center Speedbird 302 Level 340"

"Our normal radios are OK, Jim. Did you hear that BA
aircraft transmission? But we've still got the low voltage
warning on the right 28V DC system."

"Jane, I think we really need to be talking direct to Miami
so that we can tell them what we are doing and they can tell us
if there any other aircraft in our vicinity. I know our satellite
radios are out but can't we use HF radio? The aircraft were
delivered with the equipment. I know the sets were very noisy

and it was difficult to choose the correct frequency for the time of day but with single side band it was usable."

"Jim, they removed the HF sets last year. We don't have to have them any more now we've got satellite radios and ADS C."

"Well it looks as if they got it wrong."

"Jim, isn't it possible to cross connect the electrical supplies from one side of the aircraft to the other by manually operating some of the switches in the roof?"

"It's a bit complicated, Jane, but you're right. We should have a go. The instructions are displayed by the electronic flight bag."

"But the display isn't working. You'll have get the manuals from the library shelf behind us."

There was a long pause and I paged forward.

"Jane, I've got the book open now. You had better check that I am selecting the correct switches. We can't afford to make a mistake."

I heard them going through the manual bit by bit and carefully selecting the switches in the correct sequence. However, the cross connecting clearly hadn't worked at all.

"You know what I think Jane. I think the No. 1 engine low voltage TRU fault wasn't a TRU fault at all. There is clearly a serious switching fault in the 28V DC system. The sooner we get on the ground the better." There was a pause. "Well the navigation system still seems to be operating but the GPS has gone and the aircraft is operating on inertial gyros only. I'm going to turn the aircraft left for St Antony which is now our closest airport. Transmit a PAN call giving our altitude, heading and intentions and ask for an aircraft to relay the PAN call to Miami. When you've done that we had better try to analyse the situation in more detail."

I heard Jane transmitting a PAN call alerting other aircraft of their engine shut down and the fact that the aircraft was flying direct to St Antony from their current position at Flight Level 210. I made a note to check with Miami and try to see if that call was ever relayed to them by another aircraft. Then there was a pause of two or three minutes.

"I've just changed the Flight Management System destination to St Antony and the machine now says that it is going to take two hours and thirty nine minutes and we're going to have one hour fifteen minutes of fuel left. That's a bit surprising really as I thought we would have had more fuel. I suppose it's because we lost quite a bit of time and added on quite a bit of distance when we turned right to clear the airway before we shut the engine down. I'd better update the passengers."

A pause.

"I can't get the passenger address system to work. It sounds as if it is trying to work and then it doesn't. Its panel shows power there but the display shows a fault. There must a partial power failure I think. Thank goodness the aircraft controls are driven directly from the frequency wild alternators without any TRUs and are signalled by fly-by-wire. Everything seems to be normal and we've got both APUs driving their alternators in reserve so flying the aircraft should not be a problem."

"But what about the fly-by-wire computer system? That uses 28V DC?"

"I know Jane, but the designers obviously must have thought of that, as that 28V DC comes from small 28V DC generators driven by the hydraulic systems. I only wish the aircraft had the old system of hydraulically powered control surfaces but apparently the electrical system saves weight." There was a pause.

"Jane, what do you think is working and not working?"

Instead of Jane answering I heard some knocking and banging noises.

"Captain, what's going on? We've lost our intercom system and most of our cabin services. We are not on full lighting and some of it seems not as bright as it should be. We can't use the PA system and we can't talk to you. None of the galley heaters are working either. There's something very strange with the electrics. I had to use the safety lock to get in without checking with you first."

I assumed that the voice I could hear was Charlotte, the cabin supervisor, and Jim then explained the situation and asked her to try to do the best she could with the facilities that were left. He asked her to come back in about fifteen minutes after he and Jane had reviewed the current position. But again Jane was prevented from discussing things with Jim, this time by VHF.

"Worldwide 442 this is Speedbird 439. Have relayed your PAN call to Miami. They asked that you try to pass further information by relay or direct to St Antony air traffic when in range. Can we be of further help? "

Jane asked the British Airways aircraft to get their operations to tell Worldwide operations what was happening and to get St Antony organised to meet the flight. No sooner had this exchange finished when Jane replied to Jim's earlier question. Her voice was very calm.

"Jim, as far as I can see half of the batteries on the left side are being charged from the No. 1 TRU being driven from the No. 1 APU alternator but the other half on the right are not being charged at all and have only about thirty minutes of power remaining or possibly less and then we shall be losing some systems. Your FMS should continue to work. However, I think we have a real problem with the pressurisation."

"Why is that a problem? It is driven directly off the No. 1 alternator."

"The actual pressurisation is but the control circuit is misbehaving and I can't change any of the settings. I have a nasty feeling we are going to depressurise as the battery voltage falls."

There was a longish pause.

"Well even if the pressurisation does fail it won't really matter. We'll all have to use emergency oxygen. What a mess. I was hoping to hide our problems from the passengers."

A pause.

"I wish I didn't have to waste my time flying the aircraft. But the auto-pilot won't cut in"

A pause of a few minutes and I paged forward.

"Jim, the voltage on the second battery system is dropping."

"I thought so. We are beginning to depressurise."

About three minutes later I could hear the cabin supervisor again but her voice sounded partly muffled.

"Captain, we're depressurising and some of the oxygen masks in the business section haven't dropped down."

"How many? Haven't you got some emergency bottles, Charlotte?"

"We've got about four bottles but I think there are about ten masks that appear to be stuck. I've tried releasing the masks manually but so far only managed to get two to fall. You'll have to descend or the passengers without masks will pass out. Let me make a careful assessment of missing masks and bottles."

I realised that they were struggling with their oxygen masks as they were trying to talk.

"Jane, I'm going to descend to 10,000 ft which should be low enough, even without oxygen. We'd better try and get a message to Miami. Hopefully we won't be down there for long. Charlotte should be able to release the masks. I think we can make St Antony if we don't climb up again but it will be tight. I'll check on the FMS when we are level."

I heard Jane transmitting the new 100 flight level but did not hear a reply.

"There are some clouds ahead, Jane, but the weather radar isn't working. I'll eyeball us round them but not sure what we'll do when it gets dark."

A pause.

"Jane, what do you think the problem is with the passengers' masks? Surely they should all fall down when the pressure drops?"

"They should and they should all be checked regularly as well on a maintenance check. Problem is it is a very difficult check to do. You have to seal the cabin on the ground and lower the cabin pressure. As a back up each mask has its own mechanical release low pressure catch but clearly it's proving difficult to make all the masks drop."

"Well I wish they'd get a move on. We are eating up the fuel."

There was a long pause of about twenty minutes before Charlotte returned.

"I've managed to get enough of the missing masks to drop down. We're trying to get the rest down but you can climb now if you want to."

I heard the engine opening up and there was a long pause, presumably as the aircraft was climbing.

"Well now we are level at flight level 210 the FMS says that we should be at St Antony in one hour and fifteen minutes and that we will have fifty minutes of fuel left."

"Jim, that's not too bad but there seems to be a lot of lightning about. Still now it's getting dark we should be able to avoid some of it, even without the radar."

"Yes but it's not really the way we want to go. It will cost fuel."

"Jane, who did we speak to last? Can we talk to anybody?"

"The last call was from Speedbird 439 asking us to keep Miami in the picture."

"OK. Well try if you can raise another aircraft. Use 121.5. Most aircraft keep a watch on the emergency frequency."

Again I could hear Jane calling other aircraft to act as a relay to Miami but there were no replies.

"Jane, it looks OK now for St Antony. We'll have to go there directly and hope no storms develop."

A long pause.

"The engine rpm has dropped and I've had to drop down to Flight Level 190 to get the power back."

"I noticed that. That must mean some of the tank booster pumps are not working. The engine is being starved of fuel."

There was a pause.

"Jim, how do we know how much fuel we've got?"

"The Flight Management System has added the contents of the two centre tanks and the two wing tanks. Of course, the two centre tanks will be empty since they were used first automatically and we switched the pumps off when the warning lights came on."

"But that doesn't mean they're completely empty, does it? There could be a little fuel left. We don't know which bus bars supply the power to the fuel gauging system."

"You're absolutely right and I'll turn the booster pumps on for the centre tanks just in case but I think we've got a more serious problem. My sums and the flight management system agree on the fuel remaining but they would, wouldn't they, as they use the same information? The problem is that we can't be sure the cross feed cocks are open enabling fuel to be got from the right hand tank. Worse than that, even if the cross feeds are open we don't know for sure if the booster pumps are working in the tanks. The fuel indication is completely unreliable. So Jane, regardless of the fuel tank readings, I don't see how we can rely on getting all the fuel from the tanks in to the left engine. We just don't know if their booster pumps are working because we can't rely on the pressure warning lights. Goodness knows what will happen if they're not running."

"I think the engine draws or sucks the fuel along the fuel supply lines from the tanks so it may be alright."

"Hope so, but there is clearly a fuel feed problem since I've had to reduce height. Of course normally, both engines are running and they have their own fuel tanks so that each engine can get the fuel from its own tanks. As I said, the question is 'can the left engine get all the fuel from the right tanks and the centre tanks if not all the booster pumps are working?' And what happens if the booster pumps are running and there's no fuel in the tanks?"

"Jim, it can't matter if a fuel tank is empty and the booster pump is still running. All that does is to shorten the life of the pumps."

An aircraft suddenly came on the RT.

"Worldwide 442 this is American 943. Understand you are proceeding to St Antony. Please pass your flight details for relaying to Miami."

"943 this is Worldwide 442. We estimate St Antony at 1935. Currently at Flight Level 190. Will call St Antony as soon as we are in range."

"American 943 to Worldwide 442 message copied. Will advise Miami."

There was a pause.

"Good Luck."

I wondered what Jim and Jane would have thought of the 'Good Luck!' It was meant to be kind but they clearly knew the aircraft was in great trouble. What was impressing me as I listened was how calm they were.

"Jane, the FMS says we've just got fifty minutes to go and we'll still have fifty minutes fuel. Sounds alright but it's all going to depend on how much of the fuel we can use."

A brief pause.

"You know we've really had no training in ditching at all. We're allowed to fly for over three hours on one engine and there's not even simulator training. ITAC claims on the web site that it's possible to ditch the aircraft but I'm not so sure."

"Jim, in the cabin crews' notes they use the word catastrophic several times."

"Sounds like a typical marketing/operational conflict to me. Let's hope the marketing boys are right if we do have to ditch. Anyway I bet they never considered ditching at night."

There was a pause.

"Have you noticed the radio altimeters, Jane?"

"Yes, Jim. I'm afraid none of them are working."

"If we have to ditch it's going to be very difficult to judge the flare. Incidentally because we've had to reduce altitude the FMS is now forecasting we'll only have forty five minutes of fuel assuming we can use it all. You'd better get Charlotte back up here, please."

There was a noise which was probably Jane getting out of her seat to get Charlotte. She couldn't have been away long as a similar noise re-occurred.

"Jim, I got one of the cabin staff to get her."

Again a noise almost certainly Charlotte coming back on to the flight deck.

"Charlotte, it will be touch and go whether we have to ditch. You've just got time to brief all the passengers in case we have to. Get them all to put on their life jackets now but remind them not to inflate them."

"Captain, it's not going to be easy because they're using oxygen masks."

"I know, but they won't have enough time on the descent below ten thousand to put on the life jackets."

"Captain, how much time have we got?"

"Thirty five minutes."

"We'll get started right away."

A pause but I waited without paging forward. I was too absorbed.

"Jane, we're about 90 miles from St Antony. See if you can raise Nelson Approach. Ask for a straight in on 24 and I'll position the aircraft right now. Goodness knows whether the gear will go down or the slats and flaps will work. I'll let down for a three degree approach path but we're going to have to be ready to ditch if the fuel pressure warning light comes on. Find out what the wind speed is."

"PAN PAN, PAN PAN, PAN PAN, Nelson approach, this is Worldwide 442. We are 85 miles to the north east of you at Flight Level 190. Making straight in approach runway 24. We may have to ditch. Advise when you have us on radar."

I was lost in admiration at the way Jane remembered the correct procedure and used PAN to keep the other aircraft off the air.

"Worldwide 442 this is Nelson approach. Your PAN call copied. Will advise radar contact. Cleared for straight in approach runway 24."

"Well that's something. At least Nelson knows what's going on. I wish I knew as much about the fuel situation. I've selected our transponder to emergency so they won't have to worry about identifying our echo."

A few minutes pause.

"Worldwide 442 we see you on our radar at 50 miles approaching centre line. You are cleared for a straight in approach on runway 24. Surface wind 150 degrees five knots."

"442, Roger. We have started our descent."

"Glad the wind is light."

"Nelson Approach, this is Air France 591 maintaining 15,000 ft."

"Air France 591 we have an emergency and the airfield is closed. What will be your intentions?"

"591 to Nelson Approach, we would like to go to Antigua."

"Diversion to Antigua approved. Maintain heading and altitude change to Antigua approach and stand by for clearance."

"Nelson, 591 copied. What is the problem? Can we help?"

"591 negative. Please change to Antigua approach for clearance. They are expecting you, cleared down to 8,000 ft."

A very brief pause and then

"Lufthansa 334 to Nelson Approach, on frequency request ILS clearance for 24."

"Lufthansa 334 please clear this frequency and call Antigua. We have an emergency and the airport is closed."

"Lufthansa 334 roger."

Suddenly I could hear the sound of the engine winding down.

"Jim" Jane sounded very alarmed. **"The fuel pressure warning light is on and the engine rpm has dropped to 1,400 rpm. The engine isn't able to get the fuel from the right tank."**

"OK we'll definitely have to ditch. The fuel cross feeding can't be working. I'm having to nose down to keep the speed up and I'm throttling back some more to prevent the engine going out and to keep the flying controls working. Keep an eye on the APUs in case they run out of fuel first though they should be alright as they have their own fuel reserve header tanks. I'll try to get as close to the island as possible. Tell the tower what we're doing."

"MAYDAY, MAYDAY, MAYDAY, Worldwide 442. we can't make the Nelson runway. We're going to have to ditch. Will be turning on to 150° just before ditching. Anticipate we will be ditching four miles short of St Antony, just to the south of centre line."

I listened spellbound and appalled.

"Jane, we're still showing about 3,200 kilos. Is there nothing we can do?"

I sensed it was a rhetorical question.

"Thank good we're below cloud now not that it is much help. All I can see are the lights of St Antony and the runway in the distance."

A brief pause.

"I'm going to hold this heading until 800 ft and then turn on to 150 degrees for touch down. At 1,200 ft I'll call for the flaps. Let me know what happens."

The aircraft must have carried on down and I heard Jim calling for the flaps.

Jane called. **"They're not moving."**

"Yes they are. I can feel something. The indicators are probably not powered up. Try the landing lights."

"I'm turning finals for ditching"
"Full flap. Good Lord, one of the landing lights is working."
A pause.
"I think I'll start the flare now."

There was a brief silence followed by a terrible noise and then silence. I couldn't move or do anything for quite a long time. I pressed the fast forward button but there was nothing. I decided to play the whole thing again, stopping to take notes. Bob came in just as I was finishing. He put a finger in front of his lips and we left the room. Downstairs Bob set the alarm and locked the building.

"OK. I know it's late but let's go for drink, Peter. Follow me and we'll go to the Harrow in Petersfield. It's not too far and worth the journey."

We managed to find a table and ordered some drinks.

"What do you think, Peter?"

"I'm shattered. I think it is quite the most horrifying flight deck recording I've ever heard."

"I agree. Terrifying."

Neither of us said anything for a few minutes.

"I think you have been very kind, breaking all your rules and letting me hear that recording."

"Well it's a sort of thank you for all your help." He looked at me. "Not that Hull Claims won't be thanking you, I imagine. Worldwide should never have taken the aircraft."

"It's incredibly lucky that the voice recording worked in spite of the electrics being in a complete mess."

"Yes, it is. The rest of the data in the module was mostly rubbish after the engine shut down."

"Well we've still got to dot the I's and cross the T's. At least we know that it was fuel starvation when they still had some fuel. We don't know exactly what the electrical fault was. Have you copied it to ITAC? I imagine that Jimmy Benson will be able to work out what probably happened after the No1 low voltage 28V TRU was switched on."

"Yes, we sent it straight over. Haven't had an answer of course. Too early in the morning. We know the aircraft depressurised and we now know why they had to go to low level for a bit."

"Bob, is the salvage complete?"

"Yes it is. Why do you ask?"

"I wondered what sort of condition the roof panels were in? If it were possible to learn which masks didn't drop?"

Bob looked at his watch. "Do you want to talk to Tom?"

"You do it. I want to keep out of this. Ask him if there is anything strange about the panels at the front of the aircraft."

"Let's do it from my car. It's far too noisy here."

We finished our drinks and got into Bob's car. He dialled Tom's mobile and brought him up to date.

"Tom, is it possible to learn anything about the oxygen masks from the wreckage? Is it possible to tell if any of them were still jammed up and didn't drop?"

I couldn't hear Tom replying but he was obviously giving Bob a data dump.

"How many were jammed?"

Another reply.

"I see. A total of four, in the business section. Wait a moment, say that again."

Bob listened intently.

"Very interesting. Thanks a lot."

Bob looked at me. "Tom says that some of the metal trim surrounding the oxygen mask stowages in the business section were physically damaged even though the masks had come down."

"Well that would explain why there was a commotion in the business section. The cabin crew were clearly trying to free the masks. Helen told me that one of the stewards in the business section wanted a screwdriver, presumably to try to force the masks out."

"Agreed. Of course the big question is why they ran out of fuel when they had sufficient fuel left."

"Bob, Jimmy Benson told me that they don't have to design for manufacturing failures. Faults in production. I think the reason why the left alternator couldn't drive its 28V TRU is that there was a mechanical fault on the right bus bar which caused all sorts of problems like services to be shed, GPS, satellite radios, feeds to flight data recorders and all sorts of other things. It was quite a sophisticated fault because with both engines running there wasn't a problem but with only one engine the load shedding contactor operated, tripping supplies on the left bus bar as well as the right one. Luckily, the emergency contactor connecting the two bus bars did not operate."

"If your analysis is right, what happened then?"

"Well the fault affected not only the supplies but the warning circuits and, as I said, the crash recorders. Some if not all the fuel booster pumps must have failed plus probably some of the fuel gauging."

"Surely that wouldn't affect the engines as they can virtually suck the fuel out of the tanks."

"True on the left side in this case but, as Jim said, what about getting the fuel from the right side? We have no idea whether the cross feed cocks were open or whether the booster pumps on the centre tank and right tanks were functioning."

"Well Peter, as we've heard, the pilots at first thought they had sufficient fuel but in fact the fuel in some the tanks which did have fuel was unusable."

"I think that's right and let's give the crew their due, they worked out the problem, they warned Nelson they might have to ditch and they got the passengers to put their life jackets on."

"Yes, Peter, you're absolutely right. The crew knew that they might not be able to use all the fuel but like us they didn't know why. That of course is why they warned Nelson."

"Yes, Bob, they knew what might happen."

"Hope ITAC can come up with something concrete to support your ideas. We've got to write a report with as little conjecture in it as possible."

"Jim did the most incredible landing in the dark. Absolutely rotten that they did so well but that they and so many passengers were killed."

"I know. Too late to give him a medal. It's a terrible story."

"I'm afraid so."

I went back to my car and went home.

DAY 42

Helen arrived tired out from LA at about 7am. She showered and came downstairs.

"Well where is it?"

"Where's what?"

"My breakfast."

"But you must have been gorging first class food all night."

"You have absolutely no idea how hard we have to work. First class passengers can be hell. Last night I had a couple who took forever over dinner and barely slept before they wanted breakfast."

"Must have been their own money they were spending. What do you fancy?"

"Not you, for a start. I'll have poached eggs on toast and coffee."

She went to the front door, got the paper and mail in and then sat down.

"All over?"

"Yes and No."

"What do you mean, yes and no?"

"Which words don't you understand? We still don't know for sure exactly why the aircraft had to ditch. I'm pretty sure it was a mechanical electrical fault which, amongst other things, prevented all the fuel being used. Hence the ditching."

"Mechanical electrical? Sounds very indecisive."

"I mean there was a mechanical failure of an electrical bus bar."

"Couldn't that lead to sparking and fire?"

I looked her admiringly.

"Did I ever tell you that you are brilliant and completely wasted as a cabin attendant. You're absolutely right. You bet it could. However, you were damned lucky, my love. It clearly didn't in your case."

"What does your friend Jimmy of ITAC say?"

"Good point. Don't know yet. I haven't checked my email this morning."

I started to move.

"Well let's have breakfast first. If I let you, you would always eat and work at the same time."

While I tried to hide my impatience Helen regaled me with details of her time in Los Angeles.

"I thought you slept all the time to prepare for the return trip."

"Well you were wrong. We go out on the Town. Well, not quite. In fact we rented a car and went to Disneyland. Had a trip on the iMax show Soarin' over California. It was fantastic. I'd never been and always wanted to go."

"It is amazing. I went a couple of years ago when I was inspecting a damaged aircraft at Orange County. I was a bit worried about the safety design of the device which cantilevers the seats forward."

"That's just typical of you. You're meant to gaze in wonder not analyse the design. Did you lift your feet to avoid the ground?"

I nodded.

"Well at least you're human. Come here and let me make certain."

"But my emails?"

"B....r your emails. I haven't had coffee yet."

Helen picked up the Times. "They've copied a bit from yesterday's Mail, my hero. I'm surprised Bob Furness is still talking to you."

"Well that shows how wrong you can be."

I told Helen about my visit to AAIB, but on threat of death if she ever told anyone.

"That was sweet of him. At least he appreciates what you did."

"But he'll be even more appreciative explaining what you did in his report."

"I've never though of that."

"That's because you're lovely. May I look at my emails now?"

"No, you'd better read this letter from St Antony. It looks very official."

I took it from her. It was a letter from the Prime Minister.

Dear Mr Talbert.

I am writing to you to express my personal thanks and the thanks of the people of St Antony for all the work that you did helping us to eradicate the drug trafficking that was taking place on our Island. In addition I know that you were an enormous help to the Air Accident Investigation Board, who were acting as our agents, discovering why the ITAC 831 belonging to Worldwide Airways ditched just short of the main runway of Nelson airport.

This is the second time you have been able to help the people of St Antony since three years ago you enabled West Atlantic Airways to stay in business to the benefit of our Island.

I hope very much therefore you will agree to accept our Freedom Medal as a recognition of the services you have done to St Antony and I look forward very much to presenting the medal to you at our next investiture.

I passed the letter over to Helen.

"Well that's really lovely. Well done." She poked me, "and another honeymoon to get the medal."

"You can only have one honeymoon, darling, and we've had it already."

"Who says you can only have one? Peter, you're so old fashioned. And it wasn't much of a honeymoon anyway."

"I didn't know you were such a connoisseur of honeymoons."

"And we weren't married."

"Now you're the old fashioned one, my love, saying we have to be married to have a honeymoon."

"You were working all the time. Honeymoons when one of the couple is working don't count."

"That sounds like Partridge rules." I thought about my letter. "But you ought to be getting a medal."

She smiled. "Well I didn't tell you but I got a letter two days ago before I went to LA asking if I would accept an M.B.E in the New Years Honours List."

"Why didn't you tell me? It must be a record between being recommended and getting the award. Someone in high places must really appreciate what you did."

"It seems so unfair that I should get something for doing my job and all those people were killed."

"Absolute rubbish. You did an amazing job. Unbelievable."

Helen hugged me. "You're still lovely. Alright. Off you go to your emails and don't wake me if I'm asleep."

I logged on and saw there was an email from Jimmy Benson with a long attachment. He had analysed the data that was missing from the flight data recorder, read the report from the first officer and read the transcript of the cockpit voice recorder which AAIB had just sent him. Reluctantly he had come to the conclusion that there must have been a mechanical fault on part of the right battery bus bar but, in that case, he would have expected there to have been some arcing damage in one particular area of the electrical compartment. As an appendix there was a very long, detailed list of services that he would have expected to have failed. I noticed, reading the appendix, that all the right fuel boosters were on the list and also the operation of the fuel cross feed cocks but I realised as I went through the list that we would never know whether the cross feed cocks were open or shut at the time of the failure.

In the actual email he had referred to the attachment and remarked 'it is possible that the aircraft might have been short of fuel due to the lack of power to the right booster pumps and the inability for the pilot to operate the cross feed cocks.'

I noticed that AAIB were on the list of addressees so I was not altogether surprised when Bob Furness came on the phone.

"You were right. You've read the ITAC email from Jimmy Benson I assume?"

"What does Tom say about the electrical arcing?"

"Well he got the email while he was still in the bar last night so he went back to the hangar, woke up the guards and had a look. He couldn't be sure because he admits he is not an expert at looking at wreckage that has come out of the sea but he says there some very strange markings in the electrical bay. He looked at the first inspection report and these markings had already been commented upon."

"That's going to tidy up your report."

"Yes, thank goodness. Thanks again, Peter."

I went to my computer and composed a note to Cindy at the *Announcer* and then to Michael Noble, giving them both a short summary of what had happened. Then I started back to the kitchen but found Helen asleep in the sitting room. She heard me and opened her eyes.

"All over?"

"Yes."

She started pulling herself together.

"You've forgotten the No."

"No."

Helen managed to grin and then fired one at me.

"What did John Southern say?"

"I haven't had a chance to tell him yet but I've sent a note to Cindy in St Antony and Michael Noble in Seattle."

"You are impossible. Cindy doesn't pay your wages, nor does Michael Noble. I think you would do your job for nothing, just because you have to find out the truth. I'm going to stay here while you ring John so I can listen to you telling him what happened before you forget."

"Come off it, Helen, I'm not that forgetful."

I called John while sitting next to Helen on the settee. "I think we know the whole story now, John."

"What happened?"

"It looks as if the engine had to be closed down. They were persuaded to take the aircraft with an electrical fault when they left and, as you know, the fault was much more serious than it seemed. However, it wasn't as simple as that. If it had been, then they would have been able to make St Antony. Firstly, the aircraft depressurised due to the electrical fault and some of the oxygen masks at the front of the aircraft didn't come down. They didn't have enough portable oxygen sets and so the Captain was forced to descend to low level while they tried to get the masks to drop. The crew must have freed some because the aircraft started to climb again but obviously that wasted some fuel. They should still have had enough fuel to reach St Antony but the left engine couldn't use the fuel in the right tanks because of the fault. Very, very sad."

"That means we will only have to pay a small fraction of the insurance claim."

"John, 176 people died and some more were very badly hurt."

"I'm sorry, Peter. I didn't mean to be heartless. But this accident is financially very significant for us."

"Well how much you have to pay is between you, the airline and the lawyers. As you know the electrical fault hadn't been listed previously in the defect report as it should have been and in the circumstances therefore they probably shouldn't have taken the aircraft. However, presumably you have to cover bad manufacture."

"But the aircraft should never have taken off."

"You don't have to convince me, John. It's all up to you now. My job is finished."

"Peter, very well done. Can you let me have a full technical report as soon as possible. Also you can let me have your expenses as soon as you like. Of course there'll be a not inconsiderable bonus payment as well."

I rang off feeling rather empty and not relishing the way John concentrated on the money whilst rather pushing to one side the terrible tragedies that had and were occurring as a result of the ditching.

Helen disappeared to produce some lunch just as the phone rang. It was Ben.

"You remember Toby Makepeace?"

"The survivor who was killed with a broken neck?"

"We think we know who did it. There was a man who helped one of the stewardesses in the life raft." I grunted. I wasn't sure I wanted to hear what was coming next. "Michael Longshaw. We think he may have been involved."

"How on earth do you know that?"

"Well, Longshaw had to go to the hospital when he got out of the rescue fishing boat and as a matter of routine the hospital took a DNA sample. Well, Makepeace must have fought his killer as he had some blood on him and again the hospital took a DNA sample. Rick asked the hospital to arrange for their samples to be checked and they were amazed to discover that they had a match, not with any criminal records but with Longshaw."

"Ben, why are you telling me? I'm just a poor aviation insurance hack."

"That's not what the papers say."

"You should know better than most not to believe newspapers. You still haven't told me what's worrying you."

"Peter, did you ever talk to Longshaw? I'd be very surprised if you didn't because he was in the thick of the rescue."

"Yes, I did talk to him to find out what happened on the plane."

"We think he was on the plane for a purpose. In fact we believe he's a James Bond type character, licensed to kill."

"That sounds very dramatic, Ben. How on earth did you come to that conclusion? Brits don't do things like that. It is isn't cricket. Anyway he never mentioned it to me."

"Peter, this is very serious. We want to send him to trial."

"What's stopping you."

"He has to be extradited and the UK Foreign Office are being very awkward. Almost as if they aren't going to help, like blocking our request. We know his passport number but they won't give us any information. Could you let me have his address and telephone number?"

I tried to reply but the phone had gone dead.

Helen appeared with some food.

"What was all that about."

"I'm not sure and I don't think I want to know. You remember that survivor who was killed with a broken neck." She nodded. "Well Ben reckons that Michael Longshaw was involved."

"The flight marshal?"

"The very one. Ben had just asked me for Longshaw's address and telephone number when the phone went dead."

"Dead! You mean cut off?"

"I did wonder. Quite a coincidence. I wasn't going to give anything to Ben anyway but I suppose I was the only one who knew that."

We started eating and then Helen went into my office for a moment.

"Well, the internet is still working."

"That's my office line. Anyway how do you know?"

"I've just looked up Toby Makepeace in Google. Did you know he was the European scuba diving champion two years ago?"

"My love, I'm not sure it matters any more. I suppose you're going to tell me that his real name was Markovitch, that he was born in Russia and came to this country with his parents when he was eight years old?"

Helen looked at me as if she felt I had been hiding something. I tried to choose my words carefully.

"Look, Toby, Alvin and Hudson are all dead, Smithson is in prison and David Winston soon will be. We can't undo what has happened. Incredibly, Jim Scott managed to ditch the aircraft at night so that there were some survivors and just as incredibly you and Linda saved them. Hopefully, such an accident will never happen again. We can't do any more."

She reached over and gave me the phone.

"Yes, you can. You can ring up Michael Longshaw and tell him that if we don't get the phone back very shortly we might have to contact Cindy."

I didn't argue.

Lightning Source UK Ltd.
Milton Keynes UK
UKOW050317260113

205403UK00001B/108/P

9 780955 385667